INSTITUTIONAL FRAMEWORKS OF MARKET ECONOMIES

Institutional Frameworks of Market Economies

Scandanavian and Eastern European perspectives

Edited by

JERZY HAUSNER
Cracow Academy of Economics, Poland

BOB JESSOP
University of Lancaster, UK

KLAUS NIELSEN
Roskilde University Center, Denmark

Avebury

Aldershot · Brookfield USA · Hong Kong · Singapore · Sydney

Published by
Avebury
Ashgate Publishing Limited
Gower House
Croft Road
Aldershot
Hants GU11 3HR

Ashgate Publishing Company
Old Post Road
Brookfield
Vermont 05036
USA

British Library Cataloguing in Publication Data

Institutional Frameworks of Market
Economies: Scandanavian and Eastern
European Perspectives
I. Hausner, Jerzy
330.12

ISBN 1 85628 399 2

Printed and Bound in Great Britain by
Athenaeum Press Ltd, Newcastle upon Tyne.

Contents

Preface vii

Contributors ix

Introduction

1. Post-Socialism, the Negotiated Economy and other Western Models 3
Jerzy Hausner, Bob Jessop and Klaus Nielsen

Part 1. Theoretical Perspectives

2. Structural Competitiveness and Strategic Capacities: Rethinking State and International Capital 23
Bob Jessop, Klaus Nielsen and Ove K. Pedersen

3. Institutional Theory and the Influence of Foreign Actors on Reform in Capitalist and Post-Socialist Societies 45
John Campbell

4. Catching Up and Institutional Learning under Post-Socialism 68
Björn Johnson and Bengt-Åke Lundvall

Part 2. Scandinavian Perspectives: The Negotiated Economy

5. The Negotiated Economy: General Features and Theoretical Perspectives 89
Klaus Nielsen and Ove K. Pedersen

6. Natural Resource-Based Industries: Big Business and the Role of the State. The Case of Norway's Oil and Gas 113
Ole Berrefjord and Per Heum

7. Towards a New Swedish Model 133
Victor A. Pestoff

8. The Institutional History of the Danish Polity: From a Market and Mixed to a Negotiated Economy 169
Ove K. Pedersen

9. Private Industrial Policy in the Danish Negotiated Economy 195
Niels Åkerstrøm Andersen and Peter Kjær

Part 3. Post-Socialist Perspectives: The Polish Case

10. Trends and Perspectives in the Development of a System of Interest Representation in Post-Socialist Societies 217
Jerzy Hausner and Andrzej Wojtyna

11. Out of Corporatism Towards...... Neo-Corporatism? 239
Jaroslaw Gorniak and Jan Jerschina

12. Social Limitations for Efficient Allocation of Resources in the Post-Socialist Countries 251
Jan Czekaj and Stanislaw Owsiak

13. Impact of Political Changes in Processes Occurring in an Enterprise 263
Stanislaw Rudolf

14. Prospects for Employee Ownership in the Process of Privatizing the Polish Economy 277
Julian Pankow

15. The Drifting Society 287
Jerzy Mikulowski Pomorski

Index 295

Preface

The market is sometimes seen as nothing but a mere aggregation of individual exchanges. This is, of course, a misconception as markets and other forms of economic interaction are always embedded in a network of social institutions. The developed market economies are characterized by different institutional frameworks and several distinct 'models' can be distinguished. This is often ignored in the contemporary debates on market reforms in Eastern Europe where attempts to implant a textbook market economy 'without adjectives' are being promoted by influential domestic as well as foreign political actors.

This book explores some of the general features which are important in the process of formation and change of the institutional frameworks of market economies. This is applied to the current post-socialist situation in Eastern Europe, in particular the Polish case, and also to the Scandinavian countries which are characterized by a set of distinct institutional features. The 'Scandinavian model' is often associated with a universal welfare state and social democratic political dominance. In this context we shall stress another characteristic feature of the Scandinavian countries: the capacity to mobilize compromise and consensus through institutionalized forms of negotiation and communication between organized economic actors.

The Scandinavian countries are currently exposed to strong external pressures as a result of the accelerated economic internationalization and the European political integration. This book explores their effects, which have been substantial - especially in Sweden. However, the above-mentioned features ('the negotiated economy') are probably more immune to those pressures than other features of the 'Scandinavian model' and probably of more relevance to the introduction of market economy in Eastern Europe as well.

Most of the contributions to this book are revised versions of papers prepared for a conference in Cracow, December 6-8, 1990. The conference took place as part of an international research project 'Negotiated Economy versus Neo-Liberalism as Institutional Framework for a Market Economy - Implications for Post-Socialism'. The project is supported by the A.C.E. (Action for Cooperation in the field of Economics) programme of the Commission of the European Communities.

We shall use this opportunity to express our gratitude to the Commission for funding the project. We also want to thank the Danish Social Science Research Council, the Center for Public Organization and Management in Copenhagen, the Academy of Economics in Cracow and the Danish National Bank for its financial support. Colin Hay has performed sterling work in preparing the final typescript for publication. We are very grateful for his enthusiastic and skilful cooperation in this project.

Finally, we want to thank M.E. Sharpe Inc., New York, for permitting us to reprint three articles which appear in different forms in books published by M.E. Sharpe. An extended version of the article by Jessop, Nielsen and Pedersen appear in Sjöstrand S.-E. (1992): 'Institutional Evolution and Change. Theory and Empirical Findings'. A slightly different version of the article by Pedersen is included in the same volume while another version of the article by Nielsen and Pedersen appears in Coughlin, R.M. (1991): 'Morality, Rationality and Efficiency. Socio-Economic Perspectives'.

Contributors

Niels Åkerstrøm Andersen: Research assistent at the Center for Public Organization and Management, Copenhagen Business School, Denmark.

Ole Berrefjord: Associate professor at the Norwegian School of Economics and Business Administration, Bergen; at present political secretary of Prime Minister Gro Harlem Brundtland, Norway.

John Campbell: Associate professor at Harvard University, USA.

Jan Czekaj: Assistant professor at Cracow Academy of Economics, Poland.

Jaroslaw Gorniak: Assistant professor at Jagellonian University, Cracow, Poland.

Jerzy Hausner: Associate professor at Cracow Academy of Economics, Poland.

Per Heum: Research officer at the Institute of Industrial Economics, Bergen, Norway.

Jan Jerschina: Associate professor at Jagellonian University, Cracow, Poland.

Bob Jessop: Professor at the University of Lancaster, U.K.

Björn Johnson: Associate professor at the University of Ålborg, Denmark.

Peter Kjær: Research assistant at the University of Stockholm, Sweden.

Bengt-Åke Lundvall: Associate professor at the University of Ålborg, Denmark.

Klaus Nielsen: Associate professor at the University of Roskilde and Research officer at the Center for Public Organization and Management, Copenhagen Business School, Denmark.

Stanislaw Owsiak: Professor at Cracow Academy of Economics, Poland.

Julian Pankow: Assistant professor at the Polish Academy of Science, Warsaw, Poland.

Ove K. Pedersen: Associate professor at the University of Roskilde and Research officer at the Center for Public Organization and Management, Copenhagen Business School, Denmark.

Victor A. Pestoff: Reader at the University of Stockholm, Sweden.

Jerzy Mikulowski Pomorski: Rector and Professor at Cracow Academy of Economics, Poland.

Stanislaw Rudolf : Professor at the University of Lodz, Poland.

Andrzej Wojtyna : Professor at Cracow Academy of Economics, Poland.

INTRODUCTION

1 Post-socialism, the negotiated economy and other western models

Jerzy Hausner, Bob Jessop and Klaus Nielsen

1. Post-socialism and western models

The collapse of socialism opened a road to the introduction of a market economy and a democratic order in the Eastern European countries. The structural transformations in these countries concern among other things the setting up of an institutional framework for the market mechanism. The market is more than a mere aggregation of individual exchanges. It is itself a social institution, necessarily supported by (and embedded in) a network of other social institutions. This institutional framework includes among other things the distribution of property rights, the principles and scope of governmental intervention in economic processes, the extent of local self-management, the creation of organizations which represent interests of different economic agents and social groups, and procedures to coordinate the actions of such organizations. The institutional framework has also an international dimension involving controls on labour migration, foreign investments, trade flows, etc..

The transformation towards a market economy started long before 1989 - in particular in Poland and Hungary - and spectacular changes have already occurred, but it is obvious that the marketization of the Eastern European economies requires widespread institutional change over a very long period. The process of creating an appropriate institutional framework for the market economy has just begun. Furthermore various repercussions might be anticipated to block, delay or redirect future initiatives.

The analysis of the above-mentioned phenomena might profit from a comparative approach. The comparison between solutions and changes occurring in countries with developed market economies and those typical of post-socialist countries might facilitate better understanding of the latter. The market economy is embedded in quite different institutional settings in different Western European countries. Frequently used distinctions such as liberal vs corporatist vs etatist structures indicate the extent of the variety. Various Western 'models' seem to offer different solutions to the problems of a post-socialist future. Germany's 'social market economy', Britain's neo-liberal 'Thatcherism', 'the Third Italy', and the Scandinavian model ('the negotiated economy') are among those most frequently referred to in current reform discourses in Eastern Europe. These four models represent quite contrary/contrasting solutions regarding interest representation, the role of negotiations, consensus mobilization, etc..

In general this book considers post-socialist perspectives from a comparative perspective. In particular it focuses on Poland as one post-socialist case and on one of the above-mentioned Western 'models': the Scandinavian 'negotiated economy'. However, the book also refers to other specific 'models' or to Western 'models' in general and it also includes more general perspectives for Eastern European post-socialism such as the implications of the new trends in the global economy for international competitiveness and the economic role of the state.

2. The Scandinavian 'negotiated economy'

Different authors have stressed different characteristics of the Scandinavian 'model' or 'models': the welfare state, social democratic dominance, the political culture of consensus, the institutionalized co-operation between organized labour and capital.

We shall emphasize the characteristic forms of economic co-operation and communication which have developed in these countries through a long and unbroken period of relative social peace and institutionalized class co-operation. State, markets and organized interests have for long been intermingled to such an extent as to make traditional analytical categories largely irrelevant. An essential part of the resource allocation is currently decided neither through market exchange nor by state intervention but rather through direct co-operation and communication, and often through institutionalized negotiations, among a multitude of mutually autonomous agents. Behaviour is co-ordinated not only through prices, voting or (bureaucratic) rules but through institutional interaction of independent agents as well. Compromise and consensus are being mobilized systematically by institutional means. Expectations are formed and preferences are mobilized through institutionalized discursive processes.

We call this 'the negotiated economy' because of the importance of institutionalized negotiations as defined in a wider interactionist sense rather than a formal and narrow institutional sense. This involves communication, persuasion and opinion formation and various other forms of interaction between social partners in addition to bargaining processes around a bargaining table.

The emergence in Scandinavia of such forms of interaction and decision-making have been interpreted as a transition from a mixed economy to a negotiated economy. The concept has Norwegian origins and has been used until now only in a Scandinavian context although similar concepts have been used by others in the analysis of new institutional features in other countries. In recent years theoretical discussions have taken place and efforts have been made to apply the concept in empirical studies of the different Scandinavian countries.

One part of this book focuses on the structure and the future perspectives of the Scandinavian countries interpreted as negotiated economies. The article by Nielsen and Pedersen provides an introduction to the theory of the negotiated economy and the other articles in part two of the book apply the concept in analyses of the development of the institutional framework of the different Scandinavian market economies.

This part of the book is partly meant as a foundation for evaluating the relevance of this model in the post-socialist context. For that purpose it is necessary to evaluate not only the achievements of the past but also the future prospects. This is the reason why the book includes material on the history as well as the recent changes of the institutional framework of the Scandinavian market economies. Accordingly this part of the book can also be read as a contribution to the debate on the sustainability of the specific institutional features of the Scandinavian countries in the current era of internationalization and integration. Is this particular brand of Social Democracy sustainable in the future? And how do the different Scandinavian countries differ in this respect?

The Scandinavian countries are currently exposed to strong external pressures. However, the features associated with the negotiated economy seem to be more immune to these pressures than the other features of the 'Scandinavian model' and they are probably also, partly for this reason, of more relevance to the introduction of market economy in Eastern Europe.

The negotiated economy is not unaffected by the neo-liberal trend, the internationalization and the current world-wide demolition of state capacities for intervention (deregulation, liberalization, privatization). Internationalization implies, for instance, the demolition of existing institutional arrangements for negotiated coordination of financial markets in Denmark. In Sweden the destructive potential of internationalization is more radical. The 'exodus' of Swedish multinationals in recent years is a real blow to the renowned 'Swedish model'. Leading representatives of Swedish 'big business' (see Pestoff in this volume) have abolished the prevailing social contract and withdrawn from most of the institutions of the negotiated economy - no doubt due to their increased opportunities for exit in the new international context. It remains to be seen whether the effects will be a breakdown or a reorganization of the negotiated economy in Sweden. The introduction of new forms of negotiated cooperation at the plant level, in accordance with a new consensual vision of democracy, flexibility and upgrading of skills, at least indicates a potential for reorganization.

Internationalization does not necessarily entail subversion of the negotiated economy. It might lead instead to institutional innovation within the framework of discursive processes and negotiated coordination. One example of this is the emergence of 'private industrial policy' in Denmark (see Andersen and Kjaer in this volume). Other events also show the continuing vitality of the negotiated economy. It is characteristic that the Danish conservative/liberal government - despite prior ideological reservations - has not only relied heavily on the established institutions of the negotiated economy but has even strengthened and remodelled it in attempts to overcome situations of parliamentary stalemate (see Pedersen in this volume). Furthermore, important new trends are apparent in the evolving field of environmental policy. Traditional state regulation is replaced by coordination through such means as negotiated settlements between industrial branch organizations and the state.

The negotiated economy might actually even be strengthened in line with the gradual removal of state discretion in economic policy as an effect of the internationalization of the economy and the political integration within the EC. Coordination through discursive processes and institutionalized negotiation is not only one of the remaining possibilities for implementing national or local strategies. It might also be more efficent, but this seems to be preconditioned by the continued existence of an approximate symmetry of power among the major societal agents, absence of exit alternatives to any of them, civilization of the class conflicts, dispersion of state power, and a certain measure of nationhood and cultural homogeneity.

3. Post-socialism: Institutional reform and western models

Another part of the book focuses on the process of establishing an appropriate institutional framework for a market economy in Poland. However, we shall present a conceptual model which is relevant for other Eastern European countries as well. The model is presented in figure 1. The point of departure is the collapse of the socialist system and the resulting systemic vacuum in the Eastern European countries (I). The previous system has broken down; no other system has yet replaced it. Attempts to create more room for manoeuvre for the market mechanism and/or to introduce a democratic order co-exist with attempts to re-articulate the old structure and norms, habits, procedures and informal relationships. It is this systemic vacuum that we designate 'post-socialism'.

3.1 Search processes in post-socialism

The systemic collapse has initiated not only a search for marketization in response to the breakdown of central planning (IIa) but also three other important dynamics which influence the process of marketization. The breakdown of the political system (one-party system, party dominance over civil society organizations) has initiated a search for democratization (IIB). The disintegration of the COMECON and the removal of the political need to maintain economic and political links with what was once the Soviet Union has prompted a search for a new international role (IIc). Finally, the increasingly visible problems of the traditional extensive growth strategy (the syndrome of economic stagnation) and the breakdown - or at least weakening - of the supportive political-institutional structure have initiated a search for an intensive growth strategy (IId).

The search processes are provoked by the system collapse but they are at the same time influenced by external pressures. We shall stress two such features. Firstly, the search for a new international role is, of course, heavily influenced by the current

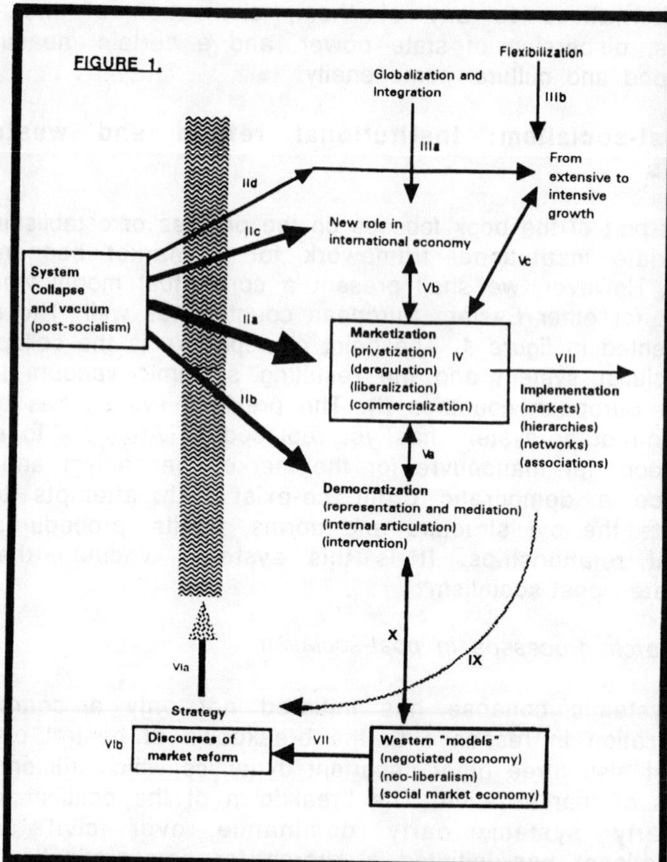

Figure 1.1 A Conceptual Model: Systemic Vacuum, Transformation Processes, Reform Discourses, and Western Models

reorganization of the international economy (globalization) and the emerging forms of international political integration (IIIa). The globalization of transnational firms, the wave of mergers, joint ventures, strategic alliances and various network forms of cooperation, the liberalization of international financial transactions and the burgeoning of new financial institutions and instruments, are among the important trends in the international economy. Among the most important political changes besides the end of the Cold War and the break up of the Soviet Union are the accelerated political integration of the European Community, the rush of other European countries to join in, and the attempt to create smaller regional economic blocs (e.g., around the Baltic Sea or in central Europe). Secondly, the attempts to move towards a more intensive pattern of economic development in Eastern Europe are occurring in a global economic context where greater flexibility is being sought in the organization of production, the labour process, the choice of product mixes, the labour market, the organization of the state apparatus and welfare services, etc.. This is sometimes summarized in terms of a transition from Fordism to post-Fordism (IIIb) but, as Jessop, Nielsen and Pedersen note in their contribution, this transition involves not only real changes in economic organization but also a paradigm shift and strategic reorientation on the part of economic and political forces. It is also linked to the rise of new technologies and new forms of competition.

3.1.1. Marketization

The main focus of interest is often directed at the search for marketization (IV). We distinguish four different forms this can take: privatization, deregulation, liberalization, and commercialization.

Privatization involves the introduction of real private ownership of means of production. In Eastern Europe this is complicated by the fact that ownership was often defined only in the vaguest manner in the former system with the paradoxical consequence that a first step in privatization is the recentralization of ownership delegated by the state to employees and management during the economic reforms of the last two decades. We distinguish three forms of privatization: (1) internal privatization (to employees and/or management); (2) external privatization (sales of shares to the highest bidders); and (3) distribution of shares to the whole population (which might take the form of national holding companies or various voucher systems).

Deregulation involves rolling back the state through removing controls, relinquishing earlier means of intervention, etc., to free economic agents from the constraining hand of the state. Thus it leads to greater formal freedom for economic agents to pursue their economic interests in the market place. This need not lead to freer, more competitive markets, however, as unfettered market forces could lead to private monopolies.

Liberalization involves creating the conditions for free markets to operate and so entails measures to prevent the emergence or survival of monopolies. Clearly the measures involved in liberalization may contradict the desire for deregulation - and vice versa.

Commercialization is aimed at the residual public sector. It involves introducing competition and market proxies in the hope of creating greater efficiency and responsiveness to consumer or client needs. In some cases this is a prelude to (or even a precondition for) subsequent privatization measures.

A specific sequence of strategic stages has evolved in relation to marketization and democratization in each country under study. In Poland deregulation was the first step in the process, followed by liberalization. Commercialization of state enterprises came next as a prelude to privatization. Likewise the search for democratization has moved from parliamentary government and political pluralism (parties, independent trade unions, etc.) to decentralization (local governments), and participatory forms of democracy (economic and industrial democracy).

3.1.2. Democratization

The process of marketization must be studied in relation to the other dynamics (search processes) initiated by the system collapse and influenced by various external pressures (see above). In particular we will focus on one of these relationships: the link between marketization and democratization (Va).

The search for democratic order has many dimensions. We distinguish three: forms of representation and intermediation; internal articulation of the state; and forms of intervention. These correspond to the input, throughput, and output aspects of democracy.

There are various sites of democratic representation: territorial (typically associated with political citizenship tied to residence within a given state territory and the right to vote for deputies in a territorially-based system of national parliamentary and/or local government constituencies); functional (based on function within the division of labour and typically associated with corporatist forms of organization); and civilian (based on ascribed or chosen identities rooted in the organization and dynamic of civil society and tied to the freedom of association and political mobilization around claims for social citizenship based on these identities). Struggles for democracy can focus on the extension and deepening of political citizenship rights, democratization of functional interest groups, or the pluralization of social citizenship and social movements. The specific sites for such struggles can also vary from central to local government, from macro-functional groups to the enterprise or production unit, from the national or macro-social 'community of fate' to the neighbourhood. Problems of representation and interest mediation occur in all spheres and at all levels. There is no guarantee that attempts to promote democratization will also promote marketization - indeed given the opposition to market forces in some areas, democratization could institutionalize resistance.

Whatever the general forms of representation in the state, a second problem occurs in terms of the overall articulation of the different state powers and capacities associated with a particular form of state. Every state has a particular hierarchy of branches, apparatuses, and administrative organs which have different representative and juridico-administrative relations to each other. Democratization must also include measures to secure the subordination of the state as a whole to democratically accountable bodies: a freely elected but toothless parliament which is unable to control the administration does not take democracy very far. Closely related to this issue is the question of the democratic accountability of functional organizations (e.g., trade unions or trade associations) and social movements (e.g., housing associations, friendly societies, or anti-nuclear movements) to their members. Again it is not hard to envisage situations where measures to secure greater democratic accountability within the state and/or corporatist bodies would hinder the pursuit of marketization.

Provided that democratic representation is effective and the state apparatus is subordinated to democratically elected organs, the forms of state intervention are less problematic. Nonetheless the struggle for democracy also encompasses the issues of open and fair government with due process, equal treatment before the law, and freedom from non-authorized discretionary decisions. Such efforts to democratize could also block or hinder marketization. To the extent that marketization is occurring in the form of the creation of a nomenklatura capitalism, for example, in which old political elites translate their political power into new market-based economic power, democratization could well prove an obstacle as ordinary citizens protest about the survival of old faces wearing new managerial caps. More generally, the requirement that decisions about marketization be subject to democratic control, freedom of information, due process, and so forth, may well delay the whole process and provoke further economic disruption.

3.1.3. Marketization, globalization and flexibilization

Two other links are also important. The search for a new international role at a time of globalization and integration influences the process of marketization (Vb). Internationalization is an important dimension of all forms of marketization. Indeed, opening up the economy to international competition increases pressures for various forms of marketization: for it intensifies competition and the need for capitalist economic rationality.

The demand for more intensive growth initiated by the system collapse and formed by the challenges of flexibility and the transition to post-Fordism have important links to marketization as well (Vc). Although markets are supposed to enhance flexibility, too much concern with marketization could shatter the delicate balance between stability and flexibility needed for trust and cooperation. Economic changes of the magnitude required cannot proceed purely on basis of market forces; they need some degree of commitment and involvement from those subject to the adverse changes which result from rapid subjection to market forces.

3.1.4. Strategies and discourses

The search processes (IIa, IIb, IIc, IId) initiated by the system collapse are embedded in structures but they are not fully structurally determined. They all involve strategic choice (VIa). The choice of strategies must, of course, be related to the existing structure of interests, behaviour and norms in the present systemic vacuum in the Eastern European countries. For instance, although the established forms of interest representation in Poland (such as branch organizations) have been weakened, they have not yet been displaced or replaced because of the institutional and behavioural inertia of economic agents. Indeed we should not underestimate the enormity of the task involved in reorganizing the Polish system, with its implications for regional transfers (deprivileging the mining industrial region around Katowice) and dissolving existing political and corporatist structures (such as the branch corporations).

The strategic dimension can be studied by investigating both the discourses of reform and the various organizations and political forces mobilized behind them (VIb). These discourses represent the specific interpretation, focus, exclusion and weighing of the different dimensions and links outlined above. The discourses often derive from and/or are justified in terms of rather simplistic interpretations of preferred Western 'models' such as the Scandinavian model, Thatcherism (neo-liberalism) and the German model (social market economy) (VII). In many cases these economic regimes are also identified with different political models, with obvious implications for the relative importance of different political forces during and after the process of democratization.

So far we have only focused on strategies, discourses of reform, and the range of possible reforms. We have not considered how these market reforms are implemented and how this might contradict the process of democratization (VIII). While there are certainly many non-state forms of economic governance (markets, hierarchies, networks, associative interaction, strategic alliances, etc.), their development and consolidation is often closely related to state forms. It is far from true that more market entails less state: often it means a different form of state. Thus we need to consider the factors which influence the choice of organizational form, constrain the particular forms of economic governance that actually develop, and connect the overall process of marketization with the parallel reorganization of the state. The discourses of reform should reflect awareness of the alternative modes of governance and the different options available in the marketization process (X).

In this context we should note that, even if one could identify the precise technical and economic reforms that the state must implement in the process of marketization, these must still be channelled through a crisis-ridden state at a time when the balance of economic and political forces both within the state and beyond it could well make narrowly conceived market reforms impracticable. In these circumstances, of course, the pursuit of such reforms must either be adapted to what is feasible and/or made contingent on earlier or simultaneous reorganization of the state. This is far from easy. For it involves an acute strategic dilemma: the structurally imposed short-term need to choose between restructuring the state to enhance its economic capacities in a period of deep economic crisis and restructuring it to enhance its democratic character in a period of growing social division. In an ideal world the state's economic capacities would be reinforced by an institutionalized, democratic compromise on the economic strategy appropriate for a post-socialist society; and the play of political forces within a (strategically selective) democratic system would be aided by the material resources produced by a successful economic strategy. But, as we have already stressed above, post-socialist economic and political processes are occurring in a systemic vacuum characterized by acute structural crises, growing social disintegration, and fast deteriorating open economies.

This poses a dilemma for which no once-and-for-all collective solution is possible: whether to prioritize the struggle for economic regeneration or that for democratization. This involves a risk that (a) some sort of solution will be imposed from above and/or from outside; and/or (b) a catastrophic collapse of societal order will provoke a retreat into localized informal markets and reliance on primordial solidarities. Any imposed solution is likely to be one that abandons an immediate search for parliamentary democracy in favour of an attempt to stabilize the economic situation. The increasing openness of the post-socialist economies will reinforce the latter solution because the need for foreign investment and credit will oblige at least partial acceptance of economic recipes from abroad. Thus any attempt to suspend parliamentary democracy and impose stabilization is likely to be supported by outside economic and political forces. But this might still be accompanied by the relocation of democratic mechanisms to the local level as firms, workers, and local political forces search for responsible market solutions to local problems by drawing on primary social relations and informal political exchanges, the development or resurgence of selective regional or national corporatist arrangements involving strategic firms and sectors, and an emerging pluralism. It would be quite premature in such a turbulent and uncertain situation to forecast what will happen in the face of the systemic and strategic vacuum which confronts the post-socialist economies. But the analyses presented elsewhere in this volume may help to provide some orientation points and material for interpreting events as they unfold.

4. Plan of the book

The book has three parts. The first part covers theoretical perspectives. The article by *Bob Jessop, Klaus Nielsen* and *Ove K. Pedersen* concerns development trends which are relevant for all countries. These trends constitute the shared background of Eastern and Western European countries. The article explores the changing forms of competition in an increasingly global economy and the associated reorientation of state activities to secure national competitiveness. Referring to figure 1 the article concerns the external pressures (IIIa and IIIb) and its strategic (VIa) and discursive (VIb) implications.

The discourses on market reforms in the Eastern European countries are in various ways influenced by foreign actors. *John Campbell* synthesizes recent institutional theories in organizational theory, political sociology and political science in his attempt to develop a model explaining how foreign actors influence the discourses of reform. He identifies three processes of such influence, collectively referred to as 'institutional isomorphism' (coercive, normative and imitative), which generate pressures for harmonizing domestic institutional features with those of foreign models. He also analyzes how the influence of these isomorphic processes is mediated by domestic political and institutional conditions. This chapter explores the different mechanisms through which Western 'models' influence the discourses of reform (see VII in figure 1).

The present recipes for institutional reform in the post-socialist countries, emphasizing full-scale introduction of private ownership and free markets, can be seen as effects of isomorphic pressures. These recipes are, according to *Bjorn Johnson* and *Bengt-Åke Lundvall*, too narrow and may seriously misguide policy-making and institutional design. Johnson and Lundvall discuss in their chapter the general problems and prospects of institutional borrowing and learning and relate them to the post-socialist reform process in Eastern Europe. They argue that the relevant economic perspective for evaluation and design of institutional settings in the post-socialist context ought to be dynamic rather than static efficiency. They consider it crucial how different institutional frameworks affect technological learning and the use of new technology. This chapter poses critical questions to the discourse of market reform (VIb), the search for marketization (IV) and the implementation process (VIII).

The second part of the book concerns perspectives for the Scandinavian 'negotiated economy'.

The article by *Klaus Nielsen* and *Ove K. Pedersen* surveys the basic features this Western model (VII). It defines the concept and presents an ideal typical model of the negotiated economy. It argues that, in the Scandinavian countries, important trends in the last decades might be interpreted as involving development from a mixed economy to a negotiated economy. The argument is illustrated with data from the Danish case. In addition the article explores the theoretical implications of the trend towards a negotiated economy - especially the challenge it poses to ideal typical conceptions in economic and political theory alike.

The article by *Ole Berrefjord* and *Per Heum* concerns features particularly important in the Norwegian case. It discusses the stae's role in relation to oil and gas - key sectors in the

Norwegian economy. The governance system which developed in this industry conforms to a long tradition in Norway regarding the organization of natural resource-based industrial activities. This is characterized as a compromise, attempting to attract industrial and managerial resources on commercial conditions, while maintaining public control over the nation's natural endowments. The article discusses features of the negotiated economies which are particularly relevant to the discourses of market reforms in those Eastern European countries where natural resource- based industries are dominant. It also highlights important features of the relationship between marketization and democratization (Va).

Concertational practices and a politics of compromise comprise important parts of the 'Swedish model' which is the best-known Scandinavian case. *Victor A. Pestoff* describes how this model is now under systematic assault by organized business. The extent of the actual de-institutionalization of the negotiated economy is examined in three areas: industrial relations; consumer, agricultural, and food policy; and housing policy. The problems facing the negotiated economy in Sweden are related to developments in the international economy. Large Swedish firms seem to lose interest in negotiations and agreements at the national level as a result of the internationalization process, and a new Swedish model might evolve as a result. This chapter raises important questions regarding the sustainability of the Scandinavian model and its relevance in the post-socialist context (VII). It can also be read as a case-study of the effects of internationalization processes on national institutional frameworks of market economies (Vb).

The article by *Ove K. Pedersen* provides a more detailed analysis of the Danish negotiated economy. It shows the capacity of the model for continuous innovation and transformation; and discusses the institutionalization of wage formation and the welfare state in the Danish case. It is shown how this has changed the state from a government-centered form to a dual form of state and, later on, to a poly-centric form of state. The new structural policy which has developed as a result of the external pressures (IIIa and IIIb) to the model, has implied another phase of transformation: a so-called drifting state has evolved. The article discusses important links between marketization and democratization (Va).

Niels A. Andersen and *Peter Kjaer* analyze some of the most important institutional innovations in the Danish negotiated economy in recent years: the emergence of private industrial policy at various levels. The focus of industrial policy has changed from subsidies to campaigns as the dominant policy instrument, and from state to private policy communities as the locus of policy formulation and implementation. Private industrial policies are identified at three levels: local and regional arenas, capital markets, and national policy. These developments are interpreted as the establishment of a particular institutional system, the negotiated economy, to ensure co-ordination by means of communication rather than coercion or economic incentives. This chapter explores the capacity of the negotiated economy for adapting to new circumstances and, indirectly, its relevance in the current context of internationalization (VII). It also indicates the variety of the available forms of implementation of market reforms (VIII).

The third part of the book concerns the perspectives of the Polish case of post-socialism.

The article by *Jerzy Hausner* and *Andrzej Wojtyna* discusses the development of systems of interest representation in post-socialism, illustrated with Polish data. The forms of representation of interests in classical socialist societies is characterized as 'state corporatism'. Formal articulation of interests occurred only through officially licensed and state controlled organizations, and the only real possibility for defence of interests not subject to bureaucratic control was based on informal family and friendship connections. The authors argue for the necessity of new forms of interest representation ('societal corporatism') as part of the institutional framework of a post-socialist market economy. However, several features tend to block the development of 'societal corporatism' and to reproduce the old structure. The chapter covers important problems in the search for democratization (IIb) and also various aspects of the relationship between democratization and marketization (Va).

The chapter by *Jaroslaw Gorniak* and *Jan Jerschina* also discusses interest representation and its relation to economic reform. They see the former economic system as constituted of three interrelated elements: permanent shortage, allocation of resources based on the political power of branch corporations, and the maintenance of power based on the distribution of resources and privileges in return for social peace. Central planning has been abandoned but the old structure of branch corporations has survived in only a slightly different form. The success of economic reform is dependent on the creation of new mechanisms for articulating and negotiating the interests of different segments of society. This involves new legal regulations, building of institutions, development of skills, and change of attitudes of economic agents.

In their contribution *Jan Czekaj* and *Stanislaw Owsiak* analyze the problems and contradictions involved in marketization (III).

The systemic vacuum is rooted in the fact that the foundations and mechanisms of central planning have not been replaced with new economic mechanisms. Post-socialism suffers from the lack of technical as well as social infrastructure appropriate to a market economy. Whereas several technical difficulties may gradually be over-come through proper regulation, the social barriers are more dangerous when it comes to building a market economy. Their chapter concludes with a discussion of the state's role in post-socialism.

The article by *Stanislaw Rudolf* focuses on the impact of political changes on the processes occurring within enterprises and vice versa. His analysis covers Polish conditions in the seventies, which were characterized by relative political and economic stability; the second half of the eighties, when political and economic changes started; and the most recent period, which has witnessed a marked acceleration of these changes. The artciles includes results from a research and development programme on structural changes in a rubber company in Lodz. Rudolf concludes that today no formal obstacles hamper the necessary organizational reforms at the enterprise level, for instance, those needed to liquidate the deeply rooted division between those who make the decisions and those who execute them. However, political changes do not impose such shifts, and only very few enterprises have actually introduced them. The article concerns very important aspects of the implementation of market reform (VIII).

The article by *Julian Pankow* also discusses the changes from the vantage point of enterprises. He focusses on obstacles to the process of privatization and the prospects for employee ownership as a means to minimize the problems and accelerate the process. Surveys on attitudes to privatization have shown strong support for the idea of privatization but a lesser willingness to participate in it. One has to reckon not only with passivity but also with resistance on the part of various social groupings, particularly the employees of the privatized plants and their organizations. Pankow's survey data suggest that linking employment to ownership has strong motivational effects. However, the privatization bill in 1990 offered only a restricted range of privileged opportunities for employees of privatized enterprises who might want to purchase stock in their companies. The article concerns important aspects of the search for marketization (II) and the implementation of market reform (VIII).

Finally, *Jerzy Mikulowski Pomorski* characterizes post-socialist Poland as a society subject to the influence of a myth of European civilization and the absence of authentic values. From the myth of a just and affluent West followed an unrealistic maximalist program of transformation. Whereas before people concentrated on biological survival, cultivation of statehood, or escaping from the public sphere to the security of private life, the current programme demands too much to stand any chance of being fulfilled. In their maximalism these societies have allowed themselves to be put to sleep by the myth of Europe, participation in which would bring justice and prosperity. Now they drift in their dream. However, new authentic values will emerge and question the myth. This awakening is seen to imply more of a problem than an interesting challenge to the West. The chapter presents a critical perspective on the influence of Western 'models' on the discourses of post-socialist reform (VII).

Part 1
THEORETICAL PERSPECTIVES

2 Structural competitiveness and strategic capacities: Rethinking state and international capital

Bob Jessop, Klaus Nielsen and Ove K. Pedersen

This paper explores some of the changing forms of competition in an increasingly global economy and the associated reorientation of state activities to secure national competitiveness. Although we try to introduce some order into the confusing and often contradictory political economy literature on competition and competitiveness, the most distinctive feature of our account is its particular approach to the state and the official discourse about competition. Thus we examine the state's structural selectivity and strategic capacities and relate these to shifts in official discourse about competitiveness. In particular we examine the changing role of the state (broadly defined) in industrial policy in a period marked by a significant redefinition of conditions making for international competitiveness. We explore the nature, preconditions, and dynamic of structural competitiveness (which involves not only nationally specific comparative advantages as well as firm-specific capacities but also the competitive implications of a wide range of institutional externalities) and also consider the politically mediated capacities to pursue national accumulation strategies. Our concern in both cases is dynamic rather than static.

1. New challenges to international competitiveness

Among the many tendencies and trends discernible in contemporary capitalism there are four which are often cited as having major implications for international competitiveness. These are the increasing impact of new technologies, the growing internationalization of the world economy, the alleged transition from Fordism to post-Fordism, and the increasingly triadic nature of the world economy. No such identification of tendencies and trends can be entirely innocent, of course; and this is particularly clear for the last two tendencies. For these are also contentious among active participants in the internationalization process itself but may well become self-fulfilling prophecies if enough economic and political forces base their action on them.

a) the rise of new core technologies as the motive and carrier forces of economic expansion and the increasing integration of different technologies in producing a given range of products as well as their application across different sectors. New core technologies relevant to the current competitive struggle include: microelectronics, telecommunications, data processing, optical technologies, robotics, new materials, renewable energy sources, and biotechnology. Their mastery is held to be critical to continued growth and structural competitiveness yet few firms are likely to have the skills, capital, and knowledge needed both for basic research and for product and process development on their own. Indeed many are so knowledge- as well as capital-intensive that they require collaboration (especially at pre-competitive stages) across many interests (firms, university, public and private research labs, venture capital, public finance, etc.), drawing on resources at different points on the globe. Such cooperation reduces competitive and technological uncertainties and helps internalize the spillover of research benefits (cf. Hughes 1989). Thus there is a clear trend towards technological cooperation among firms within each part of the triad and among distant competitors in different parts of the triad (cf. Ohmae 1985; Hughes 1989). The dynamics of technology flows, shifts in comparative advantage, and competitiveness will depend on the diffusion and absorption of new technologies and there is increasing concern about how best to transfer technology in this context. Transnational companies clearly play a key role here (and are increasingly collaborating in various forms of strategic alliance - see especially Contractor and Lorange 1988; Hughes 1989; Vonortas 1990) but there is also growing interest in most economies in state-sponsorship of technology transfer and diffusion. For, as Hughes notes, 'international technological competition is seen to have intensified firstly because medium or high technology industries are the main areas where the advanced industrial economies can expect or hope to have a competitive advantage, given the pressures of competition from the newly industrializing countries in less technology intensive products' (Hughes 1989: 276). This can be a key element in strategies for economic growth in the light of changing forms of competitiveness - with Japan being particularly advanced in its Schumpeterian and quite explicit 'knowledge-intensive industrialization' strategy. The four Asian tigers are also moving into new technologies to counteract protectionism and the threat from second-tier NICs (cf. Ernst and O'Connor 1989). But 'sunrise industry' policies are crucial to many advanced capitalist societies too and have also been taken up at the EC level.

b) another trend is the massive internationalization of financial and industrial flows involving more firms, more markets, and more countries. This tendentially homogenizes economic space as leading edge technologies are diffused, foreign direct investment is undertaken by all metropolitan powers, a small but increasing number of NICs develop their own MNCs and TNBs, and markets become international. Thus multinational firms no longer operate in a multi-domestic economy where foreign operations are run with minimal cross-national coordination via subsidiaries with their own managements, via acquisitions and mergers with limited global integration, or through cooperation agreements among otherwise independent enterprises. Instead they operate in a global economy in which operations are integrated across national borders in relation to an overall global accumulation strategy and it is hard to ascribe the firm any specific 'territoriality' owing to the complexity of its interrelationships and the global spread of share ownership with active trading in different stock markets world-wide (cf. Hood and Vahlne 1988; Petrella 1990). A reinforcing factor here is the spread of 'world markets (or markets which eventually will become such) regulated by universal standards (e.g. MAP, TOP, OSI, SNA, etc.)' (Petrella 1990: 99). Clearly this does not mean that the operations of global firms are identical from country to country nor that they are (or will ever become) equally dispersed across the globe; it does mean that they are subject to an overall strategic plan which is formulated on a global scale. In turn this has major implications for the role of the nation state and for the concept of the 'national' economy as a natural unit of the world economic order. One crucial effect is that national economic space is no longer the most obvious starting point for pursuing economic growth, technological innovation, or structural competitiveness. This is more and more reflected in the transnational strategies of firms and states alike. It is in this context that Petrella notes how 'the success of the national enterprises on the world scene is a prerequisite for the achievement and preservation of the country's technological and economic autonomy' (Petrella 1990: 102). This holds not only for advanced capitalist economies but also for the four Asian tigers and other late-comer industrializing nations.

c) a transition from Fordism to post-Fordism as the dominant model of development shaping economic and political strategies. This involves a paradigmatic shift from a growth model concerned with mass production, scale economies, and mass consumption to one concerned with flexible production, scope economies, and more differentiated patterns of consumption (on this see Jessop 1992a). This shift in the dominant techno-economic paradigm has major implications for enterprise and sectoral strategies even where Fordism was not as such previously dominant in particular branches or national economies. For it provides an interpretative framework within which to make sense of the current crisis and its disruptions to the circuit of capital and to impose some coherence on the search for routes out of the crisis. This transition is associated with a crisis of US economic hegemony (with which the Fordist paradigm is especially associated) and an emerging struggle between USA, FRG, and Japan to define a hegemonic post-Fordist paradigm. This in turn radically undermines strategies based on the 1970s wisdom that internationalization was essentially driven by US multinationals and that the state's task was to find an appropriate response to this American challenge. At stake today in international competition is the competitive struggle to switch quickly and smoothly among innovative products and processes with each new product offering better functional qualities and improved efficiency in production. It is no longer a question of competing through economies of scale in the production of standardized goods and services using dedicated production systems but of competing through the capacity to introduce flexible manufacturing or service delivery systems and exploit the resulting economies of scope. This explains why Best can describe the 'new competition' as being led by business enterprises based upon new production and organizational concepts. 'At the centre of the new competition is the entrepreneurial firm, an enterprise that is organized from top to bottom to pursue continuous improvements in methods, products, and processes' (Best 1990: 2). And this explains in turn why Mytelka (1987: 32) can justifiably claim that: 'the key to longevity has become an ability to control the transformation of the market rather than respond to changes in it' (cited in Vonortas 1990: 205).

d) the redefinition of the macro-economic global hierarchy as concepts such as European Economic Space and the Pacific Rim Economic Community are promoted to challenge the economic dominance of the US sphere of economic influence. It is far from clear that these correspond to real trends independently of their identification and active promotion in official discourses but, in so far as a range of official institutions and business strategies are premised on them, they can become self-fulfilling. Certainly they have come to play a key role in discussions of competitiveness. For our purposes the most important of these new regional concepts is the accelerated economic integration of the EC which was begun as a deliberate move to overcome 'euro-sclerosis' and to reinforce Western Europe as a 'triad power' (Ohmae 1985). The end of the cold war and the marketization of Eastern Europe are still highly uncertain new trends and will not be considered here nor do we discuss the emergence of the Pacific Rim economic region. But it is worth noting here our opinion that the growing advocacy of triad power ignores significant counter-tendencies towards the re-emergence of regional economies as well as towards a growing interpenetration of the so-called triad powers.

Each of these factors has crucial implications for the dynamics of competition and the state's role in securing competitive advantage. We will approach these in two steps. We begin by presenting some basic conceptual distinctions regarding competition, competitiveness, and competitive strategies; then we will discuss some of the implications of these trends for state functions and accumulation strategies. It is no part of our argument that competition is always and everywhere recognized as such and that those involved in competition have clear strategies towards it. For not all the conditions affecting competition are acknowledged and it operates ex post in unanticipated ways. But we do insist that competition and competitive strategy have become more and more reflexive and that there is growing concern with issues of competition. This simply reflects the truism that social agents are capable of choice and strategizing. Thus we must examine how self-conscious and reflective economic and political agents involved in these processes have become and also examine the modes of calculation they employ to this end. It will also be important to explore how far this involves second-order strategizing about how to enhance competitiveness as well as how to engage in competition with existing levels of competitiveness.

2. Competition, competitiveness, and strategies

Competition occurs on a stratified terrain rather than a level playing field: as the hierarchy of forms of competition and competitive players alters, the dynamics of competition also change. We can approach competitive hierarchies from several directions: changes in the relative importance of different markets in setting the parameters of competition, changes in the relative super- and sub-ordination of different forms of competition, and changes in the corporate forms associated with advantage in given fields of competition.

The first hierarchy concerns the relation among four types of markets: financial, industrial, and commercial markets together with emerging 'meta-markets' in the ever more important field of intellectual property right. These can be considered both within national economies (e.g., the dominance of City interests in Britain) and across national economies (e.g., the emergence of an 'international intellectual property regime' as part of the high-tech neo-mercantilist strategies pursued by the USA and Japan). Financial market transactions prompted by short-term money-making opportunities have grown at the expense of long-term industrial (or producer) interests and have engineered massive restructuring of firms through new financial instruments. Likewise, as technologies become more knowledge-intensive, access to markets in technological know-how (licenses, data-bases, patents, technology transfer, etc.) become crucial to effective competition and the appropriation of knowledge becomes a key factor in competitive success (Colombo 1988; Ernst and O'Connor 1989).

The second hierarchy is more complex and concerns the relation among different forms and/or bases of competition. Thus, as well as the conventional neo-classical distinctions among numbers of agents in markets (perfect, imperfect, monopolistic, etc.), we can also cite other, supposedly less 'pure' forms of economic interaction (such as networks or strategic alliances). To these can be added a concern with the bases on which these different forms of economic interaction operate (e.g., costs and prices, various forms of rent, state subsidies, etc.). This is not simply a question of the succession of competition forms but of their relative sub- and super-ordination. Thus, even where liberal competition survives in current capitalism, it is often subordinate to monopolistic competition (e.g., suppliers to retail chains, subcontracting to monopolies, etc.). Conversely, as new technologies, process, or product innovations become more widespread, technological rents will diminish and allocative efficiency will become more significant.

The third hierarchy concerns the corporate form assumed by the competition setters in different markets and/or forms of competition. The peak of the global corporate hierarchy is currently occupied by denationalized transnational banks and 'stateless' multinational firms (cf. Grou 1986). The leading banks now offer a full range of financial services and the leading MNCs now specialize in high-tech, high value-added groups of products (e.g., speciality chemicals, advanced transport, energy resources). Combining these hierarchies we can say that the dominant competitive forces are those which set the terms of competition in the most important market. And, as the forms of competition and competitive strategy shift, patterns of competitive advantage will also alter. In turn this implies that the state's capacity to promote competitiveness depends on its ability to pursue competitive strategies adapted to the position of the national economy and its key economic actors within the changing hierarchy.

The idea of competitiveness is conceptually ambiguous and politically controversial. Even a cursory review of the literature reveals many ways of defining and measuring it; and even the briefest acquaintance with current policy debates will indicate the political issues at stake. These points are related. For competitiveness is a discursively constructed notion with obvious strategic implications both economically and politically: different notions entail different forms of political action with different effects on the competitive positioning of firms, sectors, regions, and nations as well as on the balance of political forces within and beyond the state. The role of politics is indicated in a recent claim that worries and proposals about European competitiveness expressed by the European Commission derive more from French than German experience: for it is French rather than German industry which is uncompetitive and France which has neo-mercantilist and dirigiste traditions (Grahl and Teague 1990: 159-60). Conversely the 1992 'internal market' strategy tends to reflect more the weight of neo-conservative national governments within the European Community during the 1980s in so far as it is more neo-liberal in approach. Despite such conceptual ambiguities and political controversies, however, we will now present some elementary distinctions about competitiveness at the micro- and macro-levels.

Micro-economic competitiveness concerns firms and is measured through market share, profits, and growth. Different strategies correspond to these different indicators and will also vary with the forms of competition. Where liberal competition prevails, for example, competitiveness mainly depends on prices and cost inputs. In many branches and sectors, however, competitiveness cannot be reduced to relative costs and prices. Together with data on market share, employment levels, profits, or exports, these are now often seen more as symptoms rather than causes of competitiveness. Thus research shows that price differences are weighed against those in product quality, after-sales service, etc.. Likewise both managerial and industrial economics claim that 'firm-specific advantages', i.e., factor(s) unavailable in the short-term to competitors, are the key basis for competitiveness (Casson 1983; Dunning 1988). Such advantages are essential where monopolistic competition prevails. They might originate in production (patent rights, know-how, R&D-capacity) or marketing (design, image, knowledge of likely demand, sales networks). This has led in turn to increasing concern about input-side criteria for assessing competitiveness. The US Congress established an Office of Technology Assessment in 1978 to assess the competitiveness of US industries and this examines industry and market structures, the nature of work forces, availability of materials and components, supporting infrastructures, environment for innovation and technology diffusion, business and economic conditions, government policies and interactions with the private sector, and international trade relations (Alic 1987: 8-9). Similar ideas have been expressed in Porter's concept of the 'national diamond' of factors affecting the competitiveness of specific firms or sectors (1990). Many other studies could be cited as well to illustrate the growing recognition of the many factors which influence a firm's competitiveness.

The multidimensional character of competitiveness is even more strongly pronounced at the macro-economic level. The concept of macro-economic competitiveness is controversial since some critics deny that 'economies' can function as units of competition. They are right in so far as 'economies' are not real agents or subjects but wrong in so far as real agents or subjects do identify 'economies' as engaged in competition and act on this perception. This could occur for political or military as well as economic reasons and is closely connected to the organization of world society in and through nation-states. In this context definitions of competitiveness and their associated discourses are liable to change: mercantilist notions from the 17th century can be contrasted with 1890s imperialism or recent worries about structural competitiveness. Key indicators in recent years have been factor endowments and relative prices, costs, and exchange rates; and shares in world exports or ratios of foreign penetration of home markets. Given these concerns real subjects may seek to enhance macro-economic competitiveness either because of its perceived impact on the overall competitiveness of individual firms operating in a given national economic space or because of the repercussions of macro-economic competitiveness on other objectives - whether economic (e.g., trade balance, employment, inflation) or non-economic (e.g., electoral consequences or military capacities). Such concerns will be reflected in turn in different types of strategy to enhance competitiveness.

The dominant theoretical perceptions of macro-economic competitiveness have stressed the exclusive importance of relative prices and/or comparative advantages. Traditional international trade theory has related competitiveness to comparative advantages as shaped by factor endowments. Another approach distinguishes between comparative advantages as shaped by micro-economic factors and competitiveness as being a macro-economic problem associated with the dovelopment of prices, costs and exchange rates. Empirical studies have questioned these simplistic perceptions. Thus Kaldor (1987) has shown a 'perverse' (positive) relation between export performance and growth in relative prices or costs; and Leontief (1954) shows that the USA had net exports of labour intensive products and net imports of capital intensive manufactured goods. Various studies have shown other factors explaining the development of competitiveness. For example, Fagerberg (1988) shows that the development of market shares at home and abroad for 15 OECD countries 1961-1983 is strongly related to the ability to compete in delivery (capacity) while price- and cost-competitiveness played rather a limited role.

The macro-economic aspect of competitiveness includes not only prices, costs, and exchange rates, but also the structures which influence the capacities of firms to compete in technology, delivery, after-sales service and to develop other forms of firm specific advantages. A useful concept here is 'structural competitiveness'. The OECD sees this as 'a way of expressing the fact that, while the competitiveness of firms will obviously reflect successful management practice by entrepreneurs or corporate executives, it will also stem from the strength and efficiency of a national economy's productive structure, its technical infrastructure, and other factors determining the "externalities" on which firms build, i.e., the economic, social, and institutional frameworks and phenomena which can substantially stimulate or hamper both the productive and competitive thrust of domestic firms' (STI Review 1986: 86, 87).

The multi-dimensional character of this perception of macro-economic competitiveness is evident from a summary of the aspects of economic structure relevant to structural competitiveness (STI Review 1986, 1, 91-2). These include 'the size of domestic markets, the structure of domestic production, relationships between different sectors and industries the distribution and market power of supplier firms the characteristics and size distribution of buyers, and the efficiency of non-market relations between firms and production units'. It might further depend on 'no exaggerated conflict in the field of income distribution, price stability, flexibility, and the adaptability of all participants in the market a balanced economic structure based on small, medium-sized, and big companies the acceptance of new technology, favourable scientific and technological infrastructure and realistic requirements for risk containment and environmental protection'.

Once macro-economic competitiveness is deemed relevant, it can be targetted for action. But the definition of competitiveness, the target variables, and the strategies adopted are all discursively constituted and will vary from case to case. In some cases extra-economic factors can prove crucial (e.g., tariff and non-tariff barriers to trade, access to state subsidies); but, in so far as competition is mediated through market forces, it will depend on the struggle to increase efficiency. In the latter context it is useful to distinguish three forms of efficiency which bear on the competitive strength of economic agents. These are: a) Ricardian or allocative efficiency; b) Kaldorian or growth efficiency; and c) Schumpeterian or innovative efficiency. Ricardian competitiveness depends on efficiency in the allocation of resources to minimize production costs with a given technical division of labour and on the assumption that current economic conditions will continue. Kaldorian competitiveness depends on efficiency in the allocation of resources among available processes and products in terms of the likely impact of (re-) allocation on economic growth. And Schumpeterian competitiveness depends on efficiency in allocating resources to promote technical, product, and organizational innovations which will alter the pace and direction of economic growth (cf. Dosi et al. 1989; Hagedoorn 1989). Clearly the movement from one to another involves higher degrees of reflection; this is not just a question of cognitive powers but also of the organization of economic and political forces for reflection. For each strategic step towards a Schumpeterian competitive strategy requires a more radical approach to competitiveness: if allocative efficiency takes the technical labour process for granted, growth efficiency is oriented to alternative production techniques, and innovative efficiency is concerned with innovation in products, processes, and organization.

We suggest that there is an increasing concern with Schumpeterian competitiveness and that this is now reflected in the debate over 'structural competitiveness'. For, whereas the dominant macro-economic perceptions of competitiveness were until recently based on Ricardian or Kaldorian efficiency, the newly introduced concept of structural competitiveness points towards a Schumpeterian understanding of efficiency. This is now incorporated into OECD analyses, has become central to recent EC industrial policy, has long played a crucial role in the industrial policies of Japan, South Korea, and Taiwan, is an integral part of West German policy, etc.. Even in the USA, where allocative and growth efficiency have long been hegemonic perspectives, a concerted effort is now in train to reorient industrial policy towards structural competitiveness (Dertouzos 1988). Likewise, from a corporate strategy viewpoint, Porter's contribution can also be seen as an attempt to redirect industrial and governmental efforts from short-term, Ricardian efficiency to longer-term, dynamic, Schumpeterian concerns.

3. The state and accumulation strategies

Earlier we briefly mentioned four emergent trends in the global economy. These have clear implications for possible state functions in securing structural competitiveness and it is to these we now turn. For ease of presentation we will deal with the four trends in the same order as they were introduced above and note some possible implications. But it is no part of our argument that there is any necessary, objectively determined link between the individual trends that we happen to have identified and specific features of the current political reorganization and rearticulation of different levels of the state. Nor do we claim that these trends in themselves guarantee that states will develop the capacities to perform such functions. Indeed we have already noted that these trends can be (and are) integrated and expressed in quite different discourses and linked to contrasting strategic conclusions as different forces seek to make sense of the conflicting tendencies and counter-tendencies at work in the global economy. Given these cautionary remarks, however, we review some of the more obvious implications of the current restructuring.

3.1. Globalization and state functions

Firstly, given the growing competitive pressures from NICs on low cost, low tech production and, indeed, in simple high tech products, the advanced capitalist economies must move up the technological hierarchy and specialize in the new core technologies if they are to maintain employment and growth. States have a key role here in promoting innovative capacities, technical competence, and technology transfer so that as many firms and sectors as possible benefit from the new technological opportunities created by R&D activities undertaken in specific parts of the economy (STI Review 1986: 86). Conversely, given the budgetary and fiscal pressures on states as national economies become more open, states must shift industrial support away from efforts to maintain declining sectors and towards promoting new sectors. Alternatively, given that the new core technologies are generic and applicable to many different fields of production, states should at least intervene to restructure declining sectors so that they can apply new processes, upgrade existing products, and launch new ones. In all cases the crucial point at issue is state action to encourage the development of new core technologies and their application to as wide a range of activities as possible to promote competitiveness.

Secondly, as internationalization proceeds apace, states can no longer act as if national economies were effectively closed and their growth dynamic were autocentric. Small open economies, such as Sweden and Denmark, had already faced this problem during the postwar boom, of course; now even large, relatively closed economies have been integrated into the global circuits of capital. This is nowhere more evident in the last decade than in the USA. For the increasing concern over US competitiveness and the associated debate about the need for an explicit national industrial policy reflect the increasing exposure of a quasi-continental, broad-based, highly productive economy to competitive pressures in the global system. In particular many macro-economic policy instruments associated with the Keynesian welfare state lose their efficacy with growing internationalization and must be replaced or buttressed by other measures if postwar policy objectives such as full employment, economic growth, stable prices, and sound balance of payments are still to be secured. In some cases these policy objectives were abandoned by state managers as they placed their faith in market forces. In others new measures were taken to secure the old objectives in changed circumstances. In almost all cases states have become more involved in managing the process of internationalization itself in the hope of minimizing its harmful domestic repercussions and/or of securing maximum benefit to its own home-based transnational firms and banks. In turn this means that they must get involved in managing the process of internationalization and creating the most appropriate frameworks for it to proceed. Among the many activities included here are: introducing new legal forms for cross-national cooperation and strategic alliances, reforming the international currency and credit systems, promoting technology transfer, managing trade disputes, developing a new international intellectual property regime, or developing new forms of regulation for labour migration. This leads to the paradox that, as states lose control over the national economy, they are forced to enter the fray on behalf of their own multinationals.

Thirdly, as the dominant techno-economic paradigm shifts from Fordism to post-Fordism, the primary economic functions of states are redefined. Fordism was typically associated with a primary concern with demand management within national economies and with the generalization of mass consumption norms. This reflected the belief that Fordist mass production was supply-driven and could only be profitable when high levels of demand were maintained and markets for mass consumer durables expanded. The class compromise supporting the Fordist Keynesian welfare state also encouraged this pattern of economic intervention. But the transition to post-Fordism is prompting a reorientation of the state's primary economic functions. For the combination of the late Fordist trend towards internationalization and the post-Fordist stress on flexible production has encouraged states to focus on the supply-side problem of international competitiveness and to attempt to subordinate welfare policy to the demands of flexibility. In this sense we can speak of a shift from the Keynesian welfare state to the Schumpeterian 'workfare' state (cf. Jessop 1990b). This does not mean that the motley diversity of political regimes will disappear with the transition to post-Fordism. For the Schumpeterian 'workfare' state can take neo-liberal, neo-corporatist, and neo-statist forms depending on institutional legacies and the balance of political forces. But a general trend does seem to be emerging both in official discourse and in the de facto shifts in forms of state intervention.

Fourthly, as the forms of internationalization become more contentious and conflictual and competing strategies evolve around the triad powers, nation states must tackle not only the domestic repercussions of global restructuring but also the domestic problems emerging from the changing international balance of forces. There is a complex dialectic at work here. Alongside the trends towards globalization and the formation of supra-regional triad economies we can also see a re-emergence of regional and local economies within the nation-state. In certain respects this is associated with a 'hollowing out' of the nation-state as powers are delegated upwards to supra-regional or international bodies, downwards to regional or local states, or outwards to relatively autonomous cross-national alliances among local states with complementary interests (on these trends see, for example, Bell 1987; Dyson 1988; Sabel 1990; and Jessop 1992b). But this structural transformation is also associated with a continuing role for the nation-state in managing the changing balance of political forces entailed in the complex and contradictory process of globalization. For the nation-state is still the most significant site of struggle among competing global, triadic, supra-national, national, regional, and local forces; and social cohesion still depends on the state's capacities to manage these conflicts.

3.2. The state and competitiveness

In approaching the state's role in relation to competitiveness in a changing world economy we could logically address five issues. These are: a) the extent to which such changes derive from prior state activities and discourses and are reinforced by current actions and discourses; b) the repercussions of such changes on the state as an institutional ensemble endowed with a specific structural selectivity and strategic capacities and with a specific social and material basis; c) the state's capacities - both cognitive and organizational - to monitor and model these changes and to assess their implications for its activities and objectives; d) the state's capacities to guide these changes and promote them in the interests of structural competitiveness; and e) the official discourses which express the state's understanding of these other issues and re-orient its activities in the light of such changes. In dealing with the final issue, of course, we are examining how the state itself would answer the preceding questions as well as the strategic conclusions it draws from its answers.

In so framing these questions we assume that the state is best analyzed as a complex institutional ensemble whose capacities derive not only from its internal articulation but also from its linkages to forces beyond its boundaries. In contrast to many other accounts of state action, ours problematizes the boundaries and unity of the state as an apparatus endowed with capacities to act. We do not believe that state formation is a once-and-for-all process but argue that the state apparatus must be continually reconstituted in and through practices which endow its various (and changing) elements with a sufficient degree of internal cohesion and orient them to a common set of purposes. We relate such practices to a dominant state strategy to impose some coherence on its different parts (internal unity) and/or a dominant project to secure cohesion within the wider society (state project). In considering both aspects our approach also involves examining how state capacities are projected beyond its formal boundaries by connecting them to the micro-physics of power rooted in institutions, organizations, and interactions outside the state. State power is always and inevitably related to this 'micro-physics' but there are clearly wide variations in the extent to which the state can reflexively monitor and coordinate this dependence.

It is in this context that the changing conditions of global competition are important. For it is a crucial part of our argument that the conditions of competition have changed in ways that require a radical reorientation of state capacities and their coordination with the 'micro-physics' of power within the economy and civil society. This can be undertaken in different ways since there is no single state form or state strategy which is always and uniquely associated with successful competition. Thus liberal, corporatist, dirigiste strategies have all worked in some conditions, failed in others; strategies must be developed and adapted in relation to strategic capacities (a relation) and to changed conditions of competition. Moreover strategies which worked in the past may not work currently or be readily transferred to other cases or countries. Nonetheless, although there is a wide variety of possible strategies, a state's success in this regard depends on its having the appropriate form and capacities for a given strategy. This holds even for the apparently counter-intuitive case of the liberal, nightwatchman state. For a successful non-interventionist strategy depends on the state's capacity to insulate itself from external pressures to intervene and to restrict its own actions to those which maintain the general external conditions for free market forces. That liberal strategies do not always succeed and can fail because of the incapacity of a state to refrain from ad hoc and politically motivated interventions is exemplified below through the British case. Returning now to the main thrust of our argument we would add that state capacities to advance an accumulation strategy depend in turn on the state's second-order capacity to reflect upon and manage its capacities and to pursue strategies which secure its own internal unity. It is this which gives the political sphere its relative autonomy and means that one cannot treat politics simply as 'concentrated economics'. Indeed, the need to establish apparatus unity might well lead to policies which appear irrelevant or contradictory in relation to accumulation strategies. But, without a modicum of apparatus unity (which does not become so great as to inhibit a degree of flexibility), the state could not realize the political conditions needed to implement an accumulation strategy.

3.3. The state and strategy

Given our frequent references to strategy and strategic capacity, we should briefly define our terms. Our preferred definition of strategy involves more than purposeful action. In general it involves an overall vision of a desirable future state of affairs and a programmed path of actions to realize it. The more the pursuit of the strategy involves monitoring progress towards objectives and corresponding amendments to goals and/or means, the more reflexive it will be - especially where such reflexivity involves co-ordinating actions over different time horizons and in relation to different fields of action. In this sense it is possible for collective actors (e.g., firms, unions, states) as well as individuals to pursue strategies: the key requirement is the capacity to formulate a vision, to pursue actions related to it, and to monitor the results. Strategic capacity is nothing more (but also nothing less) than the ability to formulate and implement strategies. This can also be a property of societal systems (such as the economic or political system) as well as individuals or collective actors for, although systems as such are incapable of strategic calculation, they can be more or less conducive to effective strategizing among the individual and collective agents operating on their terrain. Indeed strategic capacity involves more than qualities of the agent considered in isolation in so far as such a capacity also reflects how agents are inserted into a wider action context. Thus the strategic capacity of a firm depends on the institutional and extra-institutional preconditions which enable the various agents within it to co-ordinate short-term incentives with long-term calculations and to subordinate their immediate self-interest to common objectives implied in the strategy. Likewise, as we have already noted, the strategic capacities of the state depend on its ability to project its power beyond its boundaries through linking up with the micro-physics of power in economy and society. And in both cases strategies must be adapted to the specific vulnerabilities of agents, systems, or other objects of action. It is in considering this adaptation that strategic capacity can be related to the ability to monitor changes in the environment and the conditions of strategic success and to learn from prior attempts to realize strategic objectives. And it is also here that one can assess how conducive different societal systems are to strategies to promote structural competitiveness.

There is a rich literature on corporate strategy but its practitioners have not extended their concepts to the state and its capacities. Our aim is to develop concepts of state strategy bearing on competitiveness and introduce our conclusions into discussion of corporate strategy. We are well aware that strategic capacity is not reducible to state capacity - even where the state has the primary role in strategy formation. One way to approach this is through the strategic selectivity of the state system. This can be defined in terms of the ways in which the specific organization of the state differentially privileges the access of some forces (representation) to formulate specific policies and secure their support within the state apparatus (internal articulation) and then to effectively implement these policies (intervention) in relation to a specific micro-physics of power (social and material bases of the state). All of these aspects must be related, of course, to the more general vulnerabilities of the targets of intervention. At stake in analyzing strategic selectivity is not only the specific institutional and organizational forms which characterize the state but also their strategic repercussions with regard both to the access of specific forces pursuing specific strategies to secure access to the state and to the strategies pursued in and through that access in relation to the wider society (see Jessop 1992b).

It is in this context that we can introduce concepts such as accumulation strategy and consider their implications for the state's role in accumulation. Just as firms may formulate and follow their own economic strategies alone or in concert with other firms, so too can states develop and pursue such strategies in relation to the national economy. Whilst the former strategies are usually analyzed in terms of forms of enterprise calculation and/or corporate strategy, the latter have been discussed elsewhere in terms of accumulation strategies. It is to these that we now briefly turn.

An accumulation strategy 'defines a specific economic "growth model" complete with its various extra-economic preconditions and also outlines a general strategy appropriate to its realization' (Jessop 1983). Thus the growth model envisaged therein must start out from the existing mode of growth and then specify how to consolidate that mode of growth and/or move to a different mode of growth. To avoid possible confusion here it should be noted that, whilst a growth model is essentially a strategic concept, a mode of growth (cf. Lipietz's term 'model of development') is more structural. For the latter term refers to the specific configuration of firms and industries in a given economic space and the modalities of their insertion into a broader (ultimately global) division of labour. In this sense the mode of growth reflects the competitive positioning (comparative and competitive advantages) of firms and sectors in the changing international division of labour and hence the position of national economies in the international hierarchy. This affects the changing balance between functional complementarities and antagonistic relations among the various economies involved in any given pluri-national productive system, i.e., how far their respective cyclical behaviours, structural crises, and general growth dynamics mesh to generate rather than block long-run growth in these national economies (cf. Aglietta 1982; Mistral 1986). For obvious reasons it also affects the prospects for domestic growth.

At any given time the mode of growth will reflect complex patterns of decline (due to competitive disadvantage), growth (due to competitive advantage), and recovery (due to effective restructuring of uncompetitive sectors). Whilst these issues are determined in the first instance by the productive circuit of capital (firm level factors), the macro-economic context is also important. It is here that the concept of structural competitiveness is so central to our understanding of growth dynamics. And this in turn points to the potential significance of state capacities and state action in promoting an accumulation strategy which enhances competitive advantage and thereby transforms the mode of growth. Indeed, as internationalization becomes an ever more dominant feature of capitalism, it is vital that accumulation strategies take account of the conditions making for structural competitiveness if they are to be successful. This is not to suggest a purely voluntaristic or decisionistic view of the state's role in accumulation - we have already noted how any strategy is conditioned both by the existing mode of growth and state capacities. It is to note that states can intervene to modify growth trajectories through skillful attention to the various social preconditions making for competitiveness.

4. Concluding remarks

This chapter has been concerned with general questions about changing forms of international competitiveness, the factors influencing increasing state concern with structural competitiveness, and how the state can be most usefully introduced into the analysis of competitiveness. Although this analysis has been developed from our interest in the changing role of the state in Britain and Scandinavia (see, for example, the studies in Jessop, Nielsen and Pedersen 1992), it has a much wider significance. Exactly the same pressures leading to growing concern with structural competitiveness and to the 'hollowing out' of the nation state can be found elsewhere in Europe, in North America, and East Asia. They are also increasingly relevant to the restructuring of the former COMECON economies. Accordingly we will now link our earlier remarks to the process of economic and political reform in Eastern Europe.

The international division of labour in which the Eastern European economies were previously involved under the dominance of the Soviet Union was not the product of pure market exchanges but was subordinate to decisive, centralized political calculation. The recent collapse of the Soviet economic empire has seriously aggravated the economic crises within individual Eastern European economies through the destruction or weakening of economic complementarities that once existed. They now find themselves deprived of old trading partners and with a pattern of specialization which is ill-adapted to their new international economic circumstances. Yet they are unable to insulate themselves from international competition and the resulting pressures for structural adjustment so that they could then either continue in the old way (which would be as politically unacceptable to the newly mobilized citizenry as, given the depth of crisis, it would be economically impossible) or else pursue some from of neo-mercantilist modernization strategy behind protectionist barriers. Nor can they meet the challenge of international competition from advanced capitalist economies head-on, however, since they are weak in relation to all four of the global trends noted above. For they lag behind in many key new technologies (the former Soviet Union is a partial exception here, especially in relation to military-industrial technologies); are insufficiently specialized to engage profitably in international (especially intra-industry) trade and typically have only cheap labour, raw materials, and some generic locational advantages to offer international investors; lack many of the key institutional as well as material conditions for flexible accumulation; and have only marginal significance in current circumstances for the creation of competitive regional economic blocs. In short, even if we discount the immediate, short-term problems involved on the road to the market, the medium-term prospects of the post-socialist economies are extremely daunting.

In this context the trajectories of the post-socialist economies will differ markedly from case to case. There are obvious differences in the advantages which individual economies (often at local or regional level and/or in regard to particular branches or sectors) can offer in the still emerging new international division of labour; and, in addition, the economic position in which they find themselves will be overdetermined by social and political developments which have their own independent logic. The prospects of retaining some control over their economic destiny depends on the capacities to sustain the coherence of the national economy in the face of growing economic and financial difficulties and the uneven impact of international competition. The key to this capacity can be found in the development of the skills, knowledge, institutions, and organizational structures both within the economy and its broader socio-political environment to adapt imported technologies to the new economic situation and national economies. In this context strategic economic and political alliances with selected partners in other economies (in the former COMECON bloc, on the fringes of the European Economic Community, and from the North American and East Asian regions) may prove helpful in creating the space and delivering some of the resources needed both for comprehensive social and economic modernization and for providing a temporary buffer against the competitive challenge from the dominant EC powers. But time is not on the side of this solution. Much more likely is the steadily growing balkanization of the post-socialist economies both individually and collectively and their selective integration-exclusion within a German-dominated European economic space.

Bibliography

Aglietta, M. (1982) 'World Capitalism in the Eighties', *New Left Review*, 136, 25-35.

Alic, J.A. (1987) 'Evaluating Industrial Competitiveness at the Office of Technology Assessment'. *Technology in Society*, 9 (1), 1-17.

Bell, D. (1987) 'The World and the United States in 2013', *Daedalus*, Summer, 1-33.

Best, Michael H. (1990) *The New Competition: Institutions of Industrial Restructuring*, Cambridge: Polity.

Casson, M. ed. (1983) *The Growth of International Business*, London: Allen and Unwin.

Colombo, U. (1988) 'The technology revolution and the restructuring of the global economy', in J.H. Muroyama and H.G. Stever, eds., *Globalization of Technology: international perspectives*, Washington DC: National Academy Press.

Contractor, F.J. and Lorange, P. (1988) *Cooperative Strategies in International Business*. Lexington, Mass: D.C. Heath.

Dertouzos, M., Lester, R.K., and Solow, R.M. (1989) *Made in America*, Cambridge, MA: MIT Press.

Dosi, G., Tyson, L.A., and Zysman, J. (1989) 'Trade, Technologies, and Development: a Framework for Discussing Japan', in C. Johnson, L.A. Tyson, and J. Zysman, eds., *Politics and Productivity: the real story of why Japan works*, New York: Ballinger, 1989, 3-38.

Dunning, J.H. (1988) *Multinationals, Technology and Competitiveness*. London: Unwin Hyman.

Dyson, K., ed., (1989) *Local Authorities and New Technologies: the European Dimension*, London: Croom Helm.

Ernst, D. and O'Connor, D. (1989) *Technology and Global Competition: the challenge for newly industrializing economies*. Paris: OECD.

European Commision (1986) 'An industrial Strategy for Europe', *European File*, 4/86.

Fagerberg, J. (1988) 'International competitiveness', *European Journal*, June.

Grahl, J. and Teague, P. (1990), *1992: the Big Market. The Future of the European Community*. London: Lawrence & Wishart.

Grou, P. (1986) *The Financial Structure of Multinational Capitalism*, Leamington Spa: Berg Publishers.

Hagedoorn, J. (1989) *The Dynamic Analysis of Innovation and Diffusion: a study in process control*. London: Pinter.

Hood, N. and Vahlne, J.E., eds., (1988) *Strategies in Global Competition*. London: Croom Helm.

Hughes, K.S. (1989) 'The changing dynamics of international technological competition', in D.B. Audretsch, L. Sleuwaegen, and H. Yamawaki, eds., *The Convergence of International and Domestic Markets*, Amsterdam: North-Holland, 269-94.

Jessop, B. (1983) 'Accumulation Strategies, State Forms, and Hegemonic Projects', *Kapitalistate 10*, 89-111.

Jessop, B. (1990a) *State Theory: Putting Capitalist States in their Place*, Cambridge: Polity.

Jessop, B. (1990b) 'After Thatcher', *New Statesman and Society*, November.

Jessop, B. (1992a), 'Fordism and Post-Fordism: a Critical Reformulation', in A.J. Scott and M.J. Storper, eds., *Pathways to Regionalism and Industrial Development*, London: Routledge, 43-65.

Jessop, B. (1992b) 'Veränderte Staatlichkeit: Changes in Statehood and State Projects', in D. Grimm, ed., *Staatsaufgaben*, Baden-Baden: Nomos Verlag (in press).

Jessop, B., Nielsen, K. and Pedersen, O.K. (1992) 'Structural Competitiveness and Strategic Capacities: the cases of Britain, Denmark, and Sweden' in S.E. Sjöstrand, ed., *Institutional Evolution and Change: Theory and Empirical Findings*, New York: Sharpe (in press).

Kaldor, N. (1987) 'The Effects of devaluations on trade in manufactures', in Idem, *Further Essays in Applied Economics*, London: Duckworth.

Leontief, W. (1954) 'Domestic production and foreign trade: the American capital position re-examined, *Proceedings of the American Philosophical Society*, 332-349.

Lipietz, A. (1987) *Mirages and Miracles*. London: Verso.

Mistral, J. (1986) 'Regime international et trajectoires nationales', in R. Boyer, ed., *Capitalismes fin de siècle*, Paris: PUF, 167-202.

Mytelka, L. (1987) The political economy of strategic partnering. Working paper. *Investment Canada*, November.

Ohmae, K. (1985) *Triad Power: the coming shape of global competition*. New York: Free Press.

Petrella, Riccardo (1990) 'Technology and the Firm', *Technology Analysis and Strategic Management*, 2 (2), 99-110.

Porter, M. (1990) *The Competitive Advantage of Nations*, London: Macmillan.

Sabel, C.F. (1990) 'The re-emergence of regional economies', in P.Q. Hirst and J. Zeitlin, eds., *Reversing Britain's industrial decline*, Leamington Spa: Berg, 17-70.

Schlieper, A. (1989) 'Case studies of Local Technology and Innovation Policies in West Germany: Success and Failure', in K. Dyson, ed., *Local Authorities and New Technologies: the European Dimension*, London: Croom Helm, 115-123.

STI Review (1986) 'Science, Technology and Competitiveness', *STI Review*, 1 (Autumn), 86-129.

Vonortas, N.S. (1990) 'Emerging Patterns of Multinational enterprise operations in developed market economies: evidence and policy'. *Review of Political Economy*, 2 (2), 188-220.

3 Institutional theory and the influence of foreign actors on reform in capitalist and post-socialist societies

John Campbell

Social scientists have recently offered two new conceptual frameworks to account for institutional transformations and major shifts in policy in Western political economies. Some researchers have shown that in the United States groups of organizational actors, including firms, unions, business associations, and state agencies, engage in a 'selection process' to solve their political-economic problems by searching for and selecting alternative institutional arrangements in collective, interactive, but not necessarily harmonious ways (Campbell, Hollingsworth and Lindberg 1991; Campbell and Lindberg 1990; 1991). Other scholars have argued that in Western Europe actors develop and engage in a 'discourse of reform' through which policy solutions are determined, often through negotiation among representatives of major social and political groups (Nielsen 1989; Nielsen and Pedersen 1989; 1991; 1990; Pedersen 1990; see also Katzenstein 1985; Schmitter and Lehmbruch 1979; Streeck and Schmitter 1985). These two lines of inquiry are similar enough that theorists have argued recently that a discourse of market reform is an integral part of the selection process currently underway in post-socialist societies in which actors are trying to reorganize their political economies (Jessop, Hausner and Nielsen 1991).

Central to the idea of a discourse of reform is the understanding that domestic actors struggle to choose from a variety of competing policies and institutional options - a struggle in which economists and other experts often play an important advisory role in identifying problems, proposing solutions, and making final choices (Nielsen and Pedersen 1990, 1991; Pedersen 1990). However, although the problems identified by these actors are occasionally of international origin, such as exchange rate, balance of payments, or trade difficulties associated with the openness of national economies, proponents of this view rarely consider how foreign actors either provide new agenda options for discourse or influence the subsequent selection process.[1] Such domestic myopia characterizes many models of institutional and domestic policy change that focus exclusively on advanced capitalist societies (e.g., Campbell and Lindberg 1991; Pedersen 1990; but see Ikenberry 1988).

Overlooking the role of foreign influence is an important omission especially if one wants to understand the discourse of market reform currently unfolding in post-socialist societies. After all, the institutional and policy choices available to domestic elites in less developed countries have often been restricted by the dependence of their countries on more advanced societies for trade and resources (Baran 1957; Evans 1985; Moran 1974). Similarly, insofar as post-socialist countries rely heavily on the West for capital, technology, expertise, and export opportunities, the West will influence the range of models of capitalism from which these countries choose (Campbell 1992).

This paper synthesizes recent institutional theories in organizational analysis, on the one hand, and political sociology and political science, on the other, to develop a model that begins to explain how foreign actors influence the discourse of reform. This paper does not suggest that we abandon the concept of 'discourse of reform', or that we reduce explanations of policy and institutional choices to the influence of foreign actors. Instead, the argument offered here is intended to complement the existing literature on the discourse of reform.

Following organizational theory, I will first identify three processes through which foreign institutional and policy models can penetrate the domestic discourse of reform. I refer to these processes collectively as institutional isomorphism. Second, drawing on literature in political sociology and political science, I will argue that the influence of these isomorphic processes is mediated by already existing domestic political and institutional conditions. By mediation I mean that the isomorphic pressure created by foreign actors is modified to a degree by domestic conditions, much as a prism refracts light that passes through it.

I will illustrate these arguments primarily with examples of the international dissemination of Keynesianism and U.S. organizational practices in business during the mid-twentieth century. Just as the spread of these paradigmatic approaches to economic policy and organizational practice were central to the rise of Fordism as a dominant institutional framework in advanced capitalist countries (Piore and Sabel 1984), the spread of Western policy and organizational models to Eastern Europe and the former Soviet Union will surely have a strong impact on the development of new institutional arrangements there. Thus, the final section of the paper explores the implications of isomorphism and mediation for the reform of post-socialist societies. In the absence of systematic data, my argument is necessarily speculative, especially for the post-socialist countries. Nevertheless, this will not detract substantially from the chief goal of this paper which is to suggest how to improve our conceptual understanding of the discourse of reform.

1. Institutional isomorphism

Contrary to those who argue that organizations develop the most technically efficient structures and practices in order to compete successfully for scarce resources (e.g., Chandler 1977; 1990; Williamson 1985), organization theorists have argued that organizations also develop their formal characteristics in order to gain political power and institutional legitimacy within their social environments (DiMaggio and Powell 1983) - occasionally even when this conflicts with efficiency considerations (Meyer and Rowan 1977). In short, organizations are concerned with social as well as economic fitness.[2] Because some organizational characteristics are more legitimate and politically acceptable than others within an environment, organizations within the same environment tend to develop similar characteristics. The process by which this homogenization occurs is called 'isomorphism' of which there are three frequently recognized types: coercive, normative, and mimetic (DiMaggio and Powell 1983). All three are useful for specifying how foreign political and economic actors influence the domestic discourse of reform.

By coercive isomorphism theorists mean a process by which a less powerful organization acquires the characteristics of a more powerful one from which it needs resources. Either the more powerful organization directly imposes its structural form and practices on the subordinate one, or the subordinate one is driven to acquire the characteristics of the more powerful organization in order to gain its approval and support. For example, Thomas Edison's firm, the Edison Electric Light Company, sought to create a market for electricity in the United States in the early 1880s. Edison's American and British financiers, led by J.P. Morgan, wanted to develop a decentralized system where residential and individual users produced their own electricity with small generators purchased from the Edison Company. Edison preferred to build a system of central generating stations that would sell electricity to users, but, with few exceptions, such as the famous Pearl Street Station in New York, was prevented from doing so by the Morgan financial group. Not until Edison was able to enlist the financial support of German banks and manufacturing firms, including German General Electric (AEG) and Siemens and Halske, who favoured centralized economic institutions in general and Edison's model in particular, was his company able to break free of Morgan's grasp and pursue the central station dream through the formation of Edison General Electric - a syndicate that manufactured and sold large-scale electrical generating equipment to local utility companies. Thus, the organization of the U.S. market for electricity was determined largely by those who financed the production of generating equipment (Granovetter 1990; McGuire, Granovetter and Schwartz 1990).

Although initially identified at the level of organizations within national economies, coercive isomorphism also operates at the international level (Djelic 1991). The U.S. federal government, for instance, pressured German authorities after the Second World War to adopt antitrust legislation similar to that in the United States in an effort to transform the German economy from one organized through cartels to one based on the U.S. model of large, autonomous, multidivisional corporations. Despite opposition from German industrial lobbies favouring cartels, the Anglo-American authorities, whose influence was bolstered by the German government's dependence on the Marshall Plan and other U.S. funds for economic reconstruction, prevailed and legislation was adopted in 1957 to restrict cartels. Moreover, several large industrial firms and banks were broken up at the order of Allied authorities (Djelic 1991; Shonfield 1965: 240). Similarly, to open competition in Japan after the war the American occupation authorities forced the Japanese Diet to rescind an earlier law restricting the spread of large retail stores (McCraw and O'Brien 1986: 108), and orchestrated land reforms that broke down the old landlord system in agriculture and increased the number of small, owner-cultivated plots (Reich, Endo and Timmer 1986: 164). In short, U.S. authorities were able to quickly push their own institutional models through the discourse of reform in these countries and into practice because domestic actors depended on them for financial resources and political support.

Two caveats are in order. First, coercive isomorphism often involves conflict and struggle. Edison deliberately sought to shift his dependence from Morgan to German finance capital in order to put himself in a position where he was dependent for resources on firms that shared his organizational vision. In other words, as long as alternative resources are available, subordinate organizations may be able through struggle to select their relations of dependence and have some influence over the process of coercive isomorphism. Second, despite the 1957 law the German economy is still more cartelized than other Western economies, particularly the United States (Lash and Urry 1987). Indeed, a modicum of cartelization and concentration in manufacturing and banking persisted and eventually grew despite Anglo-American efforts to the contrary (Shonfield 1965: 240- 50; Zysman 1983: 252-54). Similarly, in 1956, just four years after the departure of the occupation authorities, Japan restored the original law protecting small shopkeepers from the encroachment of large retailers (McCraw and O'Brien 1986: 108) and also rescinded several tax and fiscal regulations imposed by the Americans (Rukstad 1986: 312). In addition, although the occupation legally dissolved the pre-war intermarket business groups (zaibatsu), after the Americans left the Japanese government successfully encouraged the emergence of similar groups, such as Mitsubishi, Mitsui, and Sumitomo, that consisted of large firms from several unrelated industries linked through interlocks, stock holdings, and less formal interpersonal ties (Hamilton and Biggart 1988: 78; Orru, Biggart and Hamilton 1991). I will discuss later why coercive isomorphism was only partially successful in these cases. For now the point is that, contrary particularly to those versions of institutional theory that offer 'path dependent' models of institutional change (e.g., Powell 1991), the outcomes of coercive isomorphism are not irreversible.

Normative isomorphism is a process through which organizations come to resemble each other via the common education and professionalization of organizational elites, and via the growth of professional networks that span organizations and facilitate the exchange of information about different organizational models. For example, Fligstein (1990) argued that intercorporate relations in the United States were transformed during the last century from predatory trade practices, cartels and horizontal integration, to vertical integration, to product differentiation and diversification, and finally to conglomerate mergers by the spread of different managerial strategies of corporate control across firms. In the presence of new antitrust laws, the conglomerate form, for instance, spread after the

Second World War as managers who were trained in finance and who favoured short-term profits replaced those with backgrounds in sales and marketing who had preferred long-term differentiation and diversification strategies. The dissemination of new organizational models through trade and professional associations was an important part of this process (Fligstein 1991: 319-20).

At the international level, new models of corporate organization and management were transmitted from the United States to France during the 1950s as the French government created 'productivity missions' that sent French employers, engineers, managers, union representatives, economists, psychologists, and sociologists to the United States to learn how to better organize French business practices. As a result, French firms eventually adopted many American methods and organizational forms, particularly the large multidivisional firm - a model that French policy makers saw as having the additional political advantage of lying between the old inefficient form of family capitalism and the distasteful possibility of state-run socialism (Boltanski 1990). Similarly, the dissemination of Keynesianism to the policy discourse in France was facilitated to an extent by the Keynesian economists sent by the United States to advise the French government after the war (Hirschman 1989; Rosanvallon 1989: 186).

The French case also illustrates the process of mimetic isomorphism whereby organizations that are simply not sure what to do when confronted with extreme environmental uncertainty and limited information imitate the practices of other organizations that they perceive as being particularly legitimate or successful. The French chose to emulate U.S. organizational practices in part because the United States was the most successful economic model to be found after the war - a time during which the French government sought to reorganize its economy through the promotion of key industries and 'national champions' (Djelic 1991). Japanese modernizers did much the same thing during the late nineteenth century when they modelled their legal and law enforcement system on the French; their navy and postal system on the British; and their banking and educational system on the United States (DiMaggio and Powell 1983). Ironically, today U.S. firms that face intense international competition, volatile markets, and rapidly changing technologies are looking to the Japanese for new organizational models, such as R&D consortia in semiconductors and biotechnology and quality control circles in automobiles, to help them cope with the environment as effectively as the Japanese (DiMaggio and Powell 1983; Powell 1987: 73).

In fact, the French case shows how all three types of isomorphism may operate simultaneously to influence domestic discourses of reform. In addition to the normative and mimetic processes discussed above, the adoption of American organizational practices was partly inspired by Marshall Plan authorities from the United States who wanted to avoid communist and fascist alternatives in France, and who required that a group of French managers be educated to American techniques in exchange for U.S. funds to the French government (Boltanski 1990: 344) an example of coercive isomorphism. Similarly, acceptance of Keynesian advisers from the United States by the French was partly tied to Marshal Plan funding after 1947 (Rosanvallon 1989: 186). Indeed, this case illustrates how these isomorphic processes may be mutually reinforcing.

2. Institutional mediation

Recently organization theorists have recognized that the ability of actors to define reigning organizational forms in an environment is not always as straightforward as most descriptions of institutional isomorphism suggest. Instead, they argue that these processes will be influenced by the structure of the state itself, and recommend that analysts who subscribe to the theory of institutional isomorphism pay close attention to the work of political scientists and sociologists who are developing their own brand of institutional theory - one that focuses on the state as an actor in its own right and as a set of political and legal institutions that constitute an important part of the environment within which other organizations operate (Scott 1987: 509).[3]

Although only a few researchers have tried to blend these two versions of institutional theory (e.g., Fligstein 1990), several scholars have demonstrated how domestic political and economic arrangements influence the agendas of political discourse by limiting the range of options available to policy makers (e.g., Campbell 1988; Evans, Rueschemeyer and Skocpol 1985; Gourevitch 1986; Hall 1986; Katzenstein 1977). This suggests that the ability of foreign actors to influence the domestic discourse of reform through isomorphic processes is itself mediated by another set of institutional forces: the arrangement of existing national political economies of which there are several important dimensions.[4]

2.1. Political institutions

For example, Margaret Weir (1989; Weir and Skocpol 1985) argued that political institutions influenced the degree to which Keynesianism spread from Britain to other countries during the late 1920s and 1930s. Keynesianism, she claimed, quickly became an important contending policy model in the United States because the state apparatus consisted of a fragmented array of agencies, including several that were created during the New Deal, that afforded Keynesians access to the policy-making process. Thus, when a second major economic slump hit in 1937, Keynesianism was well-positioned within the federal bureaucracy to assume a prominent place on the agenda over which policy makers debated in trying to revitalize the economy. Indeed, Roosevelt's response to the recession in 1938 was based largely on the recommendations of Keynesians located throughout the federal bureaucracy. However, because the U.S. state also consisted of many powerful agencies, such as the Treasury Department and Budget Office, that were dominated by non-Keynesians who opposed deficit spending, the status of Keynesianism remained somewhat ambiguous, even during its post-World War II heyday. Indeed, after the 1964 tax cut, perhaps the peak of Keynesianism in the United States, but especially during the stagflation of the 1970s, rational expectations and supply-side theorists attacked Keynesian orthodoxy from various locations within the state apparatus, and with increasing success (Martin 1991; Salant 1989). Of course, this situation was exacerbated by the fact that neither the Republican nor Democratic parties entirely embraced a full-employment policy. Even the Democrats were frequently split over the issue due to the wavering support of Southern and agricultural interests within the party (Weir 1989). In sum, a fragmented state apparatus and the lack of a political party programmatically committed to Keynesianism influenced the degree to which this new macroeconomic policy model was available and subsequently utilized.

In contrast, Weir argued that Sweden adopted a more full-employment oriented brand of Keynesianism, and did so by 1933 - years before Keynesianism was accepted in the United States or Britain - not only because of the Social Democratic Party's dedication to these principles, but also because Royal Commissions, advisory boards, and a variety of other institutional mechanisms within the state apparatus had long permitted economists, experts, academics, and actors representing all the major social groups and political parties to raise alternative policy models and negotiate about them in the policy-making discourse. On the other hand, despite the intellectual presence of Keynes himself, it took much longer for policy makers in Britain to take Keynesianism seriously due largely to the Treasury's more orthodox views and its influence over the civil service through its ability to oversee expenditures for administration, staff, and economic and social programmesmes. Indeed, through its control over the civil service the Treasury effectively prevented Keynesians from having much influence in policy discourse until the mid 1940s - even when the Labour Party was in power in 1929 (Weir 1989, 55; Weir and Skocpol 1985, 127-28). The point is that the degree to which control over the policy agenda is centrally controlled and insulated within the state has an important effect on the extent to which the discourse of reform is permeable to new ideas of foreign or, for that matter, domestic origin.

2.2. Political coalitions

Others have suggested that cross-class and cross-sector political coalitions determine the composition of political agendas and ultimately policy outcomes. Notably, Peter Gourevitch (1986; 1989) argued that although state structures were important in channelling the power of economic interests, the primary vehicle that transported Keynesianism to the political agenda and into practice in different countries was the ability of labour and farmers to form political alliances, occasionally with sympathetic heterodox business groups, in support of such policies. In Sweden, the famous 1932 'cow trade' between the Social Democrats and the Agrarian Party created an opportunity for serious consideration of demand stimulus techniques. Similarly, the creation of Roosevelt's New Deal coalition of labour, agricultural, and progressive business groups helped elevate Keynesianism to a prominent place on the political agenda in the United States where it was often the macroeconomic policy of choice from 1938 until the mid 1970s. In Britain, by contrast, international business interests, particularly financial interests in the City, were strong, agriculture was politically weak, and labour was not very interested in demand stimulus policies until the 1940s. As a result, the necessary coalition failed to materialize and British policy makers failed to seriously consider Keynesianism until the Second World War.

Although this analytic approach focuses more on policy outcomes than on the initial generation of discourse agendas, as do those who are concerned with the impact of political institutions, such as Weir, it is clear that in some cases politicians are encouraged to submit new policy models to the discourse process at the encouragement of representatives from different classes and sectors of the economy. Indeed, one reason that neo-liberalism appeared on the political agenda and altered the terrain of debate in the United States during the late 1970s was that members of the business community, including capital-intensive manufacturers and multinational corporations that had traditionally supported the Democratic Party's brand of Keynesianism, began to favour more conservative policies. This was largely due to their shift from being 'price makers' to 'price takers' as international competition intensified and made it difficult for them to pass along the costs associated with regulatory and welfare policies to consumers through higher prices (Ferguson and Rogers 1986: Ch. 3). More recently, organized business interests in Sweden have pushed neo-liberalism back into the discourse of reform (Pestoff 1991).

2.3. Economic institutions

Domestic economic institutions also mediate the degree to which foreign actors are able to shape the discourse of reform - at least on a permanent basis. Again, Germany provides a good illustration. Although U.S. advisers were inclined to persuade politicians in the Federal Republic after World War II that they should adopt Keynesianism, their efforts were relatively unsuccessful. One reason was that the German economy had consisted for decades of highly organized industrial structures, such as cartels and informal networks among private actors, that were inimical to Keynesian-style state intervention (Allen 1989). Even when the Allied authorities dismantled these formal structures, they often re-emerged. For example, as part of their general effort to decentralize economic power, the Allies tried to impose the principle of 'state banking' where each bank was only permitted to operate in one German *Land*. However, by 1950 the Deutsche and Dresdner Banks had re-established control over virtually all of their old national branches because German policy makers, having to rebuild their devastated economy and defend against the military threat to the east, turned to the remaining informal network of banking elites who knew how to efficiently mobilize and allocate capital through centralized means and who moved quickly to do so when asked (Dyson 1986: 123).

Similarly, in Japan part of the occupation strategy for dismantling the old zaibatsu involved severing the interlocks that connected commercial, finance, and industrial capital. Yet close coordination between big banks and their major customers soon re-emerged. In part, this was an artifact of state policy that encouraged banks to lend heavily to selected industries, but it was also due to the fact that well-developed capital markets did not exist. Indeed, during the pre-war era there was little need for capital markets because much finance was provided by the big zaibatsu banks. As a result, when finance capital was needed after the war, it was natural and easy for companies to mobilize their old, but now informal, contacts and re-establish their links with banks (Eccleston 1986: 64-70).[5] In sum, first, existing economic institutions may dampen the influence of foreign actors on the domestic discourse of reform, as occurred in the case of Keynesianism in Germany. Second, the residue of recently dismantled institutions may in the long-run reverse the influence of foreign actors, as occurred in the cases of German and Japanese banking.

It is worth noting that the relatively limited adoption of Keynesian principles by the Germans, and to an extent the Japanese, was also due in part to the fact that the dominant occupation elites from the United States were members of the military who were not strongly committed to Keynesianism. In contrast, the U.S. advisers sent to France and Italy, where Keynesianism was more fully embraced after the war, were usually Keynesian-trained economists (Hirschman 1989). Thus, normative isomorphism also had important effects on these outcomes.

2.4. Historical legacies

The resurrection of economic institutions suggests that historical legacies also mediate the influence of foreign actors on the domestic discourse of reform. In their analysis of the development of the post-occupation Japanese economy, Gary Hamilton and Nicole Biggart found that the Japanese state orchestrated the return of the large intermarket business groups, reminiscent of the zaibatsu, not simply because policy makers believed that this was the most efficient way to organize production, but because it was an organizational form that was deeply rooted in traditions of loyalty, decentralization, paternalism, and cooperation that dated to the preindustrial organization of Japanese families and communities. Indeed, the intermarket business group was an organizational form dedicated to cooperation within the group and in which each member was responsible for the welfare of other firms subordinate to it. After the war, when the public's confidence in the state was shaky, policy makers pursued this approach to legitimize their economic interventions (Hamilton and Biggart 1988; Orru, Biggart and Hamilton 1991: 373-76). Likewise, another reason why German policy makers resisted Keynesianism was their perception that it would trigger inflation and increasing state intervention in a country whose memories of hyperinflation during the 1920s and then strong Nazi state control remained vivid (Allen 1989).

3. Implications for post-socialist societies

To summarize briefly, the literature exploring the processes by which political and economic actors select alternative policies and institutional arrangements through a discourse of reform has neglected the potential influences of foreign actors. Two versions of institutional theory can be blended to help rectify this situation. First, concepts from the institutionalism of organizational analysis can be used to understand the isomorphic processes by which foreign actors influence the domestic discourse of reform. Second, concepts from the institutionalism of political science and political sociology help us understand how the political and economic institutions, political coalitions, and historical legacies that exist within a country mediate the extent to which isomorphic pressures actually transform national political economies and convince policy makers to adopt new policy models.

The extent to which these processes are occurring in Eastern Europe and the former Soviet Union is not entirely clear. However, anecdotal evidence suggests that the model outlined here has some merit in the post-socialist context. First, isomorphic pressure is certainly being exerted on post-socialist countries by the West, particularly for neo-liberal alternatives. The European Community (EC), International Monetary Fund (IMF), World Bank and several Western governments have already demanded neoliberal policy and structural changes by post-socialist governments as a quid pro quo for trade and cooperation agreements. When change is not fast enough or of the right kind, aid is withheld, as it was by the EC from Rumania in 1990 (Gowan 1991/1992) and by the IMF from Poland in 1991 (Engelberg 1992). Similarly, Western governments, the OECD, IMF, World Bank, and EC have furnished post-socialist countries with dozens of experts to introduce Western policy models into the discourse of reform and to offer advice about how to implement these models (Gowan 1991/1992).

Second, domestic conditions appear to be mediating the effects of these isomorphic pressures. For instance, in late 1991 the so-called Group of Seven, that is, the United States, Japan, Germany, Britain, France, Italy, and Canada, offered the Soviet republics a

$1 billion loan and agreed to postpone another $3.6 billion in payments on the Soviet Union's foreign debt, if the republics agreed to undertake a complete macroeconomic and structural adjustment programmes, supervised by the IMF, that would include reducing massive budget deficits, cutting public expenditures, dropping price controls, restricting monetary growth, and cooperating with each other to overcome their economic problems. However, four republics, including the Ukraine, Azerbaijan, Georgia, and Uzbekistan, refused to sign the agreement for political reasons. Leaders in the Ukraine and Uzbekistan faced elections in the near future that made it difficult for them to agree to the accord. Leaders in Azerbaijan and Georgia had to deal with other internal political problems that prevented them from signing. In response, British and U.S. representatives to the talks threatened sanctions against the republics that refused the agreement and warned that holdouts would receive no economic assistance (Quinn-Judge 1991). In effect, the Group of Seven exerted coercive isomorphic pressure by offering economic aid for structural change in the Soviet republics. However, the Group's success varied, at least in the short term, according to differences in the internal political situations of the republics.

It is particularly difficult to speculate about how indigenous institutions and politics will mediate the external isomorphic pressures post-socialist countries will face because these institutions and politics are undergoing substantial change themselves. For example, given the strength of the Solidarity movement and the tendency toward neo-corporatist interest representation that emerged in Poland after 1980 (Ost 1990), one might have expected that the post-socialist government in Poland would have avoided in large part the neo-liberal policies favoured by the IMF and other foreign creditors. Instead, the Solidarity government embraced these policies. Whether the government's actions reflected temporary domestic political and institutional instability, or simply the overwhelming need for foreign economic assistance is not clear. Similarly, whether such harsh austerity policies hold in the face of strikes and other forms of protest remains to be seen (e.g., Hausner 1991). However, the point is that the isomorphic influences of foreign actors may be greater in the present period, when domestic institutions and political coalitions are in flux, than they will be later, when these factors have solidified.

If the model of institutional isomorphism applies in the post-socialist context, then it matters a great deal where Eastern Europe and the former Soviet Union get their capital, finance, technology, and expertise. If they get it from the United States, then one would expect them to develop political economic arrangements similar to those of the United States, such as large corporate hierarchies, weak unions, the absence of peak associations, limited bargaining at the national level over wages and prices, state intervention restricted primarily to regulatory and other property rights actions, and other features of neo-liberalism. However, because U.S. economic hegemony has eroded over the last two decades, these countries will also rely heavily on other sources of aid, particularly Japan and Germany. To the extent that aid comes from Japan, these countries would be inclined to develop vertical subcontracting rather than vertical integration among firms, long-term working relationships between banks and large firms within intermarket groups, weak labour unions, and the presence of some indicative planning by the state. If they get resources from Germany, then they would tend to emulate a more corporatist model with a stronger role for organized labour, at least at the firm or industry level, close ties between banks and firms, limited state intervention, but the development of relatively substantial welfare programmess. Whether Scandinavian countries will provide aid and, thus, facilitate the development of institutions prone to negotiation among business, labour, and other social groups is unclear.

On the other hand, insofar as the political economies in all of these Western countries are moving in neo-liberal or at least post-Fordist directions (Lash and Urry 1987; Streeck 1991), institutional outcomes in post-socialist countries may tend to converge, particularly if all of these countries receive substantial aid from the same international sources, such as the IMF or World Bank that favour neo-liberalism. In fact, others have noted that financial dependence on these international institutions in the past has promoted political isomorphism among nation-states in other parts of the world (Meyer 1987, 56). However, the tendency toward convergence across post-socialist countries should not be overstated precisely because domestic political and institutional arrangements will mediate the impacts of these endogenous influences. Indeed, although several post-socialist countries have embarked on privatization programmes with the encouragement of Western actors, the manner in which privatization is proceeding varies dramatically depending on the domestic situation in each country (Stark 1992).

In any case, sources of external resources may vary across economic sectors. 'Parallel investment strategies' may develop where Western investors in post-socialist societies seek investment outlets that are similar to those they have already exploited back home. Japanese capital may invest in electronics or automobiles, German capital may invest in machine tools, chemicals, and banking, and U.S. capital may invest in durable consumer goods industries. Thus, there is reason to believe that each post-socialist economy will not be characterized as typically neo-liberal, corporatist, negotiated, enterprise-group based, and so on. Rather, different sectors will take on different characteristics, as has occurred in other countries, including the United States, which demonstrates far more institutional diversity across sectors than its common neo-liberal characterization suggests (Campbell et al., 1991). Furthermore, insofar as actors in post-socialist countries are able to select between different sources of capital, technology, and expertise, as Edison did at the turn of the century, they will be able to have more control over these isomorphic processes and, in turn, will be able to manipulate them to serve the interests of dominant domestic political coalitions and elites.

However, the influence of foreign actors on the discourse of market reform in post-socialist countries need not result simply from coercive isomorphism. Managers in post-socialist industries may try to emulate the successes of their Western counterparts in ways that lead to mimetic isomorphism, as occurred in post-war France. Perhaps because the Japanese and Poles share an interest in producing steel and automobiles, Poland will be more likely to adopt the Japanese model in these sectors than the British, Scandinavian, or U.S. models insofar as the Japanese lead the Western field in these sectors. Additionally, to the extent that professional networks are already emerging between post-socialist countries and the West, such as the week-long conference between Soviet and American economists at Harvard during the summer of 1991, normative isomorphism will also come into play. Indeed, professional contacts with economists, such as Jeffrey Sachs and his associates, as well as the other Western policy advisers previously noted have already been instrumental in pushing neo-liberal macroeconomic policies to the forefront of the political agenda in Poland (Etzioni 1991).

If the model suggested here is correct, it also implies that the outcomes of the economic transformations in post-socialist countries are not necessarily going to be the most technically efficient. First, although the international economy may be moving toward greater post-Fordist flexibility, a model that many scholars suggest is a more efficient way to organize economic activity given the current volatility of world markets and technology (e.g., Piore and Sabel 1984; Powell 1987), isomorphic relations with the United States or Britain, countries that are less inclined toward flexible institutions than others, including Germany, Italy, and Japan, may induce post-socialist countries to adopt relatively backward Fordist practices. This may occur either because these countries are forced to do so by lenders, or because they choose to do so in order to attract foreign resources in the first place. Indeed, Poland's decision to follow the advice of Jeffrey Sachs and other neo-liberal economists from the United States and implement 'shock therapeutic' austerity policies may be a case in point. However, actors in post-socialist countries may also select inefficient Western models because these are the ones that they have been exposed to the most through their professional contacts with the West, or simply because they perceive them as being intrinsically desirable.[6]

A second reason why technically inefficient economic practices may dominate post-socialist societies is that historical and institutional legacies will linger and impede more efficient outcomes. The importance of such legacies is being demonstrated now in Eastern Europe where, for example, houses, apartments, land, and factories are being returned to those who owned them prior to their confiscation by the communist regimes - a process that is probably fair and otherwise socially desirable, but not necessarily the most economically efficient (Etzioni 1991). Indeed, attitudes of social justice and egalitarianism, and deep-rooted expectations about guarantied jobs and social welfare services continue to guide economic and political behaviour in Eastern Europe. In Poland, for example, some enterprise managers have agreed to take their firms private at artificially low prices in exchange for guarantied jobs and pay (Etzioni 1991). Similarly, because citizens have grown accustomed to free medical care and subsidized prices for medicines, social unrest has developed in connection with announcements that some health care would be marketized. Furthermore, those concerned about preserving social benefits for employees and preserving institutions of worker self-government have resisted privatization. Indeed, the Mazowiecki government in Poland failed to generate enough support to reform such industries as mining, metallurgy, and rail and city transportation (Indraszkiewicz 1991). Whether technical efficiency should be the primary objective of post-socialist transformations is, of course, a question beyond the scope of this paper.

4. Conclusion

I have suggested that two versions of institutional theory can be synthesized to provide a new perspective from which to view the discourse of reform. On the one hand, the model offered here complements the concept of the discourse of reform. On the other hand, it diverges with most of the regulation theory that informs recent attempts to extend the concept to the post-socialist situation (e.g., Jessop, Hausner and Nielsen 1991). Many regulation theorists suggest that institutional forms derive fundamentally from either the commodity relation, the labour capital relation, or some interaction of the two (Boyer 1990: p.13). I have suggested that institutional forms also 'derive' from the actions of actors engaged in a variety of additional political and cultural relations associated with the state, political coalitions, informal residues of past institutions, and lingering cultural traditions. Although these other factors may be related to the economic relationships that lie at the heart of regulation theory, once established these additional factors exert independent effects on the process of institutional transformation that cannot be reduced to commodity or capital-labour relations. Nevertheless, this does not mitigate the fact that the argument presented in this paper is a friendly amendment to the literature on the discourse of reform, or that there may be ways to integrate institutional and regulation theories (e.g., Delorme 1990).

Of course, substantial empirical research is required to demonstrate the usefulness of the scheme presented here for understanding the transformation of post-socialist societies. This could involve the development of detailed historical comparisons of institutional reforms as they occur in specific industries common to several post-socialist societies. One might construct detailed case studies of the development of financial, manufacturing, agricultural, health care, or other industries found in Poland, Hungary, and Czechoslovakia, for example, where infusions of foreign capital, technology, and expertise is likely, or has already started. Through such studies one could determine how foreign resources influence emerging institutional arrangements in each sector; whether these influences vary according to which foreign sources provide the resources; how indigenous political and economic institutions, political coalitions, and historical legacies, in each country facilitate or dampen foreign influences; and whether previously established informal property rights and cultural beliefs influence this process. After all, empirical research is the only way we can determine for sure how useful the ideas suggested here are for understanding institutional and policy transformations in either the East or West.

Notes

[1]On the rare occasions when foreign actors are mentioned, such as the ability of the Organization of Economic Cooperation and Development (OECD) to 'propagate' alternative institutional models, there is virtually no discussion of the mechanisms whereby these externally given models enter domestic agendas of discourse, or whether foreign actors influence which model is finally selected (e.g., Nielsen 1989: 300).

[2]For elaborations on this argument, see Scott (1987) and the essays in Powell and DiMaggio (1991) and Thomas, Meyer, Ramirez and Boli (1987).

[3]For extended comparisons between the institutional theory of organizational analysis, described above, and the new institutional theories of political science (e.g., March and Olson 1984; 1989) and economics (e.g., North 1990; Williamson 1985), see DiMaggio and Powell (1991).

[4]Although definitions of institutions are often vague (Jepperson 1991) and there is some conceptual overlap between the organizational and political versions of institutional theory (Scott 1987), organizational theorists tend to view institutions as the shared belief systems that shape organizational structures and practices. Thus, they are often concerned with understanding the phenomenological process of institutionalization whereby new belief systems come to be accepted and guide organizational activity (e.g., DiMaggio and Powell 1983; Meyer 1987; Meyer, Boli and Thomas 1987; Meyer and Rowan 1977). In contrast, political- economic theorists tend to view institutions from a structuralist perspective as sets of formally routinized and enduring patterns of behaviour that are associated with certain functional arenas within society, such as the realm of political or economic activity, and that restrict the choices available to actors operating within those institutions (Scott 1987, 499). For example, so far as the state is concerned, the policy-making process is constrained by the rules of procedure governing elections and policy formation, the regulatory, fiscal, and monetary capacities available to governments for policy implementation, and the relative balance of power among political parties, different governmental agencies, social classes, and interest groups (Skocpol 1985). In short, organizational analysts view institutions as cultural rules that give rise to formal organizations; political-economic analysts view institutions as the arrangement and structure of formal organizations themselves. For further discussion of these issues see Scott (1987) and DiMaggio and Powell (1991).

[5]The resurrection of German and Japanese financial institutions through the mobilization of long-standing informal networks during critical periods in each country's history supports those who have argued that during times of high uncertainty and economic volatility actors resort to relationships based on trust and familiarity to weather the storm - even in the most competitive markets where neoclassical theory would predict precisely the opposite response (Baker 1984).

[6]Assuming that Fordist institutional models have become technically inefficient, the adoption of these models by post-socialist actors represents a good example of what Meyer and Rowan (1977) called the acceptance of 'rational myths,' that is, organizational forms and practices that are recognized as having prestige, high ceremonial value, and legitimacy, regardless of their efficiency. Organizations often adopt rational myths, they argued, to obtain loans, donations, or investments from other organizations in their environment.

Bibliography

Allen, C. (1989) 'The Underdevelopment of Keynesianism in the Federal Republic of Germany', in P.A. Hall, ed., *The Political Power of Economic Ideas*, Princeton: Princeton University Press, 263-89.

Baker, W. (1984) 'The Social Structure of a National Securities Market',

American Journal of Sociology, 34 (4), 59-82.
Baran, P.B. (1957) *The Political Economy of Growth*. New York: Monthly Review Press.
Boltanski, L. (1990) 'Visions of American Management in Postwar France', in Zukin and DiMaggio, eds., *Structures of Capital*, 343-72.
Boyer, R. (1991) *The Regulation School: A Critical Introduction*. New York: Columbia University Press.
Campbell, J.L. (1988) *Collapse of an Industry: Nuclear Power and the Contradictions of U.S. Policy*. Ithaca, NY: Cornell University Press.
Campbell, J.L. (1992) 'Property Rights and Governance Transformations in Eastern Europe and the United States', in S.-E. Sjöstrand, ed., *Institutional Evolution and Change*, New York: M.E. Sharpe, in press.
Campbell, J.L., Hollingsworth, J.R., and Lindberg, L.N., eds., (1991) *Governance of the American Economy*. New York: Cambridge University Press.
Campbell, J.L. and Lindberg, L.N. (1990) 'Property Rights and the Organization of Economic Activity by the State', *American Sociological Review*, 55 (5), 634-47.
Campbell, J.L. and Lindberg, L.N. (1991) 'The Evolution of Governance Regimes', in J.L. Campbell et al., eds., *Governance of the American Economy*, 319-55.
Chandler, A.D. (1977) *The Visible Hand*. Cambridge, MA: Harvard University Press.
Chandler, A.D. (1990) *Scale and Scope*. Cambridge, MA: Harvard University Press.
Cox, A.W., ed. (1986) *The State, Finance and Industry: a comparative analysis of post-war trends in six advanced industrial economies*, New York: St Martin's Press.
Delorme, R. (1990) 'The State and Economic Development.' CEPREMAP Working paper No. 9102, Paris: CEPREMAP.
DiMaggio, P.J. and Powell, W.W. (1983) 'The Iron Cage Revisited: Institutional Isomorphism and Collective Rationality in Organizational Fields', *American Sociological Review*, 48 (2) 147-60.
DiMaggio, P.J. and Powell, W.W. (1991) 'Introduction', in idem, eds., *The New Institutionalism in Organizational Analysis*, 1-38.
Djelic, M.-L. (1991) 'From Mergers to the Modern Corporation.' Unpublished paper, Department of Sociology, Harvard University.
Dyson, K.W. (1986) 'The State, Banks, and Industry: The West German Case', A.W. Cox, ed., *The State, Finance and Industry*, New York: St. Martin's Press, 118-41.
Eccleston, B. (1986) 'The State, Finance and Industry in Japan', in Cox, ed., *The State, Finance and Industry*, 60-79.
Engelberg, S. (1992) 'Polish Government Completes a Budget Aroved by I.M.F.' *The New York Times*, March 10, p. A9.
Etzioni, A. (1991) 'Eastern Europe: Wealth of Lessons.' *Challenge* July/August.

Evans, P.B. (1985) 'Transnational Linkages and the Economic Role of the State, in Evans et al., eds., *Bringing the State Back In*, 192-226.

Evans, P.B., Rueschemeyer, D., and Skocpol, T., eds., (1985) *Bringing the State Back In*. New York: Cambridge University Press.

Ferguson, T. and Rogers, J. (1986) *Right Turn*: *The Decline of the Democrats and the Future of American Politics*. New York: Hill and Wang.

Fligstein, N. (1990 *The Transformation of Corporate Control*. Cambridge, MA: Harvard University Press.

Fligstein, N. (1991) 'The Structural Transformation of American Industry', in Powell and DiMaggio, eds., *The New Institutionalism in Organizational Analysis*, 311-36.

Gourevitch, P. (1986) *Politics in Hard Times*: *Comparative Responses to International Economic Crises*. Ithaca, NY: Cornell University Press.

Gourevitch, P. (1989) 'Keynesian Politics: The Political Sources of Economic Policy', in Hall, ed., *The Political Power of Economic Ideas*, 87-106.

Gowan, P. (1991/1992) 'Old Medicine, New Bottles: Western Policy Toward East Central Europe', *World Policy Journal* (Winter), 1-33.

Granovetter, M. (1990) 'The Old and the New Economic Sociology: A History and an Agenda', in R. Friedland and A.F. Robertson, eds., *Beyond the Marketplace*: *Rethinking Economy and Society*, New York: Aldine de Gruyter, 89-112.

Hall, P.A. (1986) *Governing the Economy*: *The Politics of State Intervention in Britain and France*. New York: Oxford University Press.

Hall, P.A., ed. (1989) *The Political Power of Economic Ideas*. Princeton: Princeton University Press.

Hamilton, G.G. and Biggart, N.W. (1988) 'Market, Culture, and Authority: Management and Organization in the Far East.' *American Journal of Sociology*, 94 (Supplement), S52-S94.

Hausner, J. (1991) 'The Formation of a System for the Representation of Interests', in idem, ed., *In Systemic Vacuum*? *Dilemmas of the Transformation Process*. Cracow: Cracow Academy of Economics, 43-70.

Hirschman, A.O. (1989) 'How the Keynesian Revolution was Exported from the United States, and Other Comments', in Hall, ed., *The Political Power of Economic Ideas*, 347-59.

Ikenberry, J.G. (1988) *Reasons of State*: *Oil Politics and the Capacities of American Government*. Ithaca: Cornell University Press.

Indraszkiewicz, J. (1991) 'The Formation of Economic Consciousness', in J. Hausner, ed., *In Systemic Vacuum*? *Dilemmas of the Transformation Process*, Cracow: Cracow Academy of Economics, 31-42.

Jepperson, R. (1991) 'Institutions, Institutional Effects, and Institutionalism', in Powell and DiMaggio, eds., *The New Institutionalism in Organizational Analysis*, 143-63.

Jessop, B., Hausner, J., and Nielsen, K. (1991) 'Negotiated Economy and Neoliberalism as Institutional Frameworks for a Market Economy - Implications for Post-Socialism' (see introduction to this volume).

Katzenstein, P., ed., (1977) *Between Power and Plenty: Foreign Economic Policies of Advanced Industrial States.* Madison: University of Wisconsin Press.

Katzenstein, P. (1985) *Small States in World Markets.* Ithaca, NY: Cornell University Press.

Lash, S.M. and Urry, J.R. (1987) *The End of Organized Capitalism.* Madison: University of Wisconsin Press.

March, J.G. and Olsen, J.P. (1984) 'The New Institutionalism: Organizational Factors in Political Life', *American Political Science Review*, 78 (4), 734-49.

March, J.G. and Olsen, J.P. (1989) *Rediscovering Institutions: The Organizational Bases of Politics.* New York: Free Press.

Martin, C.J. (1991) *Shifting the Burden: The Struggle Over Growth and Corporate Taxation.* Chicago: University of Chicago Press.

McCraw, T., ed., (1986) *America versus Japan.* Boston, MA: Harvard Business School Press.

McCraw, T.K. and O'Brien, P. (1986) 'Production and Distribution: Competition Policy and Industry Structure', in McCraw, ed., *America versus Japan*, 77-116.

McGuire, P., Granovetter, M., and Schwartz, M. (1990) 'The Social Construction of Industry'. Unpublished paper, Department of Sociology, University of Toledo.

Meyer, J.W. (1987) 'The World Polity and the Authority of the Nation-State,' in Thomas et al., eds., *Institutional Structure: Constituting State, Society, and the Individual*, 41-70.

Meyer, J.W., Boli, J. and Thomas, G. (1987) 'Introduction', in Thomas et al., eds., *Institutional Structure: Constituting State, Society, and the Individual*, 12.37.

Meyer, J.W. and Rowan, B. (1977) 'Institutionalized Organizations: Formal Structure as Myth and Ceremony', *American Journal of Sociology*, 83 (2), 340-63.

Moran, T.H. (1974) *Multinational Corporations and the Politics of Dependence.* Princeton: Princeton University Press.

Nielsen, K. (1989) 'Flexible Adjustment and Political Stability: The Terms of the Debate', *Scandinavian Political Studies*, 12, 297-312.

Nielsen, K. and Pedersen, O.K. (1989) 'Is Small Still Flexible? An Evaluation of Recent Trends in Danish Politics', *Scandinavian Political Studies*, 12 (4), 343-71.

Nielsen, K. and Pedersen, O.K. (1990) 'The Negotiated Economy - The Structure, the Processes, and the Instruments'. Paper presented at the Conference on Market, Politics, and the Negotiated Economy - Scandinavian and Post-Socialist Perspectives, Cracow, Poland.

Nielsen, K. and Pedersen, O.K. (1991) 'From the Mixed to the Negotiated Economy: The Scandinavian Countries', in M.E. Coughlin, ed., *Morality, Rationality, and Efficiency*. New York: M.E. Sharpe, 145-65.

North, D.C. (1990) *Institutions, Institutional Change and Economic Performance*. New York: Cambridge University Press.

Orru, M., Biggart, N.W. and Hamilton, G.G. (1991) 'Organizational Isomorphism in East Asia', in Powell and DiMaggio, eds., *The New Institutionalism in Organizational Analysis*, 361-89.

Ost, D. (1990) *Solidarity and the Politics of Anti-politics: Opposition and Reform in Poland Since 1968*. Philadelphia: Temple University Press.

Pedersen, Ove K. (1990) 'Learning Processes and the Game of Negotiation - Wage Formation and Negotiated Economy in Denmark.' Second International Conference on Socio-Economics, Washington D.C.

Pestoff, V. (1991) 'The Demise of the Swedish Model and the Rise of Organized Business as a Major Political Actor.' Conference of the Society for the Advancement of Socio-Economics, Stockholm, Sweden (see also Pestoff's contribution to this volume).

Piore, M.J. and Sabel, C.F. (1984) *The Second Industrial Divide*. New York: Basic Books.

Powell, W.W. (1991) 'Expanding the Scope of Institutional Analysis', in Powell and DiMaggio, eds., *The New Institutionalism in Organizational Analysis*, 183-203.

Powell, W.W. (1987) 'Hybrid Organizational Arrangements: New Form or Transitional Development?' *California Management Review*, 30 (1), 67-87.

Powell, W.W. and DiMaggio, P.J., eds., (1991) *The New Institutionalism in Organizational Analysis*. Chicago: University of Chicago Press.

Quinn-Judge, P. (1991) 'U.S., Allies Agree to Defer Part of Soviet Debt.' *The Boston Globe* (November 22), p. 1.

Reich, M., Endo, Y. and Timmer, C.P. (1986) 'Agriculture: The Political Economy of Structural Change', in McCraw, ed., *America versus Japan*, 151-192.

Rosanvallon, P. (1989) 'The Development of Keynesianism in France', in Hall, ed., *The Political Power of Economic Ideas*, 171-93.

Rukstad, M.G. (1986) 'Fiscal Policy and Business - Government Relations', in McCraw, ed., *America versus Japan*, 299-336.

Salant, W.S. (1989) 'The Spread of Keynesian Doctrines and Practices in the United States', in P.A. Hall, ed., *The Political Power of Economic Ideas*.

Schmitter, P.C. and Lehmbruch, G., eds., (1979) *Trends towards Corporatist Intermediation*. Beverly Hills, CA: Sage.

Scott, W.R. (1987) 'The Adolescence of Institutional Theory.' *Administrative Science Quarterly*, 32 (4), 493-511.

Shonfield, A. (1965) *Modern Capitalism*. Oxford: Oxford University Press.

Skocpol, T. (1985) 'Bringing the State Back In: Strategies of Analysis in Current Research', in Evans et al., eds., *Bringing the State Back In*, 3-42.

Stark, D. (1992) 'Path Depedency and Privatization Strategies in East-Central Europe', *East European Politics and Societies*, 6 (1), 17-51.

Streeck, W. (1991) 'Industrial Relations in a Changing Western Europe.' Third European Regional Congress of the International Industrial Relations Association, Bari and Napoli, Italy.

Streeck, W. and Schmitter, P.C., eds., (1985) *Private Interest Government*: *Beyond Market and State*. Beverly Hills, CA: Sage.

Thomas, G., Meyer, J., Ramirez, F., and Boli, J., eds. (1987) *Institutional Structure*: *Constituting State, Society, and the Individual*. Beverly Hills, CA: Sage.

Weir, M. (1989) 'Ideas and Politics: The Acceptance of Keynesianism in Britain and the United States', in Hall, ed., *The Political Power of Economic Ideas*, 53-86.

Weir, M. and Skocpol, T. (1985) 'State Structures and the Possibilities for 'Keynesian' Responses to the Great Depression in Sweden, Britain, and the United States', in Evans et al., eds., *Bringing the State Back In*, 107-67.

Williamson, O. (1985) *The Economic Institutions of Capitalism*. New York: Free Press.

Zysman, J.A. (1983) *Governments, Markets, and Growth*. Ithaca, NY: Cornell University Press.

4 Catching up and institutional learning under post-socialism

Björn Johnson and Bengt-Åke Lundvall

1. Introduction

A crucial question for the post-socialist countries in Eastern and Central Europe is whether and, if so, how they can embark on a process of catching up in economic performance in relation to the more advanced industrial economies of the OECD. That such catch-up is possible can be seen from the experience of the first decades of the postwar period when much of Wetsern Europe as well as Japan managed to close their productivity gap relative to the United States. Hitherto the catching-up mechanisms at work here have been interpreted primarily as a process of international technological borrowing and learning. In this paper we point to the importance of, and difficulties connected to institutional borrowing and learning in this process. The present recipes for institutional design in the post-socialist world emphasize, in typical neo-liberal fashion, the introduction of private ownership and free markets. We argue that this interpretation is too narrow and may seriously misguide policy-making and institutional design.

These recipes reflect the neo-classical core in economic theory. Any economic theory must build on some assumptions about the institutional set up of the economy. In mainstream neo-classical economics these assumptions are very simple and, really, rather void of empirical content: pure and competitive markets. This reflects the way neo-classical economics gives a narrow definition of its subject or area of application. It simply treats population, resources, tastes and technologies as givens, determined somewhere outside that part of society open to economic analysis.

Specifically, in neo-classical growth and trade theory, technical progress is regarded as exogenous and diffusion of economic relevant knowledge as free, not only within but also between countries. In principle, all economic units are assumed to have free and equal access to best practice techniques. It follows from this type of analysis that, if competitive markets could be, quickly, introduced into the former planned economies of eastern and central Europe, these would in a short time come to share the efficiency properties of the neo-classical model. The firms in these countries would also, costlessly, gain access to international best practice techniques and, hence, their income levels could be expected to increase quite rapidly in the near future.

But, of course, this will not be the case. Both the introduction of market mechanisms and of new technical knowledge from abroad will turn out to be complicated and difficult processes.

In this chapter we discuss some problems connected to international borrowing of both technologies and institutions[1] and relate them to the institutional and economic reform process in the former planned economies. A basic assumption behind the discussion is that knowledge has become the strategic resource and learning the most important process in the modern economy. Therefore the most interesting questions for the citizens of the post-socialist societies relate to dynamic rather than static efficiency. It becomes important to understand how the institutional setting affects innovation processes and entrepreneurial activities. Especially it becomes important to consider what might be learnt from the West regarding the role of institutional and technical change.

It is well known that in most nations only a small part of the total technical learning is really home spun. Both the product- and process innovations diffusing through most national economies are to a large extent developed in other countries.

This means that much technical learning in a national economy is relatively easy, because some of the hardest work - the development of new knowledge - has already been done abroad. This perspective was introduced into the analysis of international growth patterns in the first decades after the Second World War (Gomulka 1971). The fact that labour productivity was growing more rapidly in some national economies than in others, was presented as reflecting a process of catching up in relation to the US - which at the end of the war was the world leader in terms of technology and productivity. One basic element in this analysis is, in contrast to neo-classical assumptions, that technical knowledge does not move freely across national borders and that it takes considerable time for laggards to emulate the best-practice. Another basic element is that the existence of a technological gap does not by itself propel growth in the laggard countries. Concepts such as absorptive capacity (Gomulka 1971) and social capability (Abramowitz 1989) have been used to indicate that countries at the same productivity level may have very different prospects for catching up.

A central message in this chapter is that international differences in productivity reflect, not only the distribution of technical knowledge, but also differences in the national institutional set-ups and how well these match the technological opportunities prevailing in a certain period. Another message is that the ability of laggards to exploit international differences in productivity levels as a source of economic growth, i.e., the ability to borrow different forms of economically useful knowledge from abroad is strongly affected by the institutional set up. In the language of the catching-up analysts, many of the most important dimensions of the absorptive capacity (Gomulka 1971) and the social capability (Abramowitz 1989) reflect the national institutional set-up.

A conjecture behind the argument is that in the present era - even if there is still ample room for technical learning across national borders and for international transfer of technology - institutional learning is at the centre of international growth patterns. In the literature on third world countries the need for, and the problems with, institutional borrowing from industrialised countries have been recognised for a long time. Here, it will be argued that such a perspective has become increasingly important for the first, and, not least, for the second world.[2]

For example, the development of the European Community towards stronger economic, political and social integration brings closer together national systems which have very different institutional set-ups established through long historical processes. The construction of the single market and the economic and monetary union are examples of comprehensive projects of institutional learning. Guided by strong political forces and a well trained bureaucracy markets and their institutional frameworks of norms, rules, regulations and laws are shaped through a lengthy, complicated and conflict-ridden process, which clearly illustrates Polanyi's (1957) thesis that market economies do not evolve in spontaneous ways, but have to be deliberately and forcefully constructed and implemented. How to exploit the institutional diversity of Europe, as a source of institutional learning in this process, is a key question for present, as well as potential, members of the Community.

The erosion and collapse of the old economic institutions of Eastern and Central Europe and the attempts to build modern market economies are of course at least as significant and comprehensive as an illustration of the importance of institutional learning. In comparison with the EC project, however, it seems to be closely connected to quite simplistic ideas of institutional borrowing through an import of the institutions of private ownership and the free market from the West.

If this conjecture is correct, there is a need for a conceptual framework, helping us to understand international institutional learning. The purpose of this chapter is to contribute to the development of such a framework and to hint at its possible application to the case of post-socialist market building.

In economics, the comparison of different institutional set-ups (comparing different economic systems) has traditionally focused on the allocation of scarce resources, with tastes and technologies taken as exogenously given, i.e., on static efficiency. This is not, however, the most relevant perspective today. It is more interesting how different institutional set-ups affect technical learning and the use of new technology. This will be especially true in the post-socialist case since the opening up of the economies to international competition is an integral part of this project and international competitiveness is very much a question of dynamic, rather than static, efficiency. As a consequence, we shall focus upon how institutional borrowing and learning relates to technical innovation, i.e., to the creation and use of qualitatively new resources.

2. Borrowing and learning: technologies and institutions

The closing of the technological gap may be thought of as a simple transplantation of machinery, techniques and blueprints from firms in one country to firms in another. This corresponds to what we would call technical borrowing. For non-systemic and standardized techniques - e.g., stand-alone machine-tools - this kind of technology transfer may be possible. When it comes to non-standardized, complex and systemic techniques, technology transfer involves a much more complex process of technical learning where the receiving unit must adapt and transform both its own knowledge base and the technology, itself. This is, of course, even more true when it comes to the most creative aspects of the process of innovation - to cross-country interaction resulting in radically new products and processes.

The same distinction may be made for institutional transfer. Simple and standardized institutions may be copied from one country to another, as indicated by the term institutional borrowing. Especially, this would be the case when the institutions borrowed are of a stand-alone character: i.e., when they can be integrated without any radical consequences for other parts of the whole institutional set-up - an example might be new international conventions in international contract law affecting both the curriculum of business schools and the norms and rules of lawyers working in this area. But there are strict limits for this kind of institutional borrowing. Even extremely simple institutions will be difficult to import from abroad without a substantial element of institutional learning - that is of adapting the local institutional set-up and the institutional novelty to each other.[3] Existing institutions tend to condition borrowed ones. Due to the largely informal, culturally transmitted, part of a nation's institutional set-up, it normally tends to change rather slowly and incrementally, and new or foreign elements are often easily, and informally, rejected (North 1990). Information about new ways to communicate and interact can often be interpreted in different ways and is intensely culturally filtered.

The post-socialist countries are in a historically unique situation regarding institutional borrowing and learning. The old institutional set-up is still present because it is rooted both in specific organisations and formal authorities and in the minds of people. In addition, the knowledge about what markets are and how they actually function seems to build on neo-classical conceptions and be both crude and biased. At the same time the old order is in disrepute among the majority of the citizens and the willingness to support change is quite strong. There is a need for radical rather than incremental institutional change. In this situation, it is reasonable to assume that just copying and borrowing single institutional elements, large and small, from the western world will produce unforeseen, surprising and often unwanted results for these societies.

3. The innovation process

Innovation theory regards, increasingly, innovation as a cumulative and interactive process rather than as events, uniquely localized in time and space (OECD 1992). In a modern economy, innovation is an ubiquitous process, including both the act of creation of novelty - often through a new combination of existing elements of knowledge - and its adaptation and diffusion. But since novelty, always to some extent, is unexpected, and since far from all novelty can be economically utilized, innovation, as every creative process, is hard to understand and difficult to plan. It is not just accidental that the planned economies were low-performers when it came to innovation. Rigid and hierarchical information and communication channels constitute a hostile environment for innovation.

Economic theory tries to avoid the question of novelty by treating technical development and change in consumer preferences as exogenous in the economic process and simply refering to other disciplines, like psychology and the engineering sciences, for answers. Biological evolutionary theory, however, has been forced to tackle the problem, since biological evolution, undoubtedly, has produced novelty and since there are no other disciplines in the neighbourhood to which the question can be conveniently referred. In biology, novelty takes the form of new genetically coded knowledge; the knowledge of how to make a chicken from an egg and a hen from a chicken is an example of such coded knowledge and novelty takes the form of a new or recombined genetic code. Actually, the best answer to the general question of 'what evolves?' in both biological and social evolution is probably knowledge (Boulding 1978).

In neo-Darwinian evolutionary theory, new knowledge, or in fact any novelty, presupposes some element of chance and some kind of generation of accidental combinations.[4] Lamarckian evolutionary thinking, while allowing for the appearance of new species, emphasises learning and the inheritance of acquired characteristics. In economic evolution, the process of innovation may be regarded as involving both kinds of mechanisms. The process is Lamarckian, in the sense that new technical knowledge comes about in a cumulative learning process, but neo-Darwinian, in the sense that new combinations appear unexpectedly. In addition, in order to understand how new knowledge becomes applied, i.e., to understand how innovation is distilled from accidental occurrences and cumulative learning, and put to work in the economy, an evaluating filter or a selection mechanism is required.

Looked upon in this way, innovation is a combined process of a partly unexpected, cumulative generation of new knowledge, and selection of bits of this knowledge for application in the economy. It is important to notice that the generation of novelty and the selection and utilization of it are intertwined into one joint process. From the appearance of a new idea to the actual diffusion of a new product or process there lies, often, a long and uncertain road, along which further new combinations and adaptations are added to the initial one.

In the context of technical innovation, the institutional set-up may be regarded both as an important generator of novelty and as a selection mechanism. Since institutions, i.e., the rules and norms regulating the relationships between people, may be regarded as focusing devices determining the innovative agenda of individuals and organizations, they also shape this process both at the level of creation and utilization of technical novelty. Post-socialist economies do not need just markets and private property; they need the kinds of markets and property rights that can shape and promote innovation. There is, really, no other way to gain and sustain international competitiveness.

4. Interactive learning

Conceptually, we can regard the process leading to new knowledge and to its utilization in the economy (which, again, requires new knowledge, perhaps of a more practical kind) as a process of learning.[5] There is the learning, resulting from (re)searching, aiming at understanding basic principles and relations in nature and society, by scientists at universities, etc.. There is also the learning based upon the more goal-directed searching for new production methods, and new products and product characteristics, in the R&D departments of private firms.

As important as learning based on searching, is learning about improved processes and products as a, mostly unintended, by-product of the encountering of different problems in day-to-day economic operations, taking place in connection with everyday production and sales efforts and other routine activities. This has been treated in economic theory as learning-by-doing (Arrow 1962), learning-by-using (Rosenberg 1982) and learning-by-interacting (Lundvall 1988).

It is a basic observation in cognitive theory that human learning is a social process. Learning presupposes concepts and language, which are products of human society, and, in almost any line of human action, learning proceeds through interaction between people. Some learning is, undoubtedly, done in isolation by simple imprinting of experiences on the memory, but most economically relevant learning is done by feed-back and by conversation between people. The more complex the learning process, the more interactions it probably requires. Professional searching in universities, research institutes and R&D departments, which is characteristic for the modern economy, also involves many forms of intense interacting inside research communities and between these and other communities and individuals.[6]

There are, thus, different kinds of learning and they are all more or less interactive. The interactive character of learning means that developing common codes of communication and learning to communicate between the involved parties become of crucial importance for the dynamic efficiency of the economy.

One reason why the socialist economies had a low capability to innovate and had great difficulties in emulating new technologies developed abroad was that the system did not support interactive learning. The lack of democracy made open and honest communication between parties difficult. Communication channels between departments within firms and between different firms were often narrow, muddled and biased if they existed at all. Specifically, the centralised organizations of R&D interacted only marginally with firms as users of their results. More generally the users of new products were not given enough competence and power to influence the product development among producers. To redesign these relationships and vitalize interactive learning is a major challenge for the post-socialist societies.

5. The growing interest in institutional learning and institutional borrowing

As mentioned above, the interest in institutional or cultural learning has recently been increasing but it is, of course, not totally new in economic literature. In particular, institutional economics has treated the subject. Copeland (1981), for example, in an historical essay on the Ancient Near East discusses a number of communities which successfully borrowed organizational and communication traits from technologically more advanced communities.

At the more practical level, there are examples of periods of intensified interest for institutional borrowing. Looking back at the industrialization of Sweden, as an industrial late-comer, we find that influential entrepreneurs introduced, first, British and, later, US forms of management and organisation in Swedish plants. This may be one important reason for the success of scale-intensive engineering firms in modern Sweden.

Recently, the interest in the Japanese system of innovation has been growing. Especially, organizational and institutional traits connected to the new information- and communication technologies have been in focus. At the level of the single corporation, it has been observed that the organization, increasingly, is relying upon participatory communication and cooperation among workers, shops and departments, in contrast to traditional more hierarchical structures. At the inter-firm level, it has caught the interest that markets seem to be organized to a higher degree in Japan than in the U.S.A. and Western Europe. Loyalty and voice are important elements in the interaction, and users and producers do not change their mutual relationships, readily, when relative prices change. Japanese firms also seem to use feed-back in terms of user experiences more systematically, and in more organized ways, in innovation processes.

It seems as if this interest for the Japanese innovation system and, especially, its supposedly strong communication economies, is motivated by a presumed possibility for institutional borrowing. Such an optimistic view is not altogether without support in theory. Veblen argued that the transfer of a technique from one cultural situation to another was often not only possible, but that it also could increase the efficiency of the borrowed technique: 'The borrowed elements of industrial efficiency would be stripped of their fringe of conventional inhibitions' and 'the borrowing community would be in a position to use them...with a better chance of utilizing them to their full capacity' (Veblen 1915). It is an interesting question if the same kind of mechanism might be working when it comes to the borrowing of elements from a foreign institutional set-up. Actually, the establishment of Western-like institutions in Japan at the end of the War and the techno-economic efficiency of the Japanese system of innovation could be analyzed in this perspective.

6. Problems in institutional learning

Of course, this isolated quotation by Veblen tends to underestimate the difficulties involved in institutional borrowing. Often it is quite difficult to realise the full productivity potential of a piece of new, foreign, technical equipment, and for different reasons institutional borrowing is, often, more difficult than technological borrowing.

Since institutions concern relations between people and people, and technology, to a higher degree, concerns relations between people and things, there is usually more resistance to institutional change than to technical change. It is easier both for management and workers to accept changes in the work process which merely involve that technical things should be done in a different way than changes resulting in a reshuffling of hierarchical patterns and in the introduction of new ways to communicate. At a fundamental analytical level, this resistance reflects that institutions - understood as regularities in social behaviour - have as their functional role to shape a reasonably stable environment for learning and technical change.

A related phenomenon is that it may be easier to recognize technological than institutional problems. It is, normally, more obvious when technologies do not function or when there are unutilized technological opportunities. Technological innovations are more salient than institutional innovations and this may lead to a postponement of otherwise obvious institutional and organizational innovations.[7] In this way, institutional rigidities may accumulate in small steps over long periods, while information on the adverse effects of this relative delay of organizational change is neglected.

The non-salient character of institutional innovation is related to the problem of superstitious learning, i.e., when an outcome is credited with the wrong cause (Kogut 1991). It is obvious that it is easier to connect cause and effect correctly for technological than for institutional innovations. This again makes rejection of possible institutional borrowing more probable, especially in conflict situations, where the balance of influence and power between different groups is affected.

At a general level, managers are often aware of the risks of under-investments in the 'human factor' and clearly recognize this mistake when it occurs in other firms. When it comes to their own firm, however, they tend to avoid information on this subject. This phenomenon, of only seeing 'the mote that is in thy brother's eye', was clearly observed in Danish industry, where industrialists ascribe the general productivity fall in the middle of the eighties to organizational and institutional problems in industry, in general, but tend to see few of these problems in their own firm (Gjerding et al., 1990). Furthermore, if many interlocking persons and groups feel responsible for, or identify themselves with, a specific organizational form, they will try to postpone and resist even minor changes.

Managers may also be uninterested in organizational innovation, since it may be difficult, fully, to appropriate the generated incomes due to a lack of property rights. Patents, copy rights and trade marks serve in this function for both hardware and software technical innovations, but their are no comparable institutions for organizational and institutional innovations.

It can also be argued that the specialists on technical innovation, i.e. engineers, are educated in a more dynamic spirit than the specialists on organizational and institutional factors. In fact, stability and permanence are important ideals amongst 'transaction costs engineers', for instance amongst lawyers. These people also lack a common international, professional, language compared to technical engineers. Law, and organizational items, generally, are much more country specific than technology, which makes international interactive learning in institutional and organizational matters more difficult.

A final reason for institutional inertia, adding difficulties to institutional learning, is the enormous complexity of the institutional system of a modern economy. Lots of different institutions mingle into a complicated interrelated whole, which is rather poorly understood and, really, not very much researched.

Together, all these difficulties with organizational and institutional learning may add up to pathological patterns of behaviour resulting in a resistance to institutional change and give some truth to the idea, often erroneously ascribed to Veblen, that institutions tend to retard technological change and, thus, constitute a rigid element in social change. This is certainly not a truth without exceptions (Johnson 1988), however, and in some situations the institutional brakes turn into accelerators. For instance, if some basic institutions guarantee a certain level of social security and in other ways facilitate class- and interest-group communication and compromising, then employee resistance to organizational change may be turned into active cooperation.

In the post-socialist countries the resistance to change will be very strong for obvious and natural reasons. Without a financial basis for social policies compensating the victims of institutional change it is to be expected that institutional change involving losses of jobs, incomes and privileges will be strongly resisted. Careful consideration of the possibilities to turn resistance into cooperation is needed. The role of state policy cannot be reduced to open up the economy for private property and international competition. It must also prepare a social imbedding of the market forces and help building the institutional foundations of a learning economy. In order to propel institutional change of this kind it might be necessary to introduce elements of welfare state policies.

7. Some illustrations

All these difficulties should not give the impression that institutional borrowing is next to impossible. Institutional learning is at the centre of the combined but uneven international growth pattern and institutional borrowing is, as it has always been, an important part of this. Relative changes in international competitiveness between countries are often accompanied, and sometimes generated, by institutional innovations in one country, which then slowly diffuse to other countries through mixed processes of institutional borrowing and learning.

In fact, important parts of western economic history can be understood in terms of institutional borrowing and learning across the Atlantic Ocean, from Europe to America and back again. North (1990) underlines the critical importance of the English institutional heritage for the creation of the thriving American colonial economy, which set the stage for a new phase in capitalist development. The institutions which were shaping this early development and resulted in the institutional set-up of a new nation - for example plantations, merchants, shipping firms, family farms, town meetings and self-government, colonial assemblies, and the intellectual traditions from Hobbes to Locke - were predominantly of English origin.

More than 150 years later Europe enters a period of massive institutional borrowing from the USA. After the second world war and connected to the Marshall aid programme, productivity delegations left for the USA to study scientific management and the organisational forms which were connected to the best practice mass production technologies, which, without qualification, were supposed to be American. Not many years later the multi-divisional firm structure, introduced by du Pont and General Motors in the 1930s, with some country-specific modifications spread throughout Western Europe (Williamson 1985).

8. Conceptualizing institutional learning in post-socialism

To imply that institutional catching-up is a possibility is a provocative statement. It indicates both that the institutional set-ups of some countries are better suited to support innovation, and the exploitation of technological opportunities, than other set-ups in other countries and that these institutional set-ups can be transferred from one country to another. This involves, of course, some simplifications. First, what is a best-practice institutional set-up in one national context might work very poorly in another. Second, the institutional set-up should not be assessed exclusively from the point of view of techno-economic dynamics. How the institutional set-up affects the quality of life and the environment cannot be neglected. In fact, it may be argued that the introduction of environmental safe-guards into market mechanisms is the most necessary of all institutional learning projects in the modern world.[8]

In order to get a more realistic assessment of the potential of institutional borrowing, it might be useful to analyze countries as national systems of innovation where the economic structure and the institutional set-up are looked upon as forming systemic wholes (Andersen and Lundvall 1988; Lundvall 1992). In this perspective, we get a better understanding of when, and where, foreign institutions may be transferable from one system to another. One and the same form of work organization may, for example, function quite differently in different systems because of the cultural context.

As a consequence, it may be easier for European economies to learn from each other in this respect than from the, culturally, vastly different Japan. The differences between, for example, the Danish and Swedish systems of innovation are in fact quite considerable in spite of the similarities in cultural history and social policy and their close geographical proximity (Edquist and Lundvall 1991). To make detailed comparative studies of national systems of innovation and their institutional set-ups, when the differences cannot be explained by drastic cultural distances, might give a better basis for institutional borrowing and learning than studies involving more far-away models. In this connection the fact that there are important differences in these respects between the Central European economies, in spite of the similarities in their recent political history and their close geographical proximity, might become an important source of institutional learning.

Our conclusion is that there is a case for institutional learning based on international differences. But, in order to understand the limits and opportunities involved, we need concepts which take into account the complexity of the modern learning economy. And here, the concepts forming the core of standard economics are of little help.

First, one should take into account that diversity is an important source for learning. As a whole, there is substantial diversity in how institutions and technologies are combined in a modern economy (Bruno et al. 1991). At the same time, we know that a lack of interest in, and knowledge about, the organisational, institutional and human aspects in the innovation process can lead to substantial losses of productivity (Gjerding et al. 1990). This indicates the need for a general movement away from mechanistic models, presenting the world as homogeneous, towards evolutionary models giving differentiation, variety and diversity, as well as selection mechanisms, their proper place as both sources and results of learning and innovation.

The traditional bipolar presentation of markets versus hierarchies is not useful when it comes to understanding international institutional learning. This is true at the micro level where most markets supporting product innovations can be shown to be 'organized markets' (Johnson and Lundvall 1989). But it is equally true at the macro level where the specific mix of market regulation and planning differs between nations.[9]

In dynamic Schumpeterian approaches to comparative analysis, the role of entrepreneurship is at the centre of analysis. Here, it is important to note that new forms of collective entrepreneurship have been developing, giving the individual hero of the innovation process a less prominent role. The development of the R&D departments in big firms was recognised by Schumpeter himself. But, today, cooperation within, and between, firms and networks of firms tend to play an increasingly important role in learning and innovation. The traditional focus on competition, as the sole mode of interaction between firms, hampers the understanding of different national modes of collective entrepreneurship.

We also believe that the concept of 'national systems of innovation' has a fundamental role in defining opportunities and limits for institutional learning between countries. This concept, used in somewhat different ways by Freeman (1987) in his important book on Japan and by Nelson (1992) and Lundvall (1992), gives a different perspective on national economies from the one prevailing in the neo-classical tradition. In the neo-classical theory of international trade, the national economy is just a homestead for given 'factors of production' and this gives, of course, little help, when it comes to understand institutional learning between countries.

As a final conclusion: In order to assess the possibilities for institutional learning, the concept of social capability must be much better understood. It is necessary for the state and other collective agents in the post-socialist countries to take on broad responsibility for the social capability of society. The development of social capability will determine to which extent the post-socialist countries will be able to enter trajectories characterised by catching up. Social capability has several different dimensions. One dimension refers to the infrastructure for transport, communication and telecommunication. Of course, social capability also relates to the the production and diffusion of knowledge both through research, education and training and through developing organizational structures promoting interactive learning in connection with routine economic activities. It also involves a moral dimension. In an economy where corruption is widely dispersed and trust difficult to establish, the catching up process will be hampered both by high transaction costs and by a low efficiency of interactive learning.

Therefore a policy which promotes ruthless entrepreneurship will prove subversive for catching up - in the long term it will undermine the social capability of the national economy.

This paper has argued that the construction and support of social capability should engage economic agents in international institutional learning of a much more complex and sophisticated kind than the one reflected in the usual recommendations to introduce more private ownership and more free markets in the post-socialist countries.

Notes

1 We define institutions as sets of habits, routines, rules, norms and laws, which regulate the relations between people and shape human interaction. By reducing uncertainty and ,thus, the amount of information needed for individual and collective action institutions are fundamental building blocks in all societies. (Johnson, 1992)

2 There are several theoretical explanations for, why institutional change has become so important in the present era. In France, the regulation school has pointed to the crisis of a 'Fordist' model of accumulation and to the uncertain movements towards 'post-fordist' institutions (Boyer, 1988), while Carlota Perez and Christopher Freeman (Freeman and Perez, 1988) have analyzed this crisis as a change in 'techno-economic paradigm', reflecting the development and diffusion of information technology resulting in 'mismatches' with the existing institutional set-up.

3 The seminal work of Everett Rogers (1982) on communication of innovations is introduced by a case where 'water boiling' could not be introduced, with success, in a Peruvian village because, even this simple routine, proved to be incompatible with the norms and habits ruling in the village.

4 Mutations and sexual recombinations in standard biological neo-Darwinian evolutionary theory.

5 We are here talking about learning in the sense of creating new knowledge, not merely moving knowledge from one person to another as in ordinary education.

6 The chain-linked model of innovation emphasizing the interaction in innovation processes - including the interaction between science and technology - has recently become a standard reference in the literature on innovation (Kline and Rosenberg, 1987).

7 In Akerlof (1991) there is a discussion of the relations between salient information and procrastination effects (i.e. irrational postponement of action) in different social and economic situations.

8 This is strongly formulated in a recent UNESCO report: 'Markets, for example, will have to learn to function without expansion, without wars, without wastes and without advertising that encourages waste'. (Goodland et al. 1991)

9 That there are no pure systems was emphasized by the Swedish institutionalist economist Johan Åkerman (1936): 'Our juxtaposition of the extreme X-society and the extreme Y-society should have demonstrated fully *that such purely competitive or purely planned societies never have and never will exist.* But this is not all: We have also tried to show that both these types of society are incomprehensible as logical constructs.' (Op.cit 1936: 141, our translation).

Bibliography

Abramowitz, M. (1989) *Thinking about Growth*, Cambridge: Cambridge University Press.

Akerlof, G.A. (1991), 'Procrastination and Obedience', *The American Economic Review*, Papers and Proceedings, vol. 81 (2).

Åkerman, J. (1936) *Ekonomisk Kausalitet* (Economic Causality), Lund: Gleerups Förlag.

Andersen, E.S. and Lundvall, B.-Å. (1988) 'Small national systems of innovation facing technological revolutions - an analytical framework', in Freeman, C. & Lundvall, B-Å., eds., *Small nations facing the technological revolution*, London: Pinter.

Arrow, K. J. (1962) 'The Economic Implications of Learning by doing', *Review of Economic Studies*, June.

Boulding, K. (1978) *Ecodynamics: A New Theory of Societal Evolution*, London: Sage Publications.

Boyer, R. (1988), 'Technical Change and the theory of Régulation', in G. Dosi, C. Freeman, R. Nelson, G. Silverberg, and L. Soete, eds., *Technology and Economic Theory*, London: Pinter Publishers.

Bruno, S., Cohendet, P., Desmartin, F., Llerena, P. and Soege, A. (1991) *Modes of Usage and Diffusion of New Technologies and New Knowledge. A Synthesis Report*, Bruxelles, Commission of the European Communities, Fast, FOP 227.

Copeland, M.A. (1981) *Essays in Socioeconomic Evolution*, New York: Vantage Press Inc.

Edquist, C. and Lundvall, B.-Å. (1992) 'Comparing Small Nordic Systems of Innovation', in R. Nelson, ed., *National Systems of Innovation: A Comparative Study*, Oxford: Oxford University Press (in press).

Freeman, C. (1987) *Technology Policy and Economic Performance: Lessons from Japan*, London: Pinter.

Freeman, C. and Perez, C. (1988) 'Structural crises of adjustment, business cycles and investment behaviour', in G. Dosi, C. Freeman, R. Nelson, G. Silverberg, and L. Soete, eds., *Technology and Economic Theory*, London: Pinter Publishers.

Gjerding, A.N., Johnson, B., Kallehauge, L., Lundvall, B.-Å., and Madsen. P.T. (1990) *Den forsvundne produktivitet* (Productivity Lost), Copehagen: JOFs forlag.

Goodland, R., Daly, H., El Serafy, S., von Droste, B. (1991) *Environmentally Sustainable Economic Development: Building on Brundtland*, Paris: UNESCO.

Gomulka, S. (1971) *Inventive Activity, Diffusion, and the Stages of Economic Growth*, Århus.

Johnson, B. (1988) 'An Institutional Approach to the Small Country Problem', in C. Freeman and B.-Å. Lundvall, eds., *Small Nations Facing the Technological Revolution*, London: Pinter Publishers.

Johnson, B. (1992) 'Institutional Learning', in B.Å. Lundvall, B.-Å., ed., *National Systems of Innovation - Towards a Theory of Innovation and Interactive Learning*, London: Pinter Publishers.

Johnson, B. and Lundvall, B.-Å. (1989) 'The limits of the pure market economy', in J. Bohlin et al., eds., *Samhällsvetenskap, Ekonomi, Historia: Festskrift till Lars Herlitz*, Gothenborg: Förlaget Daidalos.

Kline, S.J. and Rosenberg, N. (1986) 'An Overview of Innovation', in National Academy of Engineering, *The Positive Sum Strategy: Harnessing Technology for Economic Growth*, Washington, D.C.: The National Academy Press.

Kogut, B. (1991) 'Country Capabilities and the Permeability of Borders', *Strategic Management Journal*, 12 (1).

Lundvall, B.-Å. (1988) 'Innovation as an Interactive Process - from User-Producer Interaction to National Systems of Innovation', in G. Dosi, C. Freeman, R. Nelson, G. Silverberg, and L. Soete, eds., *Technology and Economic Theory*, London: Pinter Publishers.

Lundvall, B.-Å., ed., (1992) *National Systems of Innovation - Towards a Theory of Innovation and Interactive Learning*, London: Pinter Publishers.

North, D.C. (1990) *Institutions, Institutional Change and Economic Performance*, Cambridge: Cambridge University Press.

OECD (1992) *Technology and the Economy - the Key Relationships*, Paris: OECD.

Rosenberg, N. (1982) *Inside the Black Box*, Cambridge: Cambridge University Press.

Rogers, E. M. (1982) *Diffusion of Innovations*, New York: The Free Press.

Veblen, T.B. (1915) *Imperial Germany and the Industrial Revolution*, New York: MacMillan & Co..

Williamson, O. E. (1985) *The Economic Institutions of Capitalism: Firms Markets and Relational Contracting*, New York: Free Press.

Part 2

SCANDANAVIAN PERSPECTIVES: THE NEGOTIATED ECONOMY

5 The negotiated economy: General features and theoretical perspectives

Klaus Nielsen and Ove K. Pedersen

1. Introduction

The concept of the negotiated economy is no doubt rather unknown outside of Scandinavia although similar concepts are used by others (Devine l988; Moore and Booth l989; Marin 1985). The concept has been formulated and developed in a Scandinavian context and until now has been used at all frequently only in the Scandinavian countries. It was coined about ten years ago in connection with a lengthy and ambitious Norwegian public investigation which sought to uncover the power relations in modern Norwegian society (Hernes l979; NOU l982). Since then theoretical discussions have taken place and efforts have been made to apply this concept in empirical studies of the different Scandinavian countries (Pedersen 1985; Nielsen 1991, 1992; Nielsen and Pedersen l988, l989a; Pedersen, Andersen and Kjær 1992; Berrefjord and Nore l988; Midttun l988; Pestoff l988a, 1988b).

In our view the negotiated economy approach is a promising new field of inquiry even if it is still in need of a coherent body of concepts and theories. Below we present some general theoretical considerations concerning trhe negotiated economy. First, we shall argue that important trends in the last decades might be interpreted as a development from a mixed to a negotiated economy. Second, we present a model of the pure negotiated economy and a method for analyzing to what extent the actually existing forms of allocation and decision making can be seen as a negotiated economy. Third, we describe some of the central features in the emergence of the negotiated economy, that is, its discursive and institutional preconditions and effects. Fourth, we argue that the emergence of the negotiated economy challenges the dominant theories in the social sciences. Finally, we analyze the specific forms of rationality of the agents in the negotiated economy, and the question whether the negotiated economy is an efficient way of allocating and (re)distributing the resources of society.

2. From the mixed economy to the negotiated economy

2.1. The ideal of the mixed economy

The concept of the mixed economy is well known and widely used, although no well established definition exists. It has mainly been used about the Western industrialized countries in the period after World War II in order to distinguish them from societies with all-embracing market mechanisms and from societies dominated by central planning and state ownership of the means of production. In the mixed economies neither the market nor the state is completely dominant. On the contrary, a balanced relationship is assumed to exist (Shonfield 1984). Prices and supplies of goods and services are supposed to be largely determined by market processes. At the same time the state and its agencies are supposed to have large capacities for intervention to secure objectives that the market would not achieve automatically.

The mixed economy might be defined as a society which is composed of a mixture of various systems of allocation (market, state, organizations, collectives, etc.). This is not wrong, of course, but in our view rather inappropriate. If you choose this definition you will be able to identify no other alternatives to mixed economies than pure ideal-type market economies or command economies. Accordingly, all presently existing societies might be characterized as mixed economies - and all possible future forms might be covered by this label too.

We consider it appropriate to define the concept of the mixed economy in a more strict and narrow way. The reason for this is threefold. First, we wish to identify the concept with the specific historical background for its propagation. Second, we want the definition to correspond to the dominant conceptions of the ideal function of the mixed economy. Third, we wish to specify the concept in such a way as to make it possible to identify recent divergent trends.

Accordingly, we wish to stress an important feature of the mixed economy which is not included in the above definition: i.e., the clear-cut division of labour between market and state; either you have market decisions by autonomous agents or decisions by equally autonomous state bodies. There is not only a balanced mix of state and market but also a clear distinction between the areas covered by the authority of the sovereign state and areas where market agents are supposed to have full autonomy. All the important social and institutional innovations of the mixed economy such as demand management and the welfare state are characterized by such a clear-cut division of labour.

The ideal of the mixed economy has been formulated in Keynesian macroeconomics and, above all, in economic welfare theory. According to this theory optimality is secured if the resources are allocated through the market mechanism provided the non-existence of market failure. However, in the case of market failure intervention by the state is required. That is: either allocation of resources by voluntary interaction of market agents, or corrective measures taken by a sovereign state. No direct cooperation is needed. A carefully designed division of labour is considered sufficient.

It is impossible to find any society that corresponds fully to this ideal of the mixed economy. Nevertheless it seems obvious that following the 1930s and especially in the first decades after World War II we experienced a development away from a market economy in the direction of a mixed economy.

It is also obvious, however, that more recent development features diverge from this trend. It has become still more difficult to delineate the borderline between market and state. Economic decisions are no longer either private or public. Now, a growing part of the allocation of resources are determined neither on the market by individual agents adapting to market changes, nor through decision-making by sovereign public authorities. Instead, the decision making is conducted via institutionalized negotiations between various autonomous private, semi-public, and public agents. The state delegates powers and participates in decision making processes without full authority. Also the discretion of private agents is restrained by the results of the negotiations. Different rationalities are combined and private and collective interests are mixed as agents engage in direct cooperation.

2.2. The negotiated economy - a definition

There are different ways to characterize these recent features and different ways to evaluate their implications. In our view they represent a transition away from a mixed economy in the direction of a negotiated economy.

We take the term negotiated economy to mean a structuring of society where an essential part of the allocation of resources is conducted through institutionalized negotiations between independent decision making centres in state, organizations and/or corporations.

As distinct from decisions made by public authorities, negotiation based economic decisions are reached on the basis of interaction between independent agents, and the relevant public authority is just one of several participants.

As distinct from authoritative decisions, negotiation based economic decisions are usually not subject to the possible use of sanctions. They are typically based on discursive, political or morally binding - rather than legally sanctioned - agreements.

As distinct from market decisions which are made by individual agents each acting separately and on the basis of given preferences and resources, negotiation based economic decisions are made through a process in which the deliberate shaping of preferences is a decisive feature.

We shall put forward the assertion that the Scandinavian countries are increasingly assuming the character of a negotiated economy. An essential part of the allocation of the productive resources as well as the (re)distribution of the output is determined neither on the market, by individual agents adapting to market changes, nor through autonomous decision making by public authorities. Instead, the decision making process is conducted via institutionalized negotiations between the relevant interested agents, who reach binding decisions typically based on discursive, political or moral imperatives rather than threats and economic incentives, even if such threats and rewards as well as persuasive measures might be essential elements of the framework around the negotiations.

We do not assert that all economic resources in the Scandinavian countries are allocated and (re-)distributed in accordance with this ideal-type version of the negotiated economy. We are even aware of the fact that, empirically, negotiated relations are of different importance in different countries, sectors and policy areas. We do maintain, however, that in our societies we experience a development away from a mixed economy in the direction of a negotiated economy as defined above. For instance, we get a mixed picture if we look at the determination of (various) prices. In some branches prices are determined by the market mechanism with no interference by the state. Other branches are characterized by autonomous price determination by market agents coexisting with state regulation, taxation or subsidizing while other prices (including free services) are set by public producers; all in accordance with the ideal of the mixed economy. Simultaneously, however, an essential part of wages, prices, interest rates and profit rates are determined through the process of the negotiated economy.

3. The approach and the model

3.1. Negotiation - an instrument for decision making

In the Scandinavian countries negotiations are widely used as instruments for decision making both in relation to allocation as well as (ro)distribution. The classical example is the labour market. Wages, working hours and other conditions of work are generally determined neither by individual market agents nor by legislation but rather through institutionalized negotiations between the collective organizations of the agents. Furthermore large investment projects are normally accompanied by negotiations between private firms and public authorities about infrastructure, sharing of risk, etc.. Either institutionalized or informal negotiations precede decision making in many different parts of the economy.

Negotiation appears to be an appropriate instrument in many different situations. It can be a preferable instrument in case of conflicts of interest especially when none of the involved parties have full control of the implementation and/or any possibility of exit. Compromise and agreement achieved by means of negotiation is an established method to handle situations like that.

However, negotiation is not only an instrument to resolve conflicts between opposing interests. It is also an instrument for achieving mutual understanding. Thus it is not only an instrumental technique for decision making; it also involves communication, compromising and achieving a consensus.

Certainly, negotiation is just one of many instruments for collective decision making. Of course, the classical instruments are the price mechanism, voting and (bureaucratic) rules - connected to the ideal-type conceptions of the market, the democracy and the bureaucracy. However, neither the economy nor the political institutions function in accordance with the ideal-type prescriptions. A mixture of many different types of instruments characterize both the economic and the political sphere in all modern societies. This mixture is often re-arranged.

The instruments might interact in a supplementary way but they might also compete, disturb and eventually supercede each other. No stable equilibrium mixture can be expected.

This instability is perhaps especially pertinent as far as the role of negotiations is concerned - in the Scandinavian countries too. In spite of a long tradition for negotiation based decision making, history in general and recent changes in particular have shown that it is always controversial how, what, and when to negotiate - if at all

Anyhow, the importance of negotiations should not be ignored. No doubt this instrument is more prevalent in the small, open economies of Europe than elsewhere (Katzenstein l985). Probably this is even more so in the Scandinavian countries which are characterized by homogeneous populations, relative symmetry of power in the capital-labour relationship, and a long history of compromising, integrating and mediating.

3.2. The negotiated economy - a model

The negotiated economy is the result of a long process characterized by the development of a multitude of institutions and inter-institutional networks - formal and informal. It is neither a coherent system nor the effect of some grand design. The negotiated economy has been constituted in an organic way by the contributions of many different actors with diverse and often short term motivations. No streamlined or ideal-type structure can be identified. On the contrary, if we look at the economic structure as a whole, we experience a muddy mixture of features from the market economy, the mixed economy, and the negotiated economy. However, we do see a general long term trend in the direction of a negotiated economy, and rather advanced states of such a structure have developed in important sectors of the economy. The following model identifies the characteristics of the pure negotiated economy.

The negotiated economy is much more than an instrument for decision making and the actual negotiations taking place around a negotiating table. These elements are parts of the overall structure of the negotiated economy encompassing the normative and institutional framework as well.

The overall structure and the comprehensive process is sketched in the figure below (Figure 3.2.1). To the left you see not only the instrument but also the institutional structure developed above,

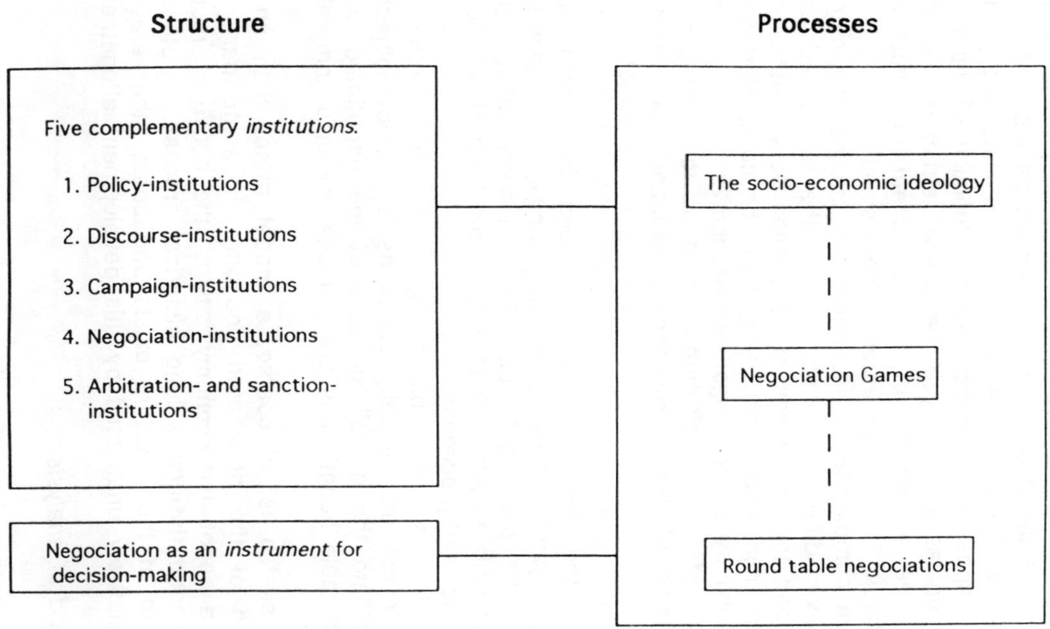

Figure 3.2.1. The negotiated economy: structure and process

around or in connection with the actual application of negotiation as an instrument for decision making. To the right you see an illustration of the comprehensive societal process where the events around the negotiation table constitute just one instance - heavily influenced by the other processual links. We shall argue that it is impossible to understand the function of the negotiated economy unless you analyze the overall structure and the total process. The application of the instrument in actual decision making should not be seen as an isolated event.

The five complementary institutions (discussed in greater detail below) cover different functions within the negotiated economy. They support the application of negotiation as an instrument, and they complement each other. They might be considered cogwheels in the machinery of the negotiated economy.

Some of the institutions attempt to mobilize mutual understanding of the socio-economic situation. This functions as an ideological (normative) framework for the negotiations. We call this the socio-economic ideology. Within this normative framework the parties involved engage in institutionalized negotiation games developing compromises on themes and procedures for the negotiations. Then in some other institutions the round table negotiations take place on the basis of the agreed upon themes and procedures.

The activities taking place around the negotiation table - whether or not this actually exists as a physical object - are integrated into the overall structure of the negotiated economy. The round table negotiations are just one link in a comprehensive process.

This sketch is, of course, a model rather than an actual description of the negotiated economy. In some parts of the economy a negotiated economy with all the above characteristics has developed through a long historical process. In other areas only a part of the structure exists and some other areas even appear relatively unaffected by this development altogether.

3.3. Method of analysis

In recent years institutional analysis has attracted a lot of interest. The social sciences have become involved in discussions of the role of institutions and the formation and transformation of institutions. The trend is perhaps most evident in economics (Hodgson 1988; Eggertson 1990) and in political science (March and Olsen 1989; Scott 1990; Pedersen, 1991).

The theory of the negotiated economy reflects a specific method of analyzing the role of institutions and the formation and change of institutions. We distinguish between the formation of the structural preconditions for the evolution of a negotiated economy, the processes for propagation, reproduction and change of the structure, and the mechanisms functioning in the processes:

- The structure comprise the legal, institutional and discursive preconditions for a negotiated economy. The legal elements consist of various individual and collective rights and obligations. The institutional elements consist of various formal institutions with different roles in the the specific institutional processes of the negotiated economy. The discursive elements of the structure constitute the normative framework; the socio-economic ideology.
- Three types of processes have been identified: (a) language games: the discursive interaction about propagation and development of the socioeconomic frame of meaning; (b) negotiation games;: the strategic interaction about formulation of preferences, interests, and rules of the game; (c) negotiations: the instrumental interaction about the formation of compromise and the elaboration of political agreements and contractual relations..
- Many forms of institutional mechanisms push the processes forward. Two forms appear especially important: conflict mechanisms and learning mechanisms. Conflict is ever present in the formulation of preferences and collective interests and the elaboration of rules and procedure for the actual 'round table' negotiations. The conflicts are verbalized. They take place within a discursive framework established through language games. Learning takes place as systematic and institutionalized testing, gathering and formulation of experiences. The discursive and institutional framework makes it possible for individual and collective agents to continuously formulate experiences in commonly accepted language codes and to propagate and change these alongside the application of alternative means.

We have identified these phenomena through diachronic as well as synchronic analyses. The intention has been to uncover (1) the formation of the structure and (2) the specific processes and mechanisms.

The diachronic part consists of description of the development of the values of selected variables through several decades. We have, for instance, described how the interpretation of various central concepts (competitiveness, inflation, flexibility) have changed, and how different policy fields (fiscal policy, incomes policy, public expenditure policy, tax policy) have been given different meanings. Another example is the description of the development of various formal organizations; how they were erected, and how their range of competence has changed. We have described the historical development of those discursive concepts and the formal units which we consider central today. We have described how the present forms have evolved.

In the synchronic part we proceed from this historical description and attempt to summarize the results in a typology of currently existing institutions with different functions. Furthermore, we attempt to identify current types of processes and mechanisms.

The ambition has been to create a method to analyze institutional history; that is, how perceptions of social reality have been constructed. Such perceptions have normative, and discursive, as well as institutional elements. The construction of a social reality can be described as the following processes: (1) some normative values (ideals) are gradually transformed into generally accepted codes of language (discourses), and (2) some discourses are gradually transformed into relatively stable (formal or informal) relations between agents (institutions). The construction of a social reality is considered the same as the institutionalization of certain values.

The diachronic analysis attempts to describe the formation of institutions as sequences of events leading from formulation of ideals to their institutionalization. Ideals are not automatically transformed into discourses, and neither are discourses automatically transformed into institutions. Not all ideals become systematized, propagated and transformed into generally accepted codes of language. Nor do all discourses become transformed into institutions. Ideals, discourses and institutions are all three created, propagated and changed through complex processes that involve struggles between and selection among alternatives. Some win and others lose.

The synchronic analysis studies the conflictual process taking place within an already established discursive and institutional framework. What are the effects of the established ideals, discourses and institutions on the behaviour of the different agents? How is it possible within the established institutional framework to propagate, reproduce and change institutions?

4. The emergence of the negotiated economy

4.1. The genesis

Most of the institutional innovations identified above with a negotiated economy did not evolve in the Scandinavian countries until the end of the 1950s. However, the institutional foundation for these innovations was established long before. In all the Scandinavian countries the tradition of institutionalized class cooperation is very strong. In Denmark this tradition dates back to the turn of the century with the establishment of a 'General Constitution' of the labour market (the 'September Agreement' of 1899) while in Sweden and Norway similar agreements were made in the 1930s. As a result we experienced a profound civilization of the class confrontation. This civilization is in our view a decisive premise for the development of a negotiated economy in the Scandinavian countries. We distinguish four phases:

In the first phase - the juridification of class relations - the peak organizations on the labour market entered into general agreements specifying the rights and duties of each party but also including acceptance of the legitimate existence of each other. Furthermore, the organizations were given autonomous rights and obligations vis-a-vis their members. The organizations were thus turned into autonomous legal subjects.

The juridification was followed by a phase of institutionalization. A highly complex pattern emerged. Private and semi-public as well as public institutions were established in order to regulate the relations between the two main classes.

This was followed by a phase of integration of the organizations into the public administration. This actually implied a transfer of public authority to the organizations enabling them to formulate policies and make authoritative decisions in connection to the labour market.

As a result of the lengthy and profound civilization of class conflict, public authority has been dispersed. It has been delegated to many different types of institutions where organizations are represented. Public authority became multicentered, thereby creating coordination problems. From the end of the 1950s until today various problems have been formulated as coordination problems. This started a fourth phase of innovative institutionalization: the coordination of decision making through discursive and institutional means.

4.2. The socio-economic frame of meaning

The existence and the autonomy of the above mentioned institutions were accepted as a basic premiss making coordination by purely legal administrative means impossible. Instead a strategy for ideological or discursive coordination was formulated and new institutions were erected to facilitate such coordination.

The main object in this process was the formulation and propagation of a socio-economic ideology: the socio-economic frame of meaning. This is a general conception of the relationships between public administration, organizations, corporations and households as part of an economic organism. The health of this organism is not automatically established. It is only created if the different agents observe a normative injunction to act in the interests of the society as perceived through the socio-economic frame of meaning. This incentive is being mobilized through many new institutions designed for this purpose. These institutions formulate problems and designate ends, means and strategies in various policy fields within the overall, normative socio-economic frame of meaning.

In particular wages or incomes policy and public expenditure policy have been formulated and propagated within the socio-economic frame of meaning. Not all policy areas have been subjected to this socioeconomic ideological conception, and the process of the negotiated economy has certainly not reached the same stage of development in all areas of potential application. Nonetheless, we claim as a justification for referring to a general trend, that macro-economic policy is increasingly assuming these contours, and that in a number of areas of policy similar although embryonic tendencies can be shown to exist.

4.3. Institutional arrangements

Since the end of the l950s five new types of institutions have developed:

- Policy institutions are public commissions and committees - usually composed along corporative lines - which formulate problems and to issue recommendations on steps to be taken.
- Campaign institutions are set up by interest organizations, corporations, public authorities or even along corporative lines in an attempt to formulate and propagate specific interpretations of problems and specific solutions in order to influence the political agenda.
- Discourse institutions are scientific or other institutions which test the consistency of the dominant conceptions and try to reformulate these into analytically coherent codes of languages.
- Negotiation-institutions are either ad hoc or permanent bodies - usually consisting of two or three parties - to outline frameworks and timetables and to reach concrete agreements by means of negotiations.
- Arbitration and sanction institutions are private or semi-public institutions which are supposed to deal with disputes and to impose sanctions in cases of violation of the agreements.

The institutions are complementary; they fulfil mutually dependent functions within a coherent process. Actually existing institutions might cover more than one function. This is the case, for instance, with the economic secretariats of the budget departments. They function simultaneously as campaign- and discourse-institutions.

Probably the five institutions exist to some extent in all Western European countries. They seem to follow from institutionalized class cooperation everywhere. It is not their existence as such which distinguishes the Scandinavian countries in this regard. It is rather their elaboration and their complementariness which have made possible a specific institutional process: the negotiated economy:

- The formation of new institutions have made it possible to formulate and propagate a specific ideological conception (the socio-economic frame of meaning) as a normative frame of reference.
- Other new institutions systematize and develop this ideological conception to constitute a rationale for individual and collective behaviour.
- Institutions mobilize and produce an elite (and to a certain extent also a popular) consensus about how to connect individual interests and socio-economic objectives.
- Within the normative framework dictated by the socio-economic ideology and the institutional restrictions imposed by general procedures and rules, a complex form of negotiation game is set into motion.
- The specific procedures and rules established via negotiation games ensure compromises and agreements in concrete negotiations between independent agents with opposite interests.

4.4. A process of institutional learning

The negotiated economy is also a learning process: in an ongoing process objectives are reformulated and experience with old means are evaluated and alternative means are formulated. This has been made possible precisely through the formation of the numerous policy, campaign, and discourse institutions. The continuous campaigning and reformulation of discourses and problems is conducted not merely by proposing a particular interpretation of the current economic situation on the political agenda. It also creates the semantic frame of reference and the discursive environment for connecting individual agency and socioeconomic objectives.

The very act of recording the experience gained by necessity involves constant reinterpretation and reformulation. Forecasts are tested and maybe falsified. Project calculations are modified. The correlation between phenomena is confirmed or denied.

Earlier approaches to problems or solutions already tried are labelled invalid, obsolete. Alternative forecasts and calculations are produced. As a result, new problems are formulated, alternative solutions are discovered, and new terms and conceptual contexts are created. The socio-economic frame of meaning is constantly being reformulated as a rationale for the understanding of society's relationships, problems and patterns of development.

This process is constantly evolving in the Scandinavian countries. Such a learning process is by no means a natural necessity. It follows from the systematic and continuous verbalization of the various conflicts of interests. It follows from the fact that the various institutions are not only capable but also forced to engage in the process. This is so not only because the socio-economic development constantly produce evidence to confirm or invalidate earlier forecasts and assumed relationships. But also because of the impossibility of avoiding a constant verbal confrontation with institutions representing opposing interests. The various participants in this confrontation are forced to analyze, comment and criticize the data, the models, the formulated problems, and the proposed solutions put forward by the other participants if they want to influence the political agenda.

5. The negotiated economy and social science

5.1. Impurity, the role of the state, and new forms of coordination

Hodgson has argued convincingly for the inevitability and necessity of impurities; different economic structures co-exist and supplement each other. It is equally inevitable that each (impure) system has a dominant economic structure as well as the fact that the state is a 'supra-regulator' of impurities: a regulator of the regulators to be found in each economic structure (1984: 220-228). The negotiated economy can be seen as a specific combination of impurities with specific forms of conflict and dominance and other 'supra-regulators' in addition to or instead of the state.

The negotiated economy is actually the historical result of a sequence of responses to the problems created by the existence of impurities. Negotiations and discursive coordination emerged, in the first place, as steps to coordinate and integrate decision-making in different structures. The juridification of the class struggle implied rights, and the subsequent institutionalization created autonomous decision-making units different from market agents and the state. The integration of the organizations into the state apparatus implied dispersion of state power and further differentiation. The negotiated economy reflects the need for integration in this institutionally differentiated system. The differentiation has made integration by market exchange or authoritative means impossible. It is instead effected or at least attempted by means of discursive processes or decision-making through negotiations.

The current complex forms of discursive and institutional coordination can be seen as measures to counteract the problems created by the co-existence of unregulated markets in some parts of the economy, regulation according to the prescriptions of the mixed economy in others, and full state discretion in yet others.

Hodgson emphasizes the necessary impurities and the role of the state as the 'supra-regulator'. The development of the negotiated economy shows that the necessary 'regulation of impurities' might produce forms of 'supra-regulation' which are different from that presupposed by Hodgson. The capacity for 'supra-regulation' is not attached to the state in the negotiated economy. It is not authoritative state planning or state regulation but rather state participation in decision-making in multi-centred structures which is the most important role of the state. The role ascribed to the state by Hodgson is actually taken over by the structured forms of interaction of the involved parties (including the state) in the institutional set-up for discursive and negotiated coordination.

5.2. The negotiated economy and economic theory

The emergent reality of the negotiated economy implies challenges to the dominant ideas within economic as well as political theory. Within political theory the constitutional interpretation of the distinction between the authority of the sovereign state and civil society still seems to dominate. In addition theories of corporatism have also gained prominence. However, none of these dominant theoretical perspectives seems appropriate in relation to the negotiated economy (Nielsen and Pedersen 1989a).

Within economic theory the debate is still dominated by the ideal-types of either the market economy or the mixed economy. Allocation of resources is evaluated either in relation to the market ideal of perfect competition or in relation to the ideal of a perfect and sharp borderline between autonomous action by market agents and supplementary or corrective measures taken by a sovereign state. The dominance of these ideals of either the market economy or the mixed economy results in blindness in relation to the coherence and the specific rationality of the negotiated economy.

The development of economic theory in the last decade does not even seem to move in that direction. Instead we have seen a lot of criticism of the established theories of the mixed economy (Keynesianism, welfare theory) based on the ideal of the market economy. For instance, the inherent assumptions concerning the capacity and the necessity for stabilization policy has been criticised by monetarism and new classical macro-economics. Also the implicit assumption in welfare theory concerning the capacity of the state for correction of market failures has been criticised by public choice theory which focuses on various government failures. Even the necessity for correcting perceived market failures has been denied by property rights theory which suggests massive extension and careful specification of private property rights as a more effective alternative.

A whole branch of theory has been developed to analyze these phenomena within the paradigm of traditional economic theory: formalized bargaining theory. Negotiations are seen as strategic games and analysed with a game-theoretical framework. Even if these contributions are no doubt helpful they are so merely in a limited sense. In game theory, the participants, the preferences, the bundle of choices (the strategies), and the outcome (dependent on the chosen strategy) are all assumed to be given rather than products of the game itself. This corresponds to the institutional reality of what we have called round table negotiations. It is not possible, however, to comprehend the processes of the negotiation games let alone the total institutional process of the negotiated economy by these analytical means. An early critique from within the ranks of bargaining theory of the application of game theory in the analysis of collective bargaining appears as relevant today as before. Stevens concludes: 'the format of game-theory analysis is such as to exclude many negotiatory phenomena of prime importance and interest' (Stevens 1963: 156).

Two basic assumptions of traditional economic theory appear problematic when studying the negotiated economy: (1) given institutions, and (2) given preferences. Neither the institutional setting (including the definition of the participants and the strategies of the game) nor the preferences of the agents can be considered given in a profound theory of the negotiated economy. Part of the institutional setting is actually an outcome of the negotiation game rather than a given framework for action. Furthermore, the formation of meaning and the moulding of preferences as a result of the formulation and propagation of the socioeconomic frame of meaning has critical implications concerning the assumption of given preferences. Of course this assumption has been challenged from many sources (Hodgson 1988: 117-144). The inadequacy of the assumption of given preferences is certainly not restricted to the negotiated economy. However, the critique appears extremely relevant - and the necessity for an alternative especially urgent - in this context. The exclusion of the formation of preferences from the theoretical horizon seems rather inappropriate in the negotiated economy, where choices and formation of preferences are integrated in one continuous process.

Traditional economic theory also ignores the problems and the effects of institutional change. This cannot be ignored when studying the negotiated economy. The institutional setting is constantly changed and constitutes a dominant item at the political agenda. For this reason it is essential to study how the institutions of the negotiated economy have been established historically. Only through such endeavours is it possible to recognize the dynamics and the functioning of this economic structure.

6. Rationality and efficiency

6.1. The negotiated economy - a power struggle

The negotiated economy is characterized by constant struggle and conflict at all levels, while simultaneously, mutual understanding is mobilized and compromises established between the conflicting parties.

The parties communicate, but they also struggle about the formulation and transformation of socio-economic experience into perceived problems, ends and alternative means. In this way the political agenda is formed around an agreed upon conception of the society at a given point of time. The preferences and expectations of the societal agents cannot be assumed given that they are constantly being formed through such an institutionalized struggle - and institutionalized communication.

In a similar way the procedures and criteria for decision making cannot be assumed to be given. There is constant struggle about the formation and transformation of institutions. On the other hand, both the discursive and the institutional results of the ongoing process constitute a framework for behaviour with more or less balanced power relations between the parties.

In other words the agents struggle not only about the results of the actual negotiations. They are also engaged in conflict - and communication - about the interpretation and the selection of problems, means and ends, and furthermore they struggle about where and how to negotiate about what. A power struggle is going on about discursive and institutional objectives as well as about the outcome of actual negotiations.

Although the overall structure of the negotiated economy appears rather stable it is for obvious reasons surrounded by controversy and challenged by advocates of alternative arrangements.

The negotiated economy is criticised from a neo-liberal position: negotiations should be substituted with market transactions because of the supposed rigidity and inefficiency of the negotiated economy due to the influence of the interest organizations. Another critique originates from an ideal-type democratic position: negotiations should be substituted with voting in parliament, which is considered the only legitimate representational form of popular rule.

Others defend the negotiated economy as a smooth and efficient procedure which guarantees the legitimacy of the decisions and the loyalty and consent of the parties involved in a process of implementation that is often decisive. According to this position many conflicts will remain unresolved if the parties behave in an un-coordinated way. Negotiations prior to the decision making are expected to prevent this from happening.

However, neither the critics nor those who sympathize with the reality of the negotiated economy seem to judge its functions from a fully satisfying conception of it. They often restrict themselves to an evaluation of the events around or closely connected to the negotiation table. They do not couple these with the processes producing the discursive and institutional framework for negotiations. If this were done the question of the efficiency of the negotiated economy appear much more complex as quite different forms of rationality are combined.

6.2. A combination of different forms of rationality

The emergence of the negotiated economy has produced a new context for rational behaviour: a combination of different forms of rationality - and not only instrumental rationality. In traditional economic theory agents are supposed to be rational in a certain sense: they choose the best possible means in relation to the predetermined goals. This assumed rationality presuppose given institutions and given preferences. When preferences (or ends) and the institutional surroundings can be considered given, it is possible to deduce the economic behaviour of the agent as a logical effect of the assumed means-end rationality. However, this is not so if moulding of preferences cannot be segregated from choices.

In the negotiated economy instrumentally rational choices are interwoven with other forms of rationality connected to discursive processes and formation of meaning. In one unbroken process the agents are confronted with different demands. They have to act rational in different ways. In round table negotiations they have to choose the means of action which are the most rational in relation to their ends within a given institutional framework. In negotiation games they also have to choose the most rational means in relation to their ends, too, with the institutional framework as the product rather than the precondition. Simultaneously, they have to act rationally in the process of formulation and propagation of the socio-economic frame of meaning. They are integrated parts of a process characterized by systematic and institutionalized interpretation of the situation, formation of meaning, and moulding of preferences. However, the different stages of the process of the negotiated economy are only partly separated in time and space. Accordingly, unambiguous behavioural conditions, stable institutional frames and given preferences cannot be assumed to exist. The agents are confronted with rather complex criteria for action in every instance of interaction in the process of the negotiated economy.

The behaviour of the agents appears irrational when judged from an ordinary instrumental point of view. However, this perception of rationality has been strongly criticised by various economists and sociologists. Recent contributions have transcended the traditional barrier between economics and sociology: 'Economics is all about how people make choices. Sociology is about why people don't have any choices to make' (Duesenberry and Preston 1960). Hodgson criticises the rationalist conception of action in economic theory. Action is seen as partly dependent on culture, values and institutions and partly dependent on idiosyncratic subjective features. Etzioni presents a similar approach: 'means selected to realize goals are often chosen partially or solely on normative-affected grounds and not on the bases of logical/empirical considerations' (Etzioni 1988: 14). Elster, too, has recently developed an eclectic approach: 'Most writers try to make do with rational self-interest as a sole motivational assumption .... Though I share their preference for a parsimonious explanation and their hesitation to get into a morass of ad hoc assumptions, I have concluded, with some reluctance, that there is no way in which the programme can be brought forward on this narrow base' (Elster 1989: 250). Thus he now believes that 'social norms provide an important kind of motivation for action that is irreducible to rationality or indeed to any other form of optimization mechanism' (ibid., 15). And he goes on to conclude that 'some forms of behaviour are best explained on the assumption that people act rationally, whereas others can be explained by .... social norms' (ibid., 97).

The irreducibility of social norms is to Elster especially striking in collective bargaining: 'Norms of equality, equity and fair division shape the outcome of bargaining generally and of collective wage bargaining in particular' (ibid., 215).

This has critical implications for the traditional theory of conflict as well. Rowe criticises what he calls the Hicksian theory which sees conflicts as exercises of naked bargaining power unaffected by normative considerations. This is contradicted by the facts that agents actually expect that normative arguments have effects, that conflicts are nearly always to some extent contained, and that conflicts are often disputes about the rights, and those very rights would be meaningless were human interaction wholly anomic (Rowe 1989: 105-108).

The co-existence of instrumental rationality and social norms is no doubt a general fact - and not only in bargaining or even collective bargaining. However, this is even more evident in the negotiated economy with its institutionalized integration of normative-affective aspects of the decision-making process.

The different forms of rationality present in the negotiated economy resemble the forms identified by Hargreaves-Heap (l989). He distinguishes three forms. In addition to instrumental rationality he mentions procedural rationality and expressive rationality. Procedural rationality is not directly related to ends. On the contrary, the rationality of behaviour is defined by the procedure or the means chosen. Expressive rationality has nothing to do with means. The rationality is connected to the process of formulating or finding ends. The formulation and propagation of the socio-economic frame of meaning introduces elements of procedural as well as expressive rationality in the negotiated economy.

The specific combination of rationality forms can also be conceived through the concepts of Habermas (l982). He too identifies three forms: instrumental, strategic and communicative rationality. While instrumental and strategic rationality are concerned with results and efficiency, communicative rationality, on the other hand, is concerned with mutual understanding and truth.

The concept of communicative rationality is perhaps the most interesting in this context. Habermas uses the concept in a prescriptive way. He imagines an idealized situation of communication without power related differences as far as admittance and influence is concerned. The interaction (the communication) is considered rational if the participants are free and equal, if they openly and publicly discuss common interests in order to achieve mutual understanding about disputed normative matters.

The formulation and propagation of the socioeconomic frame of meaning through policy, campaign, and discourse institutions is not identical with such idealized communicative interaction. The interaction between the involved parties in these institutions is not free from power related constraints. It is neither free from instrumental and strategic considerations. The campaign institutions, for instance, are meant to influence the political agenda and the preferences of the other participants in the discursive process. They engage in conflicts between different conceptions based on different interests.

In this sense it is true that 'bargaining must be distinguished from attempts to reach agreement by rational discussion' (Elster 1989: 50-51). However, several features of the discursive process in the negotiated economy resemble the ideal-type communicative rationality. Also here the participants attempt by means of verbal interaction in a continuous process of critique and self-critique to coordinate different conceptions into a mutual understanding of the current situation with its alternatives and constraints. Furthermore, the agents have to live up to certain legitimacy requirements in order to be accepted as legitimate participants in the discursive process. These requirements are not fundamentally different from the universal requirements to participants in ideal-type communication as formulated by Habermas. In the discursive process concerning the socio-economic frame of meaning the involved parties are obliged to fulfil the following requirements: (a) the arguments must be normatively correct, viewed in relation to existing value perceptions of future developments of society; (b) they must be technically credible, in relation to the prevailling professional standards and norms; and (c) they must be cognitively true, in relation to the cognitive conception of the reality it theoretically seeks to reflect.

6.3. Efficiency

Above the concept of rationality was attached to individual behaviour. We discussed the transformed context for rational individual behaviour as an effect of the emergence of the negotiated economy. Below we shall briefly approach the concept of rationality at the systemic level instead.

Is the negotiated economy an efficient way of allocating and (re)distributing the resources of society? From the point of view of a traditional economist the answer is negative. Johansen concludes the following about what he called the bargaining society:

'Bargaining will often be an inefficient decision procedure in the sense that it tends to distort the information basis for decisions, it tends to use or waste resources in the process, particularly delay decisions for reasons which are not technically necessary, it will more or less frequently lead to breakdown and failure to realize the potential gains, and threats will sometimes be carried out.' (Johansen 1978: 23)

Johansen's conclusions are well founded when the criterion of pareto-optimality is used and under the assumption of instrumentally rational agents. Bargaining processes will rarely lead to pareto-optimal allocation if you systematically omit the specific rationality of the communicative process.

However, the rationality of a system must also be related to the discursive processes needed to achieve mutual understanding of a normative frame of meaning. Certain arrangements might be considered irrational or wasteful when judged from the traditional criterion of efficiency. They might, however, appear rational as means to achieve mutual understanding.

Comparative data indicates that inefficiency is not an inescapable effect of a negotiated economy. According to Katzenstein (l985) the process of the negotiated economy (although he does not use that term) seems to be at least part of the reason for the smooth and relatively successful process of adapting to world market changes which characterizes small states in Western Europe including the Scandinavian countries. These qualities of the Scandinavian countries still seem to be intact (Nielsen and Pedersen l989b). In general flexible adjustment in Scandinavia seems to depend on its coexistence with political stability (Nielsen l989). In case of relative political instability the capacity for flexible adjustment of resources is hampered. The structure of the negotiated economy has produced a process which has shown capacity for learning and adjustment (Nielsen 1991) - although not always as fast as some might wish.

Bibliography

Berrefjord, O. and Nore, P. (l988) 'Political and Economic Policy Planning on a National Level - Exorcism and Laws of Gravity', *Scandinavian Political Studies*, 2, 103-14.

Devine P. (l988) *Democracy and Economic Planning*. Cambridge: Polity.

Duesenberry, J.S. and Preston, L.S. (1960) *Cases and Problems in Economics*, London: Allen & Unwin.

Eggertsson, T. (1990) *Economic Behaviour and Institutions*, Cambridge: Cambridge University Press.

Elster, J. (1989) *The Cement of Society. A Study of Social Order*. Cambridge: Cambridge University Press.

Etzioni, A. (1988) *The Moral Dimension. Towards a New Economics*. New York: Free Press.

Habermas, J. (1982) *Theorie des Kommunikativen Handelns. Vols. 1* and *2*. Frankfurt: Suhrkamp.

Hargreaves-Heap, S. (1989) *Rationality in Economics*. Oxford: Basil Blackwell.

Hernes, G., ed. (1979) *Forhandlingsoekonomi og blandingsadministrasjon*. Oslo: Universitetsforlaget.

Hodgson, G. (1988) *Economics and Institutions*. Cambridge: Polity.

Johansen, L. (1979) 'The Bargaining Society and the Inefficiency of Bargaining', *Kyklos*, 3, 497-522.

Katzenstein, P.J. (1985) *Small States in World Markets. Industrial Policy in Europe*. Ithaca: Cornell University Press.

March, J.G. and Olsen, J.P. (1989) *Rediscovering Institutions. The Organizational Basis of Politics*, New York: Free Press.

Marin, B. (1985) 'Generalized Political Exchange'. Firenze: European University Institute (working paper).

Midttun, A. (1988) 'The Negotiated Political Economy of a Heavy Industrial Sector: The Norwegian Hydropower Complex in the 1970s and 1980s', *Scandinavian Political Studies*, 2, 115-43.

Moore, C. and Booth, S. (1989) *Managing Competition: Meso-Corporatism, Pluralism and the Negotiated Order in Scotland*. Oxford: Clarendon Press.

Nielsen, K. (1989) 'Flexible Adjustment and Political Stability', *Scandinavian Political Studies*, 4, 297-312.

Nielsen, K. (1991) 'Learning to Manage the Supply-Side. Flxibility and Stability in Denmark, in B. Jessop, H. Kastendiek, K. Nielsen, and Ove K. Pedersen, eds., *The Politics of Flexibility. Restructuring State and Industry in Britain, Germany and Scandinavia*. Aldershot: Edward Elgar.

Nielsen, K. (1992) 'Mixed Economy, the Neo-liberal Challenge, and the Negotiated Economy', in *Journal of Socio-Economics, Fall* (in press).

Nielsen, K. and Pedersen, O.K. (1988) 'The Negotiated Economy. Ideal

and History'. *Scandinavian Political Studies*, 2, 79-101.
Nielsen, K. and Pedersen, O.K., eds. (1989a) *Forhandlingsoekonomi i Norden*. Copenhagen: Jurist- og oekonomforbundets Forlag.
Nielsen, K. and Pedersen, O.K. (1989b) 'Is Small Still Flexible?', *Scandinavian Political Studies*, 4, 343-371.
NOU (l982) *Maktutredningen*. Slutrapport. Oslo.
Pedersen, O.K. (1985) *Institutionel Historie. Om kampagnestyret forhandlingsoekonomi og koncensusplanlagt* låndannelse, Roskilde: Forlaget for Samfundsoekonomi og Planlaegning.
Pedersen, O.K. (1991) 'Nine Questions to a Neo-Institutional Theory in Political Science', *Scandinavian Political Studies*, 2, 1-24.
Pedersen, O.K., Andersen, N.Å. and Kjaer, P. (1992) 'Private Policies and the Autonomy of Enterprises: Danish Local and National Industrial Policy', *Journal of Economic Issues* (forthcoming).
Pestoff, V. (l988a) 'Joint Regulation, Meso-Games and Political Exchange in Swedish Industrial Relations.' In Marin, B. and Pizzorno, A., eds. *Generalized Political Exchange*. New York: Walther de Gruyter.
Pestoff, V. (l988b) 'Exit, Voice and Collective Action in Swedish Consumer Policy', *Journal of Consumer Policy*, 1, 1-27.
Rowe, N. (1963) *Rules and Institutions*. New York: Philip Allan.
Scott, W.R. (1990) 'Institutional Analysis. Variance and Process. Theory Approaches', paper presented at Conference on Organizations, Stockholm, August.
Shonfield, A. (1984) *In Defense of the Mixed Economy*, Oxford: Oxford University Press.
Stevens, C.M. (1963) *Strategy and Collective Bargaining Negotiation*. Westport, Connecticut: Greenwood Press.

6 Natural resource-based industries: Big business and the role of the state. The case of Norway's oil and gas

Ole Berrefjord and Per Heum

1. Natural resources, private business and the state

Norway's industrialization and economic welfare have benefitted significantly from the exploitation of natural resources. Even today, natural resources form the base for a significant share of Norway's industrial activity. For instance, as Figure 1.1 shows, approximately two thirds of Norway's exports can directly be ascribed to the exploitation of natural resources: extraction of non-renewable resources (oil, gas), production based on renewable resources (fisheries, forestry), and energy-intensive production based on hydro-electricity (metals, paper, pulp, fertilizers, petrochemicals).

The history of Norway's natural resource-based industries reveals several interesting examples of relationships between political authorities and private business, which can be considered neither consistent with the pure ideas of liberal market economies, nor with the ideas of centralized planning. One area, of course, is that identified by theorists as 'The Tragedy of the Commons' and 'The Prisoner's Dilemma' (Elster 1978). Such problems call for a collective authority to overcome the fallacies of a decentralized economy. Illustrations are easily found in the small-scale private business of Norway's farming and fisheries. In such instances, however, state participation is basically limited to ensuring the long-term interests of all participants, and is therefore never seriously questioned.

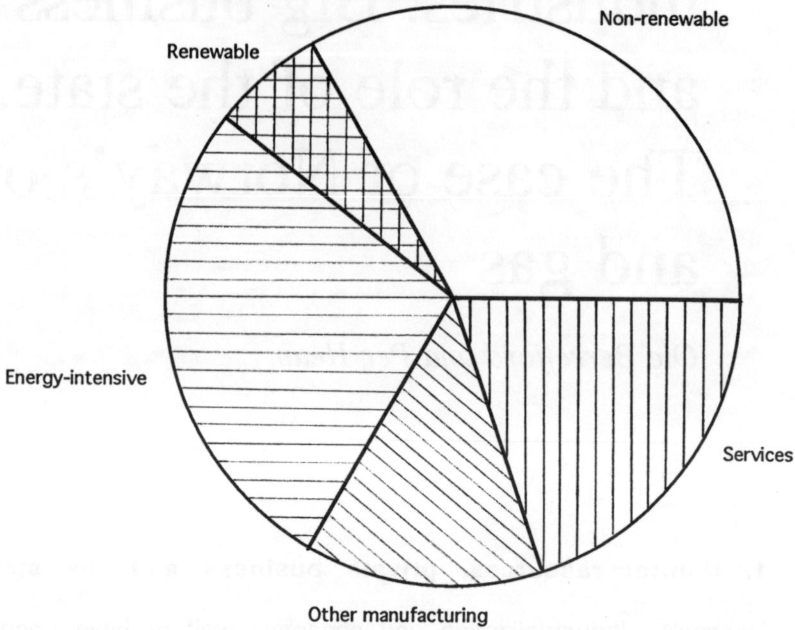

Figure 1.1: Norwegian exports by product groups, 1989

Source: The authors' own recalculation of Foreign Trade Statistics.

However, in other areas the state's role is not so universal; nor so easily grasped by conventional economic theory. In Norway, examples are found in the system regulating the exploitation of forests, water-falls and minerals. The public task has been to secure benefits and governance control for the nation, which may easily conflict with the profit interests of private business.

The system applied to such industrial activities was created during the first two decades of this century. The Law on acquisition of water-falls, mines and land, enacted in 1917, set the legal framework and the basic principles to be followed. Politically, the discussion was quite intense but it has since become widey accepted. Recently, however, as the question of international harmonization of business laws and regulations has been put on the agenda in connection with the EFTA-EEC negotiations on the European Economic Space issue, the issue has been re-opened.

Historically, the discourse on natural resource-based business has never really revolved around the issue of nationalization vs. privatization. Rather it concerned the rights of limited companies (big business) to hold land (Furre 1971). The fear was that industrial capitalists and foreign capital would take control over valuable natural resources, thereby undermining Norway's national sovereignty (attained in 1905) as well as restricting the rights of peasants to land. This led to a concessionary system executed by the state, which is still basically at work. In practice, any company that wants to buy land subject to concession - either the land is privately or publicly owned -needs to apply to the state for concession. This is also the case for any investor who wants to acquire more than 20 per cent of the shares in a company which owns property subject to concession.

This system has undoubtedly proven effective in the sense that it has allowed industrial business competence to be developed, securing the nation a position among the richest in the world. In fact, when Norway started to explore for oil and gas on its continental shelf in 1965, the same basic principles and procedures were applied as those enforced on the rights to water-falls and land half-a-century earlier (Berrefjord and Heum 1990).

In this paper, we will illustrate this system by discussing the state's role in relation to Norway's oil and gas. We start by describing the character of oil and gas activities, and present some principal considerations on the industrial participation of the state in that respect. Then we describe the main features of the legal system surrouding Norway's oil and gas, and the role it ascribes to the state.

The character of oil and gas projects, as well as the institutional structure constructed around them in Norway, imply that this business will be conducted within the context of a negotiated economy (Hernes 1978; Nielsen and Pedersen 1989). Hence, before concluding the paper, we briefly evaluate the performance of the negotiated economy regarding Norway's oil and gas, including its impacts of such a system on the distribution of power within Norwegian society.

2. Oil and gas - the question of state involvement

The government is responsible for preparing proposals to Norway's legislative power, the Storting. Thus, the state is bound to be involved in the process of creating the legal and institutional framework that will surround any new business.

The question of what role the state shall play regarding these industrial activities, however, may be answered in many different ways. Partly, the answer will reflect features that are inherent in the particular industry. Partly, it will reflect the situation prevailing during the period when the new industry is set up, building on political and industrial perceptions, and on political experience and tradition.

2.1. Features of the oil and gas industry

The fact that oil and gas are non-renewable resources raises the question of the role of the state in at least two respects. Firstly, a resource rent is normally attached to these commodities, raising the question of how it is to be distributed across the society. Solutions may differ. At one extreme, the rights to the resource rent can be privately appropriated by the companies exploiting the resources; at the other, the state may run the business itself and collect the whole resource rent. Somewhere in between lies the option of special taxation. However, no matter what solution that is chosen, the state has to decide.

Secondly, we have the question of industrial transformation. Industries based on non-renewable resources can only function as long as there are resources to exploit commercially. When resources are emptied in one area, the business moves to others. Thus, the opportunities to individual companies for long-term earnings differ from those available to the community in which the resources are currently being exploited. Either the community or the state has to prepare for this while the industry is still operating, or the community will be inclined to mobilize the state when the business has gone. In one way or another, the state will have to face the challenge of industrial sustainability.

There are also 'externalities', or impacts, attached to the oil and gas industry and to its commodities, which will call for state intervention (Johansen 1965). One aspect is strictly political, concerning oil as a key commodity in the world economy: any nation controlling a minimum reserve of oil will have to consider its strategic role in world politics, which definitely has to challenge the state.

Another aspect is the magnitude of industrial oil and gas projects. The development of offshore oil and gas resources requires large-scale capital projects, which obviously may have a wide variety of effects on substantial parts of a small economy such as Norway's. These effects will not be included in ordinary business calculations. So, if they are to be considered at all, this has to be done by public authorities.

Altogether, this means that there are certain features connected to oil and gas, which clearly imply that not only the legislative power of the state, but also the executive is likely to become involved in one way or another.

2.2. Situational factors

The likelihood of the state becoming involved in the potential oil and gas industry, also followed from the fact that the Norwegian state is the property holder of the areas which held a potential for oil and gas: Norway claimed sovereignty over the continental shelf as late as 1963, and no private property rights had been granted to the ocean or seabed areas. Of course, the land could be sold, or auctioned to business interests. This would have implied, however, that the state would be losing control over resources, which - if discovered - could have significant consequences to society. Besides, this would not have been consistent with Norway's political tradition. Consequently, there was never an issue whether the state should keep these property rights or not.

Last, but not least, the major issues at task have to play a role when choosing the governing system to be applied. One aspect of the prevailing situation back in the 1960s, is rather self-evident: no one knew then whether the area contained any oil or gas, or whether such resources could be commercially exploited. The first task, therefore, was to have the possible exsistence of oil and gas rejected or confirmed. This was not, however, the only task which the system would have to deal with. It also had to sustain options for the nation to solve different, and to some extent unknown, tasks in the future.

The fields in which these tasks most probably would turn up, could, however, be identified. If oil and gas were revealed, three questions could be taken for granted: one being how operations of the industry could benefit the society; another how integration of a new industry into the present economy should take place; and, thirdly, how long-term revenue generation in the society could be ensured after the resources had been exploited. There are, in fact, no simple or non-controversial answers to those questions. Besides, it seemed useless to devote much time and work to construct a new system to govern the exploitation of resources that might not even exist. Rather it would serve the purpose if relevant models that had proven effective in the past could be applied.

This is where political traditions play a role. In Norway, the concessionary law of 1917 regarding water-falls and land provided just such a model. This law had been constructed to support the idea of political sovereignty regarding resource-based industrial activities conducted by big business. This was also relevant in the prevailing situation: Norway did not possess the necessary industrial competence to discover the secrets of Norway's oil and gas. Those who could do so were foreign oil companies, featuring the largest business corporations in the world.

3. The governance system of Norway's oil and gas

3.1. Basic principles and institutional structure

The basic economic principle governing Norway's oil and gas has been, since it all started in 1965, that the resources shall be exploited on a commercial basis. Politically, the basic principle has been that these resources, and the industrial activities needed to exploit them, should benefit the society as a whole (St.meld. nr. 25, 1973-74). These principles are embodied in the legal framework surrounding oil and gas in Norway. Of course, this framework has been revised as experience has been gained. However, the basic principles and institutional structure have remained the same. Legally, Norway's oil and gas operations are founded on the Petroleum Law of 1985, which is a coherent presentation of several acts that had been passed until then. This law states that all rights to oil and gas on the continental shelf belong to the state. The state, however, does not possess the competence needed to exploit these resources. Thus, the rights to oil and gas are transmitted to oil companies through a concessionary procedure. This transaction, delegating the rights to oil and gas from the state to oil companies, is a key factor in understanding the system governing Norway's oil and gas. The state puts together a licence group, usually consisting of 3-6 oil companies, which acquires these rights. The rights are exclusive, but not eternal. They are limited in space and time. Within the state organization, two separate institutions have been established: a Ministry of Petroleum and Energy to execute policies decided upon in the Storting; and a Petroleum Directorate to be responsible for enforcing safety and environmental precautions, as well as to advise the government on questions regarding exploration and extraction. Beside the group of oil companies, the ministry, the directorate and the Storting are the major actors in Norway's oil and gas sector.

3.2. The concessionary system: basic lines of thought

It is not the purpose of the concessionary system, or the tasks assigned to the state, to nationalize or socialize the petroleum industry. Rather the purpose is to attract professional competence to exploit these resources, while maintaining political control over the country's national endowments. In practice, the continental shelf has been divided into blocks, according to the lines of latitude and longitudes Usually the transaction between the state and oil companies covers one block at a time. If oil and gas is not revealed within a period of 6-10 years, the rights have to be returned to the state. However, if exploration proves the existence of oil or gas in the transacted area, the companies are granted a time-restricted ownership right to these resources, limited to varying periods up to thirty years. This system has the advantage that it promotes exploration in the areas where the state wants exploration to take place: the oil companies holding the rights to the area, will not like to return it to the state, unless they feel pretty certain that it does not contain commercial reservoirs of oil and gas. Further, the system allows the state to take advantage of improved knowledge concerning the resource potential on the shelf in general, and of opportunities which new technology may offer. New areas may be opened for exploration incrementally, whereas returned blocks may be retransacted to other oil companies which consider the potential differently from the former licence holders. In other words; the system reduces loss-risks to the state caused by false judgement or inferior knowledge. In addition, the system is constructed to let the state enter into negotiations with all companies signalling an interest to take part, in order to promote the public point of view. This is not to say, however, that the public interest is easy to define, nor that it is a straight-forward task to sort out how the public interest most efficiently can be met. Actually, this ambiguity is perhaps the main explanation behind the introduction of a negotiating procedure.

In this regard, the prerequisite of commerciality has been an important bottom line. By choosing to enter into relations with several oil companies, the state has avoided the danger of having to rely on the competence and capabilities of only one. Besides, being in a position to grant preferences to companies individually, the state has promoted a set of domestic-based companies, which are capable of executing the commercial operations of oil and gas. After an introductory period of 10-15 years, Norway's oil and gas industry consisted of Norwegian-owned and foreign-owned companies. This has provided transparency and reciprocal check-points for outsiders. Likewise the establishment of the state-owned oil company (Statoil) is supposed to provide the state with checks vis-à-vis private business, and vice versa.

Statoil's position is, however, predominant. It participates in all licences granted since 1973. Originally, Statoil held at least 50 per centof the shares in each of these licences, implying that Statoil's view more or less had to become the decisive vote in the licence group. This caused an extensive political debate in the early 1980s, which was brought to an end by dividing Statoil's share into one part belonging to Statoil, and one directly to the state. Statoil's share now varies between 12 and 50 per cent, with 20 per cent as the most frequent. The state's direct financial involvement is usually 30 per cent.

Such shares are still large by Norwegian standards. Thus, the voting rules in the licence group have also been changed to avoid the domination of one company: Normally the state is not supposed to use its direct financial involvement to vote, leaving it to the oil companies in the licence to reach an agreement A decision, then, requires mobilization of a minimum share of the ownership rights, and it has to be supported by more than one of the owners in the group. To prevent a stalemate, the state's direct financial involvement may be activated. However, this option has not been executed in any licence so far.

3.3. The concessionary procedure

The concessionary procedure granting oil companies time-restricted rights to oil and gas in limited areas on the continental shelf, is a key mechanism in the governance system of Norway's oil and gas. Here conditions are set to regulate how the participation of oil companies is to take place, and procedures are lined out to make sure that these conditions are met.

So far, there have been 13 licensing rounds in Norway. The number of blocks that are concessioned has varied for each round, while the procedure followed has been basically unchanged. For each licensing round the Storting has to decide on which areas are to be included. Then, the Ministry of Petroleum and Energy announces the licensing round, and oil companies are invited to apply for ownership rights in areas where they want to take part.

When applying, the oil companies have to explain how they regard the prospects for each block in which they have interests. They also have to present a work plan for exploring the block, and to clarify how far they will allow the state to increase its share in the licence if commercial extraction of oil and gas is to take place. Also, their readiness to include Norwegian firms for supplying goods and services needed for developing oil and gas fields, have to be accounted for.

The Ministry of Petroleum and Energy, then, evaluates the applications and applicants, and enters into negotiations with those the consider the most competent and serious applicants. According to the Ministry, this requires that the applicant has the necessary competence to participate in offshore petroleum activities in a safe manner, that the applicant has sufficient financial strength to take part, and that the applicant has not earned a bad reputation from earlier participation in Norway.

During these negotiations, the Ministry discusses with each applicant the work plan described in the application, the company's offer of a sliding scale for the state's direct financial involvement, and the applicant's willingness of entering into commitments regarding industrial benefits. Considering the outcome of these negotiations, the Minister of Petroleum and Energy suggest to the government cabinet for which areas concessions ought to be granted. Further, the Minister proposes which oil companies shall form the licence group in each of the blocks, the distribution of ownership shares between these companies, and the one to be the operator for the group. The cabinet makes the final decisions on these matters through a Royal Decree.

However, before the Royal Decree is finally issued, the oil companies have been informed of the outcome of these considerations and have stated whether they agree to participate on the conditions offered. This means that they explicitly have to agree to the terms and to their ownership position in the licence groups. These terms include the obligation to keep the Petroleum Directorate informed about the results of the exploration activities. They also prescribe how the licence holders are to proceed if commercially exploitable oil or gas resources are discovered.

3.4. Business and the state: division of labor and responsibility

To summarize, we may link the roles of oil companies and the state to the chain of different operations that constitutes oil and gas production. It starts with preliminary seismic studies, proceeds through drilling exploration, field development, and finally production. There is a division of roles and responsibilities between oil companies and the state throughout this chain of operations (Berrefjord and Heum 1983). The state holds initial control through its property rights, whereas oil companies are held responsible for all commercial operations. At certain mile-stones, or decision-points in this process, the state and the companies in question enter into very different forms of relationship depending upon the specific stage of operations involved.

This division of labour, responsibility and operational power is exercising a significant influence on the performance of the oil-and-gas-based industry in Norway. In this national context it is also important to recall that at each point in time, only parts of the continental shelf are subject to this governing procedure. New areas are gradually released for exploration. Some areas are returned to the state, and in others production or preparation for extraction take place. Then, over time weaknesses in the system may be corrected, or the practice may be adjusted to shifting conditions beyond national control, either because of significant changes in oil prices or changing prospects regarding the oil and gas potential on the continental shelf.

4. A negotiated economy

4.1. The negotiated economy - duality at the business level

The governance system of Norway's oil and gas, is obviously based on frequent interactions between the oil business and the state, often generating broader political processes and participation. Thus, the concept 'The Negotiated Economy', which was introduced by the Norwegian Power Study (e.g., Hernes 1978), seems relevant to characterize the system.

Later, Berrefjord, Nielsen and Pedersen (1989) have defined the negotiated economy in macro terms as a society, where resources to a large extent are allocated through institutionalized negotiations between separate decision-making bodies of the state, of interest organizations, and of companies. Through this interaction, a common perception of the challenges at task is developed, efforts to cope with them are discussed, and compromises are negotiated. These may concern actions within the current institutional framework, or changes in the framework as such.

The negotiated economy concerns the governing of economic activities. Thus it is important to the performance of the economy, including questions of efficiency and of income distribution (Berrefjord and Heum 1984). However, even though it affects all members of the society, not everybody can be included in the discursive processes constituting the negotiated economy.

When focusing on business operations and on participation in thenegotiated economy at the business level, sheer company size itself dictates that market transactions are replaced by procedures exercised within company hierarchies, including internal negotiations included (Coase 1937; Williamson 1975). Externally, negotiations will show up in interactions between companies, and between companies and public authorities.

Based on empirical studies in the 1970s, the Power Study documented that the frequency of a company's external interactions with other companies and with public authorities tended to increase with company size (NOU 1982:3, chapter 5). Small companies were not included in these discursive processes (Schjelderup 1980).

Picturing the business community along three dimensions:

1) company structure,
2) inter-company relations, and
3) company-government relations,

these findings lead to the thesis of a dual economy. One group of companies, represented by the upper box in Figure 4.1.1 , participates directly in the negotiated economy. The other group in the lower box - resembling relational characteristics of perfect competitive markets - is left to adapt to the repercussions of the negotiated economy.

The oil and gas industry is a prominent example of such a politicized business, typically operating in the interface between market processes and political decisions. Thus, oil companies are not likely to limit the pursuit of their self-interest to market efforts; they will engage in politics as well.

As far as Norway is concerned, the oil and gas industry has mainly emerged after the empirical surveys, on which the Power Study was based, had been conducted. This may indicate that the oil and gas industry has strengthened the negotiated character of Norway's business. It is also a fact that production in general in Norway has become significantly more concentrated during the 1980s (Berrefjord, Heum and Tvedt 1990). However, there are reasons to believe that there are capacity and efficiency restrictions regarding the relative magnitude of negotiations in an economy. Therefore, we have research projects under way to investigate how the negotiated economy of Norway has changed over the last two decades, and the decisive factors behind these changes.

4.2. Performance of a negotiated economy: Norway's oil and gas

Earlier we assumed that any system governing an oil and gas industry has to deal with at least four major issues: to ensure

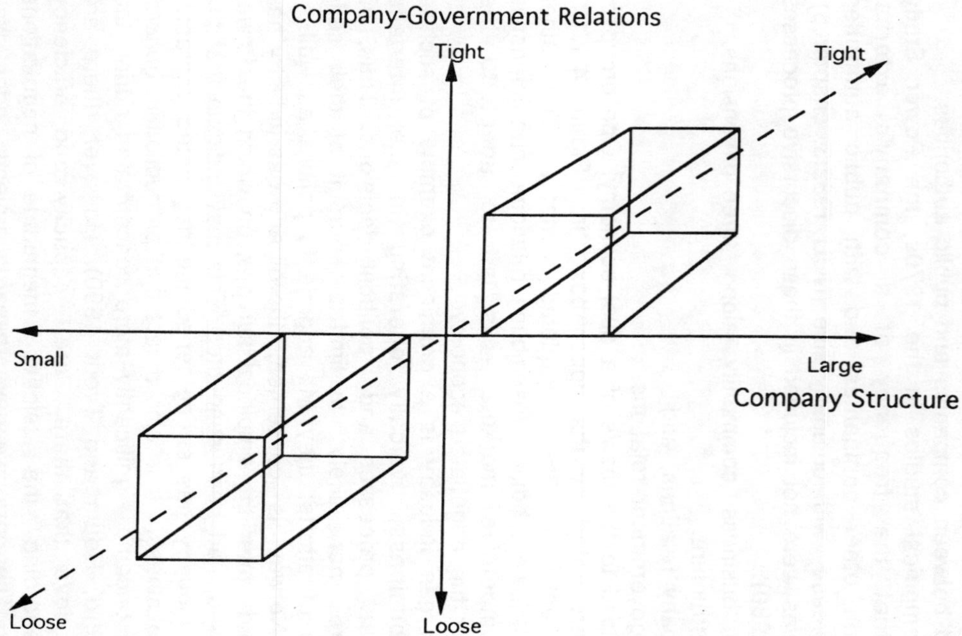

Figure 4.1.1: Political organisation of the business community

Source: NOU 1982, 135

exploration; gain social benefits if resources are revealed; integrate the new business into the prevailing economy; and promote transformation of the resource rent into long-term revenue sources. Consequently, the performance of the system and procedures, which were created to govern Norway's oil and gas, ought to be judged according to how they have coped with those issues.

Regarding exploration, the system was based on granting experienced and financially strong oil companies exclusive, but time-restricted, ownership rights to all oil and gas in limited geographical areas. This has definitely proven successful. Of course, it is not the system that has provided Norway with affluent oil and gas resources. The system, however, has allowed these resources to be revealed efficiently when the society became aware of their possible existence.

In other areas of the world, oil companies may possess exclusive rights to areas, which have not been restricted in time. Then, exploration takes place when it fits into company plans, not when it suits the society in which the areas are located. In Norway, the incentive system has been created so that the company interest in conducting exploration coincided with the interests of society. It should, however, be mentioned that disappointment regarding the oil and gas potential in Norway was emerging when the first discoveries were made in the late 1960s. This prevented oil companies from withdrawing. However, if this had become the case, it would not have been due to the system governing these activities, but to lack of competence among the companies tracing oil and gas in this area.

Regarding social benefits, the basic elements of the governing system comprise the concessionary procedure and the practice of allowing only parts of the continental shelf to be included in a licensing round. Doing so, the risks of being cheated are reduced: no one who wants good long-term relations with the property holder can base their business on fooling him into unfavourable, or unreasonable, deals. In fact, the system may be characterized as incremental, allowing the state to adjust its demands and ambitions to the experiences that are to be gained.

The discoveries of huge oil and gas resources proved the high potential for oil and gas in Norway at a time when oil business was subject to nationalization in many parts of the world (Sampson 1975). This attracted the interests of oil companies in Norway. It also increased the power position of the state, a position that was further strengthened due to the development of oil prices during the 1970s and early 1980s.

This, of course, has affected the tax level applied on the industry, allowing the government to seize a significant share of the resource rent. In turn, this has benefitted public finances, and possibly the welfare of citizens through the financing of public services.

The power position of the state, further allowed it to demand assistance from foreign oil companies in developing Norwegian-based industrial competence in the fields of oil and gas. Statoil started from scratch when it was established in 1972, to become fully operative a decade later. So has also been the case with Norsk Hydro, and is becoming the case with the third Norwegian oil company, Saga. Doing so, the state could execute control by drawing on the competitive forces which the companies placed on each other, and by comparing the performance and results of one company - or group of companies - with that of others.

Considering the achievements of the Norwegian-based oil companies, it seems fair to conclude that the negotiated economy has been rather successful in developing Norwegian-based industrial competence in this area. This seems to be the case in related business in manufacturing and engineering, in financing and insurance, in shipping-based operations, and research, as well, which also have been promoted through the concessionary procedure. Some uncertainty is, however, attached to this conclusion, as the industry so far has only proven its competitiveness internationally to some extent. Thus, we cannot rule out the possibility that the business competence developed, is inferior according to international standards. Still, other explanations are also justified: the business is rather young, and it has been more than fully employed to serve the offshore oil and gas industry at home. The incentive to expand abroad has, therefore, been rather weak.

Nevertheless, it cannot be denied that state efforts to attain direct industrial benefits have also been manifested in demands which have proved rather short-sighted: it serves, for instance, no purpose to have oil companies investing in industrial facilities in certain regions, which they hardly use. Oil companies, however, considered these outlays as a cost element, which had to be compared with the possible substantial costs of being reluctant to invest. As the investments were tax deductable, the costs were low for the company after all. In reality, the state had to pay most of the bill by having to face lower tax revenues than otherwise would have been the case. This is something the state has become increasingly aware of, however, since the oil price collapsed in 1986. Thus, despite mistakes and foolish moves, we think the negotiated economy of oil and gas in general has proven successful in coping with the question of attaining social benefits.

The third area in which the achievements of the negotiated economy in Norway's oil ans gas ought to be considered, is the integration of the emerging oil and gas industry into the existing economy. In essence, this mainly boils down to the question of deciding on the aggregate level of oil and gas activities in the Norwegian economy. The state's initial control over the areas in which oil and gas may be hidden is of minor importance in this respect, as no one knows in advance what may be discovered. The major instrument for the state is rather its legal authority to intervene in company plans, for instance regarding the time schedule for developing and producing the oil and gas they have discovered. Also, Statoil, as a 100 per centstate-owned company may be instructed to carry through projects which the state finds reasonable for public purposes.

However, this legal authority may easily conflict with the bottom line of commerciality on which Norway's concessionary system is based. It may also contradict other objectives which the state wants to pursue: how can the state promote exploration in new areas, if the licence holders are not allowed to produce what is already discovered? So, in practice, this authority ascribed to the state has been of minor value.

The oil price collapse in 1986, clearly showed that Norway's economic development had become severely exposed to the fluctuations in the oil price (Heum 1987). However, to cope with the effects of lower oil prices on the domestic oil and gas industry, a new tax-regime was introduced. This substantially reduced the level of 'government take'. Combined with increased company efforts to cut costs, and to try out 'new' and cheaper technology, Norway already faced another boom of its oil and gas activities by 1987. This led the government to consider postponing some of the suggested field development plans proposed by licence holders.

It was a widely shared view - also in the oil and gas sector - that lower activity levels than expected would be beneficial to the industry and to the society. However, within the sector, everybody also thought that fields other than theirs ought to be postponed. Strong interests were mobilised to support each single project, while there was no mutually accepted understanding of how to select between them. In this context, the legal authority of the state to decide on the matters proved of no value: all projects which the companies forwarded were sanctioned by the respective authorities.

This story is not peculiar to a negotiated economy. Rather it illustrates a problem that applies to collective decisions in general: when few are strongly affected by the outcomes of a decision, they tend to be better organized, and hence in a better position to promote their interests, than those less directly affected. Even if a given outcome would mean that those vaguely affected had more to gain than those strongly affected had to lose, decisions tend to come out in favour of the latter. In this way short-sightedness tends to overrule long-term considerations; special group interests tend to outweigh the concerns of the society as a whole (Hernes 1980).

This also raises another question: the power of the oil and gas segment vs. the public interest. As business, public administration and politicians dealing with oil and gas frequently interact, they develop common frames of reference and a mutual understanding as to what is not, decisive across the private and public spheres of the industry.

An 'oil-industrial-complex' evolves, which evidently is strong when outsiders try to confront it (Berrefjord 1983).

Such industrial complexes across the private and public sphere are no ideosyncratic phenomenon regarding oil and gas. It also tends to evolve regarding other industries and sectors of the society (cf. Midttun 1989). In consequence, the state cannot be considered a homogeneous actor. Rather, we face a fragmented, or segmented, state (Egeberg, Olsen and Saetren 1975). This means that the task of integrating a new industry like oil and gas into the prevailing economy, is reduced to a question of what the segment itself finds appropriate, considering the opportunities to the industry. At the project level, this implies that the state may become involved in business matters, in such a way that it turns out to advocate the interests of companies and the industry rather than the public interest (Berrefjord, 1990). Considered in relation to macro-political governance, i.e., in terms of the integration of the oil and gas industry into the prevailing economy, it is our view that the negotiated economy has not shown itself more successful than other systems with less state participation.

The final major question, of transforming oil and gas into other assets which may ensure Norway's income in a long-term perspective, originates in the fact that oil and gas are non-renewable resources. Of course, the magnitude of transformation needed will depend on how far oil and gas revenues keep up current levels of welfare. In this respect, however, it is almost unquestioned that the expansion of oil and gas activities in Norway, has had severe crowding-out-effects on other domestic business operating in international markets (Berrefjord and Heum 1990a).

As things stand today, it seems likely that oil and gas cannot provide growth in domestic welfare for more than another 4-5 years. Some time later, probably in the period 2000-2010,

Norway's annual volumes of oil and gas production will have to come down. Bearing in mind that it is a complex and time-consuming task to develop competitive industrial competence, the transformation issue is already highly relevant.

However, when it comes to transformation, it is evident that the state and the oil companies do not play on the same team. Companies will consider investment opportunities all over the world to secure their long-term earnings, whereas a major part of the transformation issue has to concern industrial investments in Norway. When Norway's oil and gas no longer offer the necessary profit opportunities to the companies, they will seek oil and gas resources in other parts of the world. The oil companies cannot be expected to contribute in transforming Norway's industrial base.

This implies that the negotiated economy applied on Norway's oil and gas, has provided Norway with an option, which would not have existed if the oil and gas industry had been left to private interests alone. As the state is the major collector of the operating result from Norway's oil and gas industry, the state also holds the prime responsibility for initiating transformation of the nation's oil wealth. In other words; it is furnished with a financial base to deal with a more general question: how the state can promote industrial transformation and economic growth (Berrefjord and Heum 1984a). This is, however, no easy task, meaning that only the future will tell to what extent Norway was able to take advantage of this most favorable option.

5. Concluding remarks

In this paper we have discussed the role of the state in relation to Norway's oil and gas. The governance system applied in this industry accords with a long political tradition in Norway regarding the organization of natural resource-based industrial activities. This system is neither consistent with the pure ideas of liberal market economies, nor with those of centralized planning. Rather it is a 'compromise', attempting to attract industrial competence on commercial conditions, while maintaining public control over the nation's natural endowments.

The system is not perfect. It has been able to solve some crucial tasks, while others remain unsettled. However, neither of the pure systems, leaving it all to the business or to central authorities, would be likely to prove more efficient. Probably the business-based system would have been less flexible in relation to changing market conditions.

Bibliography

Berrefjord, O. (1983) 'Industrial Policy Frameworks in the 80's', *Bergen Conference on Oil and Economics: Oil and Industry - Are They Compatible?*, Bergen, Bergen Bank.

Berrefjord, O. (1990) 'Public Projects and Corporate Behavior - A Negotiated Economy in Norway', Paper presented at the *Second Annual International Conference on Socio-Economics*, Washington D.C., March 16-18.

Berrefjord, O. and Heum, P.. *Oil Politics* (in Norwegian), Oslo: Tiden Norsk Forlag, 1983.

Berrefjord, O., and Heum, P. (1984) 'Offshore Petroleum Activities and the Development of the Political Economy in Norway', *Peuples mediterraneens*, 26, Paris.

Berrefjord, O., and Heum, P. (1984a) 'Economic Growth on the Agenda. How Governments Can Contribute in Promoting Economic Growth and Industrial Transformation', Bergen, *The Institute of Industrial Economics*, Report No. 44.

Berrefjord, O., and Heum, P. (1990) 'Political Governance of the Petroleum Industry - the Norwegian Case', in Bergesen and Sydnes (eds.) *Naive Newcomer or Shrewd Salesman? Norway a Major Oil and Gas Exporter*, Oslo, The Fridtjof Nansen Institute.

Berrefjord, O., and Heum, P. (1990a) 'Oil and the Industrial Base of the Norwegian Economy', in Bergesen and Sydnes (eds.) *Naive Newcomer or Shrude Salesman? Norway a Major Oil and Gas Exporter* Oslo. The Fridtjof Nansen Institute.

Berrefjord, O., Heum, P., and Tvedt, K-O. (1990) 'Norway: On the Track of Long-Term Balanced Growth?', ETLA, IFF, IUI and NOI *Growth and Integration in a Nordic Perspective*, Bergen, NOI-Report nr. 125.

Berrefjord, O., Nielsen, K., and Pedersen, O-K, (1990) 'Negotiated Economy in the Nordic Countries - an Introduction', in Nielsen and Pedersen (eds.) *Negotiated Economy in the Nordic Countries*, Kobenhavn, Jurist- og Okonomforbundets Forlag.

Coase, R. (1937) 'The Nature of the Firm', *Economica*, Nov.

Egeberg, M. Olsen, J., and Saetren, H. 'The Organized Society and the Segmented State', *Kirke og kultur*, No. 5 and 6.

Elster, J. (1978) *Logic and Society: Contradictions and Possible Worlds*, New York, John Wiley & Sons.

Furre, B. (1971) *Norway's History 1905-1940*, Oslo, Det Norske Samlaget.

Hernes, G. (ed.). (1978) *Negotiated Economy and Mixed Administration*, Oslo, Universitetsforlaget.

Hernes, G. (1980) 'What Leads the Leaders', *Samtiden*, No. 1-1980.
Heum, P. (1987) 'Stabilization Efforts in an Independent Oil Exporting Country - the Case of Norway', Bergen, *The Institute of Industrial Economics*, Notat No. 4,.
Johansen, L. (1965) *Public Economics*, Oslo, Universitetsforlaget.
Midttun, A. (1989) 'Negotiated Economy in a Heavy Industry Sector: The Norwegian Hydro-Power-Industrial Complex in the 1970s and 1980s', in Nielsen and Pedersen (eds.) *Negotiated Economy in the Nordic Countries*, Kobenhavn, Jurist- og Okonoforbundets Forlag.
Nielsen, K. and Pedersen, O-K. (eds.) (1989) *Negotiated Economy in the Nordic Countries*, Kobenhavn: Jurist- og Okonomforbundets Forlag.
NOU (1982:3) *The Final Report from the Power Study*, Oslo.
Sampson, A. (1975) *The Seven Sisters*, London:,Coronet Books.
Schjelderup, L. (1980) 'Small Firms in a Large-Scale Business Society', a publication from the Power Study in Norway, Oslo, Universitetsforlaget.
St.meld. nr. 25 (1973-74) *The Role of Petroleum Production in the Norwegian Society* , Oslo: Ministry of Treasury.
Williamson, O. (1975) *Markets and Hierarchies: Analysis and Antitrust Implications*, New York, Free Press.

7 Towards a new Swedish model

Victor A. Pestoff

1. Introduction

Concertational practices and the negotiated economy have long been seen as the hallmark of the politics of compromise in Sweden. Strong trade unions in coalition with the ruling Social Democrats have developed the welfare state into a 'people's home' with unique features. The Swedish model is now under systematic assault by organized business. Business challenges many, if not most, features of tripartite concertational practices, the negotiated economy and the welfare state in Sweden today.

This paper explores the role of business in reorganizing and restructuring Swedish economic, political and social relationships. Three substantive areas are chosen to illustrate the extent of de-institutionalization of concerted practices and the negotiated economy. These are industrial relations; consumer, agricultural, and food policy; and housing policy. In these and other areas business is calling for a return to the market.

The problems facing concertational practices and the negotiated economy in Sweden are related to developments in the international economy. Large Swedish firms are at the cutting edge of European eonomic integration and are helping to internationalize the Swedish economy. But in doing so, they are also internationalizing themselves and Swedish politics. As the international level grows in importance both economically and politically, Swedish business quite naturally loses interest in developments, agreements and negotiations at the national level as well as in concertational practices and the negotiated economy.

2. Recent changes: the tip of an iceberg

The Swedish parliamentary elections of 1991 introduced two new parties into the Riksdag. The Christian Democratic Union is one of these. It received 7.1 per cent of the votes in its first mandate from the electorate after almost 30 years of fighting unsuccessfully for a seat in the Riksdag. The other new party in 1991, New Democracy, was just 30 weeks old when it made its breakthrough in the Riksdag, with 6.7 per cent of the vote.

Both these non-socialist parties contributed to a dramatic swing to the right in the Swedish electorate. The Social Democrats suffered their greatest loss and the lowest level of support (37.6 per cent) since the introduction of universal suffrage at the begining of the 1920s. The parties of the right, by contrast, made their greatest gains since that time. The non-socialist coalition government formed after the 1991 election is led by Carl Bildt, the chairman of the Conservative Party, and this is also the first time that this party heads a government since the 1920s.

These facts reveal a dramatic change in Swedish politics, particularly since news from Sweden is often equated with 'business as usual', 'everything is very much the same', etc.. Dramatic as these changes may be, they are only the tip of an iceberg. There is more to come and more important, there is more than meets the eye. Swedish business is not playing its usual role and Sweden is not simply at a crossroads: she has already embarked upon an entirely new path. It is one leading from the Swedish model with a universal welfare state to a new model which might be referred to as a workfare state.

Given these dramatic changes, both apparent and anticipated, it is important to examine how and why they came about, since they raise more general problems about political and institutional change. More specifically, how do traditional institutions change in a very stable society, one without great social tensions? What is the role of politics and political choice in bringing about such dramatic changes? What role did/does public discourse play in bringing about change in Sweden?

What can the concept of the negotiated economy contribute to our understanding of institutional change, of how and why it occurs? The negotiated economy provides the basic institutional framework of the traditional Swedish or Scandinavian model(s). It posits a public dialogue between social partners (labour and capital), but one which assumes symmetry of resources and access to institutions for campaigns and discourse. If no symmetry of power exists, can the institutional base of the negotiated economy adapt and survive, or will it erode and wither?

What will the reaction of the major social partners be to fundamental changes in the negotiated economy? If one of them gains ascendancy while the others decline, will it be possible to create a new model and strike a new balance between them, or will the stronger exploit its position to dismantle the negotiated economy? Will the politics of compromise be replaced by the politics of conflict? How will the losers react? Will they acquiesce or pursue a strategy of attempting to defend or regain their old position? Will they meet changes in the negotiated economy in a defensive, adaptive or offensive manner?

Moreover, is it possible to pursue a neo-liberal strategy without dismantling the existing welfare state? Is it possible to introduce a new political model without de-institutionalizing the old one? How will the old institutions react, and will they oppose such changes? The dramatic contemporary developments in Sweden can thus serve to illustrate some major issues for research on the politics of civil society and the welfare state in the new integrated Europe at the turn of the century.

3. The privileged position of business in market economies

Numerous economists, political scientists and sociologists have documented and discussed the privileged position of business in market economies (Berrefjord *et al.*, 1982; Berrefjord and Hernes 1989; Galbraith 1984; Heckscher 1946, 1951; Key 1942, 1958, 1961; Lindblom, 1977; Lundberg 1989; Olsen 1965, 1982, 1991; Sailsbury 1984; Schmitter, 1989; Streeck 1989, 1991; and Vogel, 1989). Others underscore the importance of various channels of influence other than voting in democratic societies (Hirschman 1982 and Rokkan 1966). These widely repeated observations should lead to business receiving much more attention in academic circles.

Although business has not yet been subject to much systematic scrutiny, it is an important political actor in Sweden, perhaps *the* most important. In area after area it appears that Swedish business has embarked on a policy of radically changing established economic policies and political patterns in one of the most well-developed welfare states in the world. In brief, Swedish business wants to replace concertational practices in economic and social policy with market forces and to replace the politics of compromise, which has historically been associated with the Swedish model, with the politics of confrontation.

The main business interest association, the Swedish Employers' Confederation, rightfully conceives of itself as 'the driving force in changing the system'. Its adamant rejection of central collective bargaining initiated a reaction which brought down the Social Democratic minority government in February 1990. More recently SAF spelt out a detailed plan for the complete privatization of the welfare state by the turn of the century. It also announced its withdrawal from the governing bodies of most public administration boards throughout Sweden, including those dealing with labour market policy. SAF repeatedly demands that all forms of industrial negotiations and regulations be replaced by market forces.

Galbraith argues that conditional power is most influential in the age of organizations. It is exercised by changing beliefs, i.e., through persuasion, education or social commitment (Galbraith 1984: 213). Patrik Engellau, director of a consultant firm frequently engaged by SAF for its opinion campaigns said that '(i)deological dominance is more secure than domination with the help of tanks and bayonets. Whoever has the priority of interpreting reality has power' (1988).

Power in a social relationship, according to Weber (1969: 37), is 'the possibility of imposing one's will on other persons in spite of their opposition'. Political scientists often see power in terms of person 'A' getting person 'B' to do what 'B' would not otherwise have done (Dahl 1957: 202). The presentation below is related to the question of who exerts power in Sweden today, a question that receives no clear or concise answer in the Swedish Power Study (Pettersson, 1990).

Because of SAF's increasing influence, our focus here is confined primarily to employer organizations, rather than political parties or trade unions. This is motivated in part by Sainsbury's comprehensive survey of the challenges facing the Social Democratic Party and the Swedish Confederation of Labour (L0) in the 1980s (Sainsbury 1991). In part, during the heyday of the Swedish model, most social scientists limited their study of power to labour unions and the Social Democratic Party (see, for example, Korpi 1978 and 1981). With the dramatic decline of this model and the autumn elections, it seems more relevant to turn our attention to other social actors normally ignored by social scientists, e.g., business interest organizations and employer organizations. Previously, they were rarely subject to academic scrutiny. But this no longer seems justified.

We will, therefore, devote much of our attention below to the struggle over the institutions and forms for interaction between various social actors. These institutions and forms comprise the structures and the rules of the game of economic, political and social interaction. Whoever decides what structures are relevant, what rules apply, what games will be played, in which arenas and with which players, can significantly determine the outcome.

This struggle is conceived as an interactive process, in which organizations attempt to change their environment at the same time that they are constrained by the latter (Aldrich and Stern 1983; Aldrich and Staber 1984; Pestoff 1987, 1988b, I990b and I991a; and Schneiberg and Hollingsworth 1991). Changing the environment takes a long time and is not something achieved without sacrifices nor a long-term strategy. Thus, the view that organizations are merely a product of their environment and that they must always adapt to changing circumstances or fail in their pursuit of power is rejected here. It is not merely a question of supply and demand, where demand determines supply. Intensive marketing of new ideas can create demand for them (Pestoff 1988c), just as with new products. At the bottom line politics makes a difference and Swedish business interest associations provide a good example of this (Pestoff 1988b, I990b, I991b).

Much of the presentation below concerns the discourse about institutional change, rather than a detailed study of change itself. This is motivated by two considerations. Firstly, several authors underline the importance of public discourse, not the least discourse associated with the negotiated economy. Thus, they include both campaign and discourse institutions among the five institutional features of the negotiated economy. Secondly, the Swedish discourse calls for far reaching institutional change aimed primarily at removing many of the very institutions of the negotiated economy and welfare state, i.e., aimed at their de-institutionalization. Thus, at the micro level, the main change comes with the disappearence of an institution, rather than its reorganization. At the macro level it is nevertheless possible to speak of reorganizing the negotiated economy and welfare state. This should be kept in mind when we turn our attention to a special feature of Nordic democracies, i.e., social bargaining as manifest in the negotiated economy.

4. Reorganizing the negotiated economy

The negotiated economy (see the introduction and the chapter by Nielsen and Pedersen in this volume) is not a permanent institutional arrangement, but a process which is subject to constant change. A restructuring of the negotiated economy can be found in numerous policy areas in Sweden. Certain aspects of the negotiated economy have been subject to criticism, primarily by organized business. Some of its institutions have been curtailed or phased out in traditional policy areas, while certain of its features have taken root in new areas. This chapter examines the experience of Sweden in reorganizing the negotiated economy in industrial relations, consumer, agricultural and food policy, and housing and rent negotiations, while industrial investments and building projects, which corroborate this development, are dealt with elsewhere (Pestoff I991b).

4.1. Industrial relations

Centralized collective bargaining is the implicit core feature of the model proposed by Nielsen and Pedersen. The core features of their model are most institutionalized in industrial relations of small, but highly developed economies of the northern European countries, although Katzenstein (1985) sees some similarities with other small European countries. The institutional history of the negotiated economy is synonymous with the development of the institutions of central collective bargaining, based on the historic compromises between the peak organizations of employers and trade unions in the four Nordic countries.

Elvander (1989) provides us with an overview for the 1970s and 1980s of variations in the development of collective bargaining in these four Nordic countries. Central collective bargaining is a basic feature of industrial relations in Sweden and of the 'Swedish model'. In its heyday the Swedish model relied primarily on bi-partite patterns, and agreements were negotiated between strong unions and a highly centralized employer organization. Government intervention became unnecessary after the 1938 Saltsjöbaden Basic Agreement between SAF and LO, which laid down the the procedures for collective bargaining in Sweden and was designed to limit industrial conflict.

Politics re-entered the scene with the radicalization of the late 1960s and early 1970s. A series of legislative proposals, known as the 'Democratization of Working-Life' gained broad support in the Riksdag in the 1970s. They concerned diverse issues like work environment regulation, co-determination, work-related accident insurance, etc.. However, this changed one of the axioms of the Swedish model; that decisions were to be reached on the basis of consensus and compromise, rather than competition and confrontation. Decisions made under the former style of conflict resolution are subject to strict demands of unanimity, whereas legislative decision-making is subject to majoritarian rules. Consensus and compromise provided both the employers and unions with a veto over any changes (see Pestoff l990b for more details). Thus, SAF renounced the Saltsjöbaden Agreement in 1976, once the Co-determination Act was enacted. The Social Democrats also began to consider a proposal for wage-earner funds in the mid-1970s at the request of the trade unions. SAF and other business interest organizations openly and bitterly opposed such plans.

The politics of Saltsjöbaden were formed during a period of Social Democratic hegemony, but the 1976 election radically changed this. The first non-socialist coalition government in more than 40 years altered the preconditions for co-operation between SAF and LO, and also between them and the government. Suddenly, the trade unions, rather than the employers, were forced to negotiate without political support or guarantees from the government (Söderpalm 1980). SAF soon presented a catalogue of demands that were to neutralize much of the labour-market legislation passed during the radical years of the early 1970s (Bresky et al. 1981).

SAF repeatedly complained that this legislative package changed the balance of power in the labour market and called for reinstating the old balance. In order to achieve this, labour's ability to extract benefits through political exchange had to be curtailed. If, as Pizzorno (1983) argues, labour under-exploits its power in the labour market in order to achieve political influence, then it must be convinced to redirect its efforts back to the labour market.

Major labour market conflicts, after decades of labour peace might help to refocus labour's attention on its 'essential' responsibilities and functions. In 1977, under the first post-war non-socialist government, SAF planned to lockout 220,000 salaried employees for two weeks, but a major labour market conflict was averted. However, SAF's new leadership became convinced that the entire bargaining system needed to be revised, but realized that many of its members did not share this perspective. Changing long-term habits in a highly institutionalized system poses an enormous pedagogical problem. Thus, Curt Nicolin, the Chairman of SAF, decided that the existing machinery for collective bargaining needed to be ship-wrecked before it would be scuttled. In 1980 Sweden's largest labour market conflict erupted. Nearly three million workers were locked out by their employers or on strike for a few weeks in the Spring. The majority of the workers involved were employed in the private sector. The Chairman of SAF reassured his members on the eve of the lockout, that this was 'an investment for the future'. Labour market conflicts have recurred periodically since then, though on a smaller scale.

Crouch (1990) analyzes the development of collective bargaining in several western countries after 1968. Decentralizing collective bargaining, he argues, restores the initiative in industrial relations to management. This asserts the importance of the company level, where they dominate the balance of power, as opposed to the industrial or national level, where large unions operate in their preferred milieu (ibid.). In Sweden the employers embarked upon a policy of decentralizing collective bargaining in 1981, after initiating its centralization in the mid-1950s.

After more than ten years of struggle, centralized bargaining was finally laid to rest as a relic of the past in February 1990, through the systematic efforts of the Swedish Employers' Confederation. The government called for negotiations at the Haga castle near Stockholm in an attempt to give the Swedish model of concertational practices in labour relations a new lease of life. The unions all agreed, but SAF refused. Its adamant refusal to discuss the reinstatement of centralized collective bargaining incidentally lead to a major political crisis, which resulted in the only resignation of a Social Democratic government in the entire post-war period. The following week SAF relieved the Director of the Negotiations Division, who had been in office since the early 1970s, of his responsibilities.

SAF's Chairman, Ulf Laurin, made the following statement concerning collective bargaining on 16 February 1990:

> 'I am convinced that SAF's role during the I990s will be more significant for Swedish business than until recently. After a long-term illness, the 'Swedish model' is dead. The historic decision made by SAF on 2nd February means that there is no return. The course for our wage policy is totally clear. It is focused upon decentralization - with the intent of providing a dominant role for firm level bargaining.' (*SAF tidn.*, 16.02.90).

More recently he stated that collective bargaining had left the central level for good (*Svenska Dagbladet*, 05.11.90). 'The time of central direction (in labour relations) is past. The future role for trade unions is found at the local level. That is where tough and bright trade unionists are needed' (ibid.).

However, the Chairman of Sweden's Metal Workers' Union, Leif Blomberg, recently stated that much of the conflict on the labour market finds its origin in the fact that SAF has scuttled its collective bargaining division (*Dagens Nyheter*, 20.02.91). He continued:

> 'People (in SAF) who supported the 'Swedish Model' have been replaced by spokesmen for the market. We have never been

> farther from the Saltsjöbaden Basic Agreement than now. SAF is emphasizing political opinion formation rather than taking responsibility for wage formation....Neo-liberals, who have the US and UK as their ideal, don't give a damn about wage differentials and inequality increasing at a catastrophic rate (ibid.).

He concluded that the trade union movement has been weakened by the lack of an interlocutor for negotiating. The new role of the trade unions in the l990s must be to emphasize opinion formation. The unions must, according to him, become a countervailing power to SAF's political ambitions (ibid.).

Previously concertational practices were typical of most walks of Swedish industrial relations, not just of central collective bargaining. The interrelatedness of various segments of Swedish industrial relations has been analyzed in terms of generalized political exchange, in which each segment or policy area is conceived of as an independent meso-gamo (Pestoff l990b). There is a high degree of similarity in the central features of the various segments of Swedish industrial relations, as seen in collective bargaining, work-environment regulation, co-determination, labour-market insurance, wage-earner funds and lay representation on the governing boards of central public administrative agencies. The meso-game in each of these areas or arenas is interrelated to that of the others. Each follows its own particular logic and rules of the game, but their outcomes are nevertheless all interdependent on each other (Pestoff 1990b). A stalemate in one arena can easily spill over to another.

Many, but not all, of the institutional features of the conceptual model of the negotiated economy, as spelled out by Nielsen and Pedersen, are, or at least were, present in Swedish industrial relations between the late 1930s and the late 1970s. Class co-operation was, however replaced by class confrontation in Sweden, starting in the early 1980s. This was in line with the new strategy adopted by the dominant group in the Swedish Employers' Confederation, the Association of Engineering Employers, who organize most of the large Swedish multi-national firms, such as Volvo, ABB, Electrolux, and Ericsson.

It should be kept in mind that SAF and many other business interest associations (BIAs) do not adhere to democratic principles in their internal decision-making, but rather to market principles, which seems quite logical. Rather than granting all member firms one vote each, their statutes are similar to those of companies, where the number of shares determine the proportion of votes. Thus, the statutes of most BIAs in Sweden provide for strictly graduated voting rights according to the amount of dues paid. This assures large firm dominance in SAF's decisions.

BIAs were spurred on by the introduction of the wage-earner funds in 1983, which they adamantly opposed. They are now actively pushing for the de-institutionalization of most aspects of Swedish industrial relations, in an effort to undermine labour's political position. De-institutionalization means that many of the general, and even some of the core, features of the model of the negotiated economy have disappeared, or will do so in the foreseeable future in Sweden.

The importance of the de-institutionalization of Swedish industrial relations should not be underestimated, as they alone provide the core features of the full-fledged model of the negotiated economy. The decline in the importance of central collective bargaining and the deinstitutionalization of industrial relations imply an uncertain future for the negotiated economy in Sweden. Yet, it seems too early to conclude that the negotiated economy also ceased to exist with the final demise of the Swedish model for collective bargaining in February, 1990. We need to consider changes in other policy areas or arenas that might confirm or disavow this new pattern in Swedish concerted practices and the reorganization of the negotiated economy. Developments in consumer and agricultural policy as well as housing policy corroborate the pattern noted for industrial relations.

4.2. Consumer policy

Swedish consumer policy has been analyzed in terms of the negotiated economy (Pestoff 1989a, l990a). It has an institutional history and development of its own, starting at the beginning of the 1940s and running until present (Pestoff 1984b, 1989a). It too is based on a bi- or tri-partite configuration of principal actors, i.e., consumers, producers and the state. It attempts to shore up the organizationally weaker consumers and pit them as a countervailing power against the organizationally superior interests of business and commerce. It can be divided into five phases, including the present decentralization phase (Pestoff 1988a, 1989a, l990a).

Some, but far from all, of the institutional features of the model of the negotiated economy were found here. In particular, few if any of the structural requirements and institutional arrangements outlined by Nielsen and Pedersen were observed. Those that existed were either primarily associated with the labour market bodies or they were public institutions designed to promote official Swedish consumer policy. Thus, the functions of the five complementary institutions for policy, discourse, campaign, negotiation and arbitration or sanction were either undertaken by public institutions or they were absent.

The processes of the negotiated economy were only evident in a rudimentary fashion. There were few specific efforts to mobilize and promote a particular socio-economic ideology of bargained consumer policy in Sweden. The few existing efforts in this vein were mostly associated with parliamentary commissions on consumer policy between 1968 to 1971 and again 1982 to 1985. One of the 'independent' think tanks of private business did, however, conduct a major drive to question the aims and methods of Swedish consumer policy and called for its replacement with market forces. Together with the Federation of Swedish Industry, it published five books between 1978 and 1981 severely criticizing official consumer policy in Sweden.

However, no discourse or campaign institutions articulated the interests of Swedish consumers, because none exist. The efforts of private business were only brought to a head and temporarily routed when the Social Democrats returned to power in the early 1980s. They initiated a new parliamentary investigation of consumer policy, which served to remove the debate from the public arena and confine it to the Parliamentary Committee on Consumer Affairs. The latter combined the functions attributed to discourse and campaign institutions with its policy functions, in an attempt to reach a negotiated compromise on the future of Swedish consumer policy. Its final report, Hushållning för välfärd (Planning for Welfare) provided the premises for renewing Swedish consumer policy (SOU 1985:32).

Similar developments are seen in terms of agricultural and food policy as well as with regard to the use of price freezes. The same business-financed 'independent' think-tank, SNS, initiated a public debate about both of these types of regulation. Again, several pamphlets put this issue on the public agenda and generated enough interest and concern to result in major policy reformulations. Consumers were, however, unable to express their concerns and interests, as they lack discourse and campaign institutions. The public authorities responsible for consumer policy must therefore deal directly with these business critics of negotiated consumer policy without the help or support of independent consumer organizations.

Similarly, the negotiation games and the round table negotiations between organized business and consumers usually take place under the auspices of public consumer policy and in connection with the public agencies responsible for it. More important, many of the arenas for round table negotlations instituted in the history of Swedish consumer policy have now ceased to function as bargaining arenas. Thus, several of the institutional arenas for bargaining, described in detail elsewhere (Pestoff 1989a, 1990a), either no longer exist or have recently been radically curtailed. Not only has the Home Research Institute, which brought together consumers and producers in an effort to develop new home products between 1944 and 1957, disappeared. The annual food price negotiations between farmers and consumers, which took place between 1953 and 1990, terminated in 1991. Sweden has now opened her borders to imported food stuffs in an effort to adapt to the new GATT agreements anticipated in this area. Negotiated Swedish food prices will thus be replaced by world market prices.

Another area of importance for the negotiations which characterized Swedish consumer policy in the post-war period is that of price control and price freezes. They normally involved detailed negotiations between public authorities and individual firms or their representatives. The business community, through its discourse and campaign institutions, had criticized the policy of price freezes of distorting market signals for over a decade. They achieved their objective at the end of the 1980s, when it was decided that the instrument of price freezes will no longer be employed. Once again we can note a return to the market.

Thus, many of the features and institutions associated with negotiated consumer policy in post-war Sweden are disappearing and being replaced by the market. It becomes necessary to question whether Swedish consumer policy can illustrate the negotiated economy in the future.

4.3. Housing

Sixty per cent of Sweden's population lives in single family dwellings, but this, however, represents less than half of the households. Many families with young children prefer living in villas, while older persons often live alone in apartments. Public housing makes up about one-quarter of the multiple-family dwellings, while co-operative housing provides accommodations for another 16 per cent. Both landlords and tenants are well organized and have negotiated with each other about rents and improvements of apartments for decades in Sweden.

Private landlords, co-operative housing and the municipal housing companies each have their own negotiating organization for bargaining with tenants, who in turn are organized in the National Federation of Tenants' Associations. Private landlords usually belong to the Swedish Federation of Rental Property Owners, while municipal housing companies belong to the Swedish Association of Municipal Housing Companies. Rent negotiations have determined annual increases in rents, the overall level of rents and the need for improvements in the standard of apartments since the end of the last world war.

Rents were regulated for several decades after the end of WW2. Furthermore, the standard of newly built apartments was influenced by national building norms. Both the organized landlords and tenants are represented in the policy institutions for housing policy in Sweden. Negotiations between the municipal housing authorities and the local and regional branches of the National Federation of Tenants' Associations set the norm for annual rent increases, as rent laws prescribe that municipal housing firms should be price leaders and as they cover a considerable proportion of the dwellings. General housing and building policy in Sweden is normally determined by parliamentary commissions.

The debate about housing is highly technical and the participants are therefore usually specialists. Some of the specialized institutions called for by Nielsen and Pedersen's conceptual model are found in this area. Policy institutions are normally parliamentary commissions. Discourse and campaign institutions are not specifically related to housing nor the building sector. Nor do we find a symmetrical relationship between the partners. Forces associated with private profit interests, which desire to return to the market, appear at present to dominate the debate.

Regional rent courts together with the national rent court provide a system of institutionalized arbitration and sanction, similar to that of the labour Court and the Market Court in Sweden. These are bi-partite bodies, with an equal number of members chosen among representatives of the landlords' and renters' organizations, plus a 'neutral' legal counsel, who chairs meetings. The National Federation of Tenants' Associations represents private individuals, while the National Association of Retailers represents small shop owners as renters. Swedish Federation of Rental Property Owners, the building and tenant co-operatives and the Swedish Association of Municipal Housing Companies represent different categories of landlords, according to the needs of individual cases.

Turning to the processes of the negotiated economy once again, we find that only one actor seems more capable of actively participating in the development of a socio-economic ideology concerning housing. Once again the 'independent' think-tanks of private business play an important role in the debate about housing and rent policy. They recently published several pamphlets designed to initiate a debate about public housing and rent policy, calling for a return to market forces in housing matters.

The National Federation of Tenants' Associations has issued a debate book of its own, which decries the lobby activities of interests promoting the liberalization of rent policy and adjustment of rents paid by private individuals for housing to market forces. However, renters seem incapable of sustaining the debate or of mounting a full-scale campaign to protect the existing system of regulations and negotiations.

Implicit in such attempts to change the socio-economic ideology concerning rents and housing policy is a desire to eliminate negotiations as an instrument of decision-making. Once again it seems that the objective of the critics of the present system of negotiations is to de-institutionalize it and return housing issues and rents to unbridled market forces. This in turn also implies the termination of negotiations as an institution for allocating and redistributing resources derived from rents for personal housing.

A major reorganization is underway in numerous economic and political arenas, including industrial relations, consumer and agricultural policy, housing policy, etc.. It aims at restructuring the negotiated economy in Sweden by de-institutionalizing it and returning to the market. Organized business is the main promoter of the reorganization of the negotiated economy in Sweden. It is therefore necessary to look more closely at the political activities of the prime mover among business interest associations, the Confederation of Swedish Employers (SAF).

5. SAF's role in reorganizing the Swedish political economy

Swedish business demonstrates a unique capacity for collective action compared with business in other industrial societies (Pestoff 1988b, 1989b). There are nearly 1,000 business interest associations (BIAs) in Sweden, compared to fewer than 100 trade unions. Swedish BIAs have several unique features compared with those found in other countries. These include a high degree of vertical integration and extreme centralization, both of which facilitate a unique degree of hierarchical co-ordination, manifest in 'meta organizations', a phenomenon unknown in other polities (Pestoff 1988b, 1989b). Ownership is also important for membership and various categories of owners, such as private, public and agricultural or consumer co-operative, belong to their respective employer organizations and trade associations (Pestoff 1988c).

The BIAs for private business collaborate extensively in politics. They have developed an elaborate and sophisticated strategy for influencing political decision-making in Sweden far beyond industrial relations. SAF recently announced that it intended to unilaterally withdraw its representatives from the governing bodies of several hundred public authorities. It now emphasizes lobbying and opinion formation, as opposed to the more traditional channels provided by parliamentary ad hoc investigations, the remiss system and lay representation of the governing bodies of public authorities.

This strategy, which started as a defensive one in the early 1970s, had by the early 1980s become more offensive. Formation and manipulation of public opinion and parliamentary lobbying are now seen as the key to political and economic influence in the future.

Thus, the Chairman of the Swedish Employers' Confederation (SAF), Ulf Laurin, made a pronouncement to his members, under the headline that 'a new SAF was in the making' (*SAF tidn.*, 16.02.90). He concluded his statement about SAF's future by noting that:

> 'The center of gravity in SAF's work has shifted (from collective bargaining) to idea and opinion formation. It is ideas that change the world. (If) SAF can ... successfully propagate tomorrow's thoughts then its role will be larger than ever. SAF is the driving force in changing the system. A new SAF is in the making ' (ibid.).

SAF and other BIAs for private business have developed an extensive network of joint committees, meta-organizations, independent think-tanks, ad hoc campaign organizations, etc., for pursuing their political objectives. Many campaign and discourse institutions are prominent in this network, emphasizing the importance attributed to conditioned power.

Although the statutes of most business interest organizations in Sweden adhere to political neutrality, private business has traditionally shown a clear preference for non-socialist parties, in particular the Conservative and Liberal parties. Previously, this used to be expressed through direct campaign support. Now the election cycle in SAF's expenditures indicates another, but not contrasting pattern of support. In the early years and again more recently private business maintained a chilly, if not negative attitude in public to the Social Democratic Party.

Considerations of space prohibit a detailed presentation of SAF's relationship to political parties. It is however worth remembering the origin of SAF. It was a reaction to the political activities of Swedish workers, not to their union efforts on the labour market per se, that brought businessmen together and crystallized in the creation of SAF. In the Spring of 1902, workers in Sweden participated in the three-day Political General Strike in support of universal-suffrage proposals made by the socialists and discussed in the Riksdag. Employers responded by creating SAF a few months later (SAF, no date). According to H. von Sydow, one of SAF's first leaders, it was employees' political manifestations in 1902 that induced employers to band together (as quoted in Bresky et al., 1981:23).

The period following the Social Democratic victory in 1932, the reaction to it by Swedish business and their renewed opposition to Social Democratic policy after the end of WWII are dealt with by Sîderpalm (1976). He discusses such phenomena as the 'Club of Directors' which galvanized opposition to the new Social Democratic government. It mobilized the business community's political efforts, and gave direct financial support and advice to the Conservative and Liberal Parties during the 1936 parliamentary election. Immediately after the end of hostilities in Europe, private business organized its opposition to Social Democratic intentions of extending war-time economic planning at the end of WWII to meet the expected economic depression. This opposition was known as 'Planhushållnings motstandet' (PHM) or the Opposition to Economic Planning, and tried to bring about a defeat of the Social Democrats in the 1948 election.

SAF's expenditures demonstrate an unusual pattern in the post-WW2 period. For 40 years SAF's expenditures have followed an election cycle, with significant temporary increases every fourth year between 1948 to 1968 (De Geer 1986) and then every third year from 1970 to date (Pestoff 1989). It should be recalled that Sweden went from a four year mandate period to a three year one in 1970. A few examples will serve to illustrate SAF's and other BIAs' growing engagement in election politics in Sweden.

The Swedish Nuclear Energy Referendum of 1980 bears witness to the extent and intensity of that involvement. The Riksdag approved a grant of 36 million Swedish crowns (M SEK) to finance voter information about the three alternatives in the referendum. Alternative One, which favored the unrestricted use of nuclear energy, was backed by the Conservatives and received 8 M SEK. Alternative Two, which called for phasing-out nuclear energy by 2010, was supported by the Liberals and Social Democrats and got 10 M SEK. Alternative Three, which called for the immediate termination of nuclear energy, received 18 M SEK and was backed by the Center Party and the Communists.

The Free Enterprise Committee for Energy Information was started by SAF, the Federation of Swedish Industry (SI) and other BIAs for private business less than one year before the referendum in support of industry's demands for continued use of nuclear energy. This committee contributed an additional 20 M SEK to Alternative One, giving it the same amount of resources as those granted by the Riksdag to the other two alternatives in the referendum.

Business interest associations spent between 55 and 60 M SEK in 1982 against the wage-earner fund proposal of the Social Democrats and LO, which called for limited public ownership of the shares of stock companies, on the grounds that it would open the doors to a full-scale socialization, something which was denied by the Chairman of the Social Democratic Party, Olof Palme. All five Riksdag parties together spent 69 M SEK on the election campaign (Hansson 1984). SAF had intended to pass the baton to the non-socialist parties as it normally did in the spring, but changed its mind, and maintained the anti-fund (and often anti-Social Democratic) campaign, until election day. Then, following the Social Democratic return to power, the leading BIAs formed an ad hoc group known as the '4th October Committee', to continue the struggle against the wage-earner funds (Hannson 1984). They also helped to finance Marknads Alternativet for Sverige (MAS) (the Market Alternative for Sweden), which coordinated the three non-socialist parties' plans to abolish the Wage-Earner Funds. Its first Managing Director, Bengt Westerberg, later became Chairman of the Liberal Party.

SAF justified this participation throughout the entire 1982 election campaign by complaining that the non-socialist parties did too little too late about the wage-earner funds. The retiring Chairman of the Liberal Party, Ola Ullsten, noted afterwards in a press conference that political parties should be the leaders, not merely followers in the political debate (*Svenska Dagbladet*, 20.09.83). The latter would be an unfortunate state of affairs according to Ullsten. He also criticized organized business and the conduct of its anti-wage-earner fund campaign (ibid.). The next day, SAF's rebuttal appeared. It criticized the non-socialist parties for their tepid involvement in the anti-wage-earner fund propaganda during the 1982 election campaign, stating that if they had done more, SAF would not have found it necessary to make such efforts (*Svenska Dagbladet*, 21.09.83).

A few years later the Managing Director of SAF, Olof Ljunggren, launched a scathing public attack on the Prime Minister, Olof Palme in the major conservative daily newspaper, *Svenska Dagbladet*, in February 1986. He maintained that Palme had strongly criticized SAF in public (21.02.6). He accused Palme of systematically striving to weaken SAF's position as a bargaining agent and as a business interest association for a number of years. The balance of power in the Swedish labor market had changed drastically, owing to the efforts of the Palme Government, to the detriment of employers (ibid.). The Co-determination Act (MBL), which was passed in 1976, with broad parliamentary support in both blocks, is cited as the prime example of the Palme Government's misdeeds. He concludes by accusing Palme of political hypocrisy and 'shedding crocodile tears on behalf of low-paid groups' (ibid.).

Palme's reply, two days later, distinguishes between SAF's two roles, i.e., as an employer organization and as a political pressure group (*Svenska Dagbladet*, 23.02.86). He recommends SAF to stick to the first, and goes on to criticize it in the second. He mentions that SAF plays an active role in other organizations like NAFO, Timbro, NPT, NEF and the 4th October Committee, and also SAFs role during the 1982 election campaign, etc. (ibid.). Ljunggren's rebuttal a few days later demanded an official apology from Olof Palme (*Svenska Dagbladet*, 01.03.86) but, alas, too late: an assassin had ruled out that possibility some hours earlier. Such open hostility between the Chairman of SAF and the Prime Minister was not only new, but quite simply unconceivable during the era of labor peace issued in by the Saltsjîbaden agreement.

Sweden has practiced minority parliamentarianism during most of the period following WW2, although not normally of the extreme form found in Denmark. When the war-time Grand Coalition broke up it was replaced by the Red-Green Coalition that lasted until 1957. Then the Social Democrats formed a minority government until 1976, when the non-socialist parties took over power. Of the four non-socialist coalitions that ruled during the next six years only two had a parliamentary majority, one of which was by a single vote. When the Social Democrats returned to power in 1982, it was once again as a minority government.

Most forecasts and polls led to the expectation of a tied-race between the socialist and non-socialist blocks in 1988, with the Environmentalists holding the balance of power in the Riksdag. The election results differed so greatly from expectations, that Prime Minister Ingvar Carlsson enthusiastically pronounced in a victory statement that the Social Democrats could count on sitting safely in the saddle another ten years.

The new Social Democratic government set out in 1989 on a major tax reform that secured the support of the Liberal Party in the Riksdag. Then the government, under the leadership of the Minister of Finance, Kjell Olof Feldt, embarked on a policy of reviving the Swedish Model and centralized collective bargaining. He invited representatives of SAF, LO and TCO for discussions at the Haga castle near Stockholm, in January 1990. The purpose was to ascertain their stance on a new formula for coordinating collective bargainig at the national level. They were given ten days to two weeks to discuss certain proposals and planned to meet again in mid-February.

Both the central trade union organizations, LO and TCO were positive to the government's efforts, but SAF's executive board rejected the very idea of continuing the talks. On 2 February SAF refused to participate in any further meetings at Haga, thereby aborting the government's efforts. The Minister of Finance, Feldt, countered by presenting a crisis package for the labor market which, however, caused a public outcry, mainly from trade unionists. This in turn led to his resignation and a government crisis. The Social Democratic Prime Minister, who just little more than one year previously felt safe in the saddle, was forced to hand in his and his government's resignation, the only example of the Social Democrats resigning in the post-WW2 period.

The Social Democrats formed a new government, with a new Minister of Finance, a few weeks later. Its crisis package had been rejected by popular outcry, and it was weakened by its resignation and the loss of its popular Minister of Finance. The non-socialist parties had no alternative economic crisis package, but SAF presented one via the mass media in February. Many of SAF's demands for economic changes were passed by the Riksdag during the Spring session in 1990, including the shelving of certain social reforms, e.g., an additional week of paid vacation for all workers and an extension of paid maternity leave from 15 to 18 months. The Social Democrats turned to various non-socialist parties to obtain the necessary majority in the Riksdag for these crisis measures. Other SAF proposals were passed in the Fall of 1990 or Spring of 1991.

For the last decade and a half SAF has devoted approximately 15 per cent of its annual expenses to political activities. Now that SAF has disavowed centralized collective bargaining and has openly stated that idea and opinion formation have become SAF's primary activity, this proportion can be expected to grow sharply. In 1988 Swedish BIAs for private business spent nearly 200 M SEK for their political activities. SAF contributed more than three-fourths of this amount (Pestoff 1988b and 1989b). In comparison, all five of the established parliamentary parties combined had a similar amount at their disposal for political campaigning in the 1988 Riksdag elections (ibid.).

SAF conducted extensive promotion campaigns about the New Europe in the Fall of 1989, another in the Fall of 1990 and envisioned a third, if necessary (Beckman et al., 1991). Its campaign in the Fall of 1990 compared Swedish economic growth with that of a number of European Community members. Comparisons with England, Denmark, Germany and Spain were all to the detriment of Sweden, although sometimes at the expense of the facts (see Lingqvist, *Dagens Nyheter*, 07.11.90). This 1990 European campaign cost over 6 M SEK, a sum which was waved away as 'small peanuts' by the director of SAF's public relations division (Beckman et al., 1991).

SAF's campaign in the Fall of 1990 coincided with a balance of payments crisis and the Prime Minister announced that it intended to seek membership in the European Community, as one measure aimed at regaining the confidence of Swedish business. At the Social Democrat's Annual Convention, just a few weeks previously the party had decided to defer a final decision on the matter. SAF was more than pleased with its campaign and the government's pronouncement. Thus, it decided that a third EC campaign was not necessary.

Given its political ambition, SAF probably spent between 200 M SEK and 250 M SEK for idea and opinion formation in 1991. Ulf Laurin calculates expenses for SAF's information campaigns at 40 to 45 per cent of its current budget (*SAF tidn.*, 17.05.91). The combined budgets of the established political parties probably did not come to that amount in the 1991 Riksdag election. This has led some critics to equate SAF's activities with those normally associated with political parties (Vogel, *Dagens Nyheter*, 12.01.91).

SAF is the moving force behind numerous joint committees for private business. One of the more prominent and active ones, Naringslivets fond, the Free Enterprise Fund, commissioned a commercial firm, Samhallsrad AB, in the mid-1980s 'to investigate and make proposals for a new constitution' for Sweden. The proposal was presented in 1988, as *En ny grundlag - a Proposal* (A New Constitution - A Proposal), in a newly started publication series called Medborgarnas offentliga utredningar (the Citizens' official Investigations), published by Timbro. The series title paraphrases *Statens offentliga utredningar* (the National Official Investigations) or the reports from parliamentary ad hoc investigations. The proposal for a new constitution was presented as the work of 'a group of engaged citizens', who belonged to a project called en nya välfärden (the New Welfare), not as commercially remunerated work.

This proposal for a new constitution included numerous features that replicate American politics. Among others, the following can be noted; a single member simple majority electoral system, binding referenda, direct elected head of state, a constitutional or supreme court, a bill of rights, a division of powers between the branches of state, and free (=commercial) radio and TV. The proposal also includes special Swedish features, like limiting the size of the parliament to 151 members, eliminating the four per cent lower limit for qualification as a party in the Riksdag, constitutional limits of 50 per cent for personal taxes, constitutional protection for the right of ownership, etc.. This proposal was marketed through press conferences and a series of seminars devoted to various aspects of the new constitution. One seminar per month during the Fall of 1988 and Spring of 1989 covered such topics as the constitution, citizens' free rights, the Riksdag - the first pillar of state, the government - the second pillar of state, and the Constitutional Court and other courts - the third pillar of state. Well-known politicians, professors of political science, and journalists were among the chosen few who were invited to comment on these topics. Suddenly, favorable articles appeared in the press, while members of the Riksdag wrote proposals supporting certain features of this commercial proposal for a new constitution. Under the guise of the New Welfare, SAF and NAFO show how far they want to go in reforming the rules of the game in Sweden. They intend to stop short of nothing less than an entirely new constitution, one which is largely an import.

SAF has sponsored a tax-payers' association for several decades, Skattebetalarnas föreningen. Tax-payers are one of the groups that Olsen claims are notoriously difficult to organize; unless, of course, someone is willing to help them (ibid.). SAF has also engaged itself directly in extensive opinion campaigns aimed at cutting personal income taxes. 'Half left' (in your paycheck) was one the main slogans during the last five years. The Social Democratic government initiated a major tax reform in 1989 with the objective of limiting personal income taxes to 50 per cent.

The New Welfare also proposed a new tax system in the second number of the MOU series, called Sänkt skatt för alla (Tax Reductions for Everyone). They consider the most sweeping tax reform since the end of WW2 as only a first step. Using the slogan 'reduce taxes for a new welfare', they are establishing local branches of a new 'popular movement' bearing its name, the New Welfare. Thus, they see propagandizing for an entirely new tax system as the most significant way to attract new members. The New Welfare wants to replace the existing welfare system of social transfers paid via taxes, with one where each and every household would be responsible for financing their own welfare. Tax-payers would thereby be able to decide for themselves how their income is spent, rendering the system 'more democratic'. This would create greater incentives and generate greater investments and thus, result in greater welfare, we are told. In brief, they propose to decrease the total tax level from 57 to 40 per cent of GNP.

One of the members of the executive committee of the New Welfare, Ian Wachtmeister, tried in vain to obtain a majority for his proposal of turning New Welfare into a new political party, i.e., a neo-liberal protest party. After failing, he started the party New Democracy together with a well-known amusement park director. Their political platform stems primarily from the reports produced by the New Welfare. In several TV interviews with Ian Wachtmeister during the 1991 election campaign, he referred to the tax proposal mentioned above. He normally carried a copy of it with him to the TV studio. After a mere 30 weeks New Democracy received 6.7 per cent of the popular vote and gained 25 seats in the Riksdag. This spectacular feat can partly be explained by the fact that much of the ground was prepared by the New Welfare's campaigns and reports. Although New Democracy is not formally included in the four party bourgeois coalition government that took over power in October, 1991, it has voted for their proposals in almost all cases.

SAF has been calling for the privatization of state-owned companies and social services for a decade. It signaled a stepping up of its earlier efforts with the disclosure, in a recent interview with Ulf Laurin, the Chairman of SAF, that it had a secret plan for 'privatizing Sweden by the turn of the century'. It spells out what should happen month by month, starting in the Fall of 1991: In November 1991 the Riksdag would decide to immediately terminate the Wage Earner Funds. In January 1992 a sweeping sale of whole or partly state-owned companies and public utilities would begin. One month later nearly one million public utility apartments would be sold. At the same time the ambulance, fire fighting and library services would be privatized through contract bidding, etc.. Social services like day care, schools, health care and elderly care would be opened to private competition. Only the police, courts and defence are absent from SAF's detailed timetable for returning to the 'night-watchman state' (*Svenska Dagbladet*, 05.11.90).

'Someone must promote deregulation' (and privatization), says Laurin. 'Politicians don't dare stick their necks out as much as we can.' SAF no longer sees a non-socialist government as a necessary condition for realizing its plans. 'Given the expected mass slaughter of social democratic holy cows, a Social Democratic Government could also deregulate, privatize and make changes. The first steps are under way', he concluded (ibid.).

SAF nominates representatives to scores of governing boards of public administrative bodies at the national, regional and local levels. The practice of providing various interest group representation in this fashion is known as lay representation. It took root at the beginning of this century, but gained importance after the end of WW2. SAF actively promoted the extension of this institution of balanced representation for decades. In the early 1980s, after developing new channels of influence and new techniques for promoting its interests, such as lobbying and opinion formation, SAF began to express doubts about the future of lay representation.

A series of debate books were published by a well-known private business 'think tank' and included experienced debaters. A parliamentary ad hoc commission was mandated to review the role of lay boards in public administration. Its proposals and the subsequent minor changes passed by the Riksdag did not entirely satisfy the demands of SAF. Therefore in 1985 SAF's executive board decided that SAF should promote the termination of corporative traits in Sweden. SAF continued its campaign against lay boards with debate articles in the daily newspapers, conferences and seminars (SAF 1990).

SAF's executive board took up the issue of organizational representation on lay boards and corporatism again in September 1990 and January 1991. It demanded that interest organizations should no longer be represented on the governing boards of public administrative bodies. It also decided that SAF would no longer participate in most of the lay boards where it was represented as of the end of 1991 or beginning of 1992. Thus, on 14 February, 1991, SAF's Managing Director, Göran Tunhammar, sent a letter to the Prime Minister, Ingvar Carlsson, stating that SAF intended to withdraw unilaterally from all public administrative bodies related to labour market policy.

He stated that neither SAF nor other interest organizations in the future should be permitted to nominate lay representatives to the governing bodies of public administrative bodies. His letter to the Prime Minister concludes that the government should take steps to change the composition of the governing boards of public administrative bodies.

SAF reassures anxious members that withdrawal from the institution of lay representation will not in the slightest diminish its influence. SAF will continue to give advice and council to public administrative bodies. SAF will also promote the interests of private business in many other ways, including lobbying activities, opinion formation, etc. (*SAF tidn.*, 01.02.91). It criticizes other interest organizations for wanting to live in symbiosis with public authorities.

Lay representation institutionalizes the rules of the game of the politics of compromise. It relies on a numerically balanced representation, which gives an equal number of seats to employer and trade union representatives or producer and consumer representatives (Pestoff 1984, 1898a, l990b). By refusing to nominate employer representatives, SAF realizes that a vacuum will be created and clearly hopes that trade union representatives will no longer be permitted to nominate lay representatives. The Social Democratic government's reaction was to review possibilities of reinforcing the existing system either by a law forcing SAF to continue to nominate representatives or to replace them by retired businessmen.

There are additional illustrations of SAF's campaigns and the advent of employer organizations as a major political actor, such as commercial radio and TV and proposed membership in the European Community, but due to limits of space they will not be discussed here.

6. Problems facing Sweden after the demise of the Swedish model

We noted that one of the actors in the Swedish negotiated economy often appears to be pushing for a return to the market, and is calling for measures which would de-institutionalize the negotiation structures and processes which have been established in Sweden in the post-WW2 period. Although it may be conceived of as a challenge to tripartite concertation and the negotiated economy, this observation is also open to numerous interpretations.

The extent of this challenge depends upon the actions and reactions of other major social actors, like the trade unions and political parties, in particular the Social Democratic Party and the government. Do trade unions and the political elites have a clear understanding of the problems facing the negotiated economy and concerted practices? The statement mentioned above, made by the Chairman of the Metal Workers Union, Leif Blomberg, indicates a growing awareness of the problem. But, do they have a strategy and the resources to promote the defense of Sweden's negotiated economy and concerted practices? Or are they going to acquiesce to a reorganization of the negotiated economy?

One major difference between social actors is their view of the nation-state and the importance attached to it. There is a general tendency for the nation-state to lose importance to other levels of decision-making in Europe (Micheletti 1991; Gidlund and Sorlin 1991), but this has different implications for the social actors. Both the regional and international levels appear to be gaining in importance at the expense of the nation-state (Micheletti 1991; Gidlund and Sorlin 1991). In spite of worker and trade union internationalism, the nation-state remains the most significant level for the promotion of labor's interests (Streeck l991b). Thus, the importance of the nation-state is decreasing more rapidly for capital than labor. Swedish business is clearly a major actor in the trend toward internationalization. Swedish business is the most concentrated and probably one of the most internationally integrated of any European country (Pestoff and Ronit 1990).

Swedish business bought more European firms during the first half of 1990 than did businesses from all other countries of the world combined, and more than twice as much as American firms did during the same period.

An investigation of the associative action of business in advanced industrial societies shows that Sweden has the highest rate of economic concentration in all sectors chosen for study (Pestoff and Ronit 1990). A study of economic growth in the Nordic countries demonstrates that the share of the ten largest manufacturing firms of the total value added was twice as large in Sweden as in Norway or Finland and three times more than in Denmark in 1982 (Oxelheim, IUI, 1984). The fact that firms are considerably more concentrated in Sweden than in the neighboring Nordic countries is also illustrated by table 6.1 below. It shows growth in the share of employment of the largest manufacturing firms in the Nordic countries. Sweden not only shows the highest concentration in both catogories, but also the highest rate of increase in concentration.

Table 6.1: Growth in share of employment of the ten/thirty largest manufacturing firms in total manufacturing employment between 1974/75 and 1986/87 (per cent).

	Denmark		Finland		Norway		Sweden	
Firm Size	1974	1987	1975	1987	1974	1987	1974	1986
10 largest	11.6	15.8	22.3	34.3	16.9	31.9	41.0	58.6
30 largest	20.8	27.2	40.1	61.5	27.7	44.4	59.3	85.3

Source: Firm Dynamics, as presented in ETLA et al., 1990, Table 1:8, p. 34.

Another measure of economic concentration is found in the number of firms each country has in terms of the 500 largest firms in Europe. In absolute terms Sweden ranked fourth, while in per capita terms Sweden came second, just after Switzerland (Pestoff and Ronit 1990, and as shown in Table 6.2 on the next page). In both cases the economies of these two small countries demonstrate a high degree of economic concentration.

Table 2: Economic and Demographic Concentration in Western European Business and Commerce in 1989

	Firms per mil.		Big Firms		Population**	
Country (n=15)	Ratio	Rank	Nos.*	Rank	Nos.	Rank
Switzerland	4.66	1	31	5	6.65	11
Sweden	4.24	2	36	4	8.50	9
Finland	3.63	3	18	8	4.96	13
U. Kingdom	2.24	4	128	1	57.20	3
W. Germany	1.52	5	94	2	61.99	1
Netherlands	1.42	6	21	6	14.83	6
France	1.34	7	75	3	56.16	4
Belgium	1.01	8	10	10	9.93	8
Norway	0.95	9	4	12	4.23	14
Austria	0.79	10	6	11	7.62	10
Denmark	0.58	11	3	13	5.13	12
Ireland	0.57	12	2	14.5	3.51	15
Spain	0.41	13	16	9	38.81	5
Italy	0.33	14	19	7	57.52	2
Portugal	0.19	15	2	14.5	10.47	7
			Total = 465***			

* = Source: **Veckans affärer**, nr. 42, 17 Oct. 1990, 68–81. Europe's 500 largest businesses, not including banks, holding companies or insurance companies, rank-ordered according to 1989 value of sales.
** = Estimates of 1989 mid-year population (millions) from Monthly Bulletin of Statistics, United Nations, January 1991.
*** = 34 of the 500 largest firms in Europe which are of non-European ownership have not been included in this table: USA (22), Japan (6), Turkey (5), and Canada (1). Luxemburg (with one firm) has also been excluded in this table because of the relatively small size of its population.

The negotiated economy, concertational practices and neo-corporatism are national phenomena, most staunchly supported by the trade unions and Social Democrats in the Nordic countries. Economic integration and the internationalization of the Nordic countries puts pressure on them to reduce public spending, which in turn curtails their national sovereignty. Variations in the rate of economic integration and internationalization should also be reflected in different rates of reorganization and restructuring in the negotiated economies, concertational practices and neo-corporatism of these countries.

Streeck (1989 and I991b) and Schmitter and Streeck (1990) argue that organized labour lacks both the strategy and resources available to business for participating in decision-making in the European Communities. Nor are the institutions of the EC favorable to bi- or tri-partite participation in decision-making. Lobbying by multi-national firms and/or by the European branch organizations of organized business, without the participation of labour or consumers, seems to be a more realistic development, at least in the short-term. Treu confirms this analysis, and speaks of regime or policy shopping by large multi-national firms, i.e., of choosing to invest in countries with less costly and more flexible social benefits (Treu 1992). Streeck refers to this phenomenon as social dumping (1991b). Economic internationalization can thus include a political dimension which has implications for the balance of power at the national level.

Although Sweden is not (yet) a member of the EC, Swedish firms have been on the cutting edge of European integration and they are helping to internationalize economic transactions. But in the process of doing so they are of course internationalizing themselves and Swedish politics as well. As the European level grows in importance both economically and politically, they quite naturally lose interest in developments, agreements and negotiations at the national level. They naturally feel less constrained by and concerned with political solutions and economic bargains at the national level. They are less committed to finding specific national formulae and more interested in finding flexible, internationally applicable solutions that fit with a number of nation-states where they operate. To the extent that the negotiated economy is a specifically Scandinavian or Nordic phenomenon, it can therefore be expected to lose support and importance in the near future, as business opts for more general market-oriented solutions to the problems they face in several countries.

It has, however, been argued from a macro-economic perspective that 'structural competitiveness' requires a long-term strategic perspective (see Jessop et al., in this volume). Porter's comparative study of the competitive advantage of nations (including Sweden) focuses on the multidimensional nature of competition between nations (Porter 1990). It goes much farther than the relative price of the factors of production, or labor and social costs. He concludes that the presence of sophisticated and demanding customers in the home market, the existence of industrial clusters of international-oriented firms, and an institutional structure appropriate for promoting competition are all necessary for providing a nation with the necessary structural competitiveness (Porter 1990; Porter et al., 1991).

6. Conclusions

The power of private business manifests itself in numerous ways as discussed here. Private business clearly understands the importance of conditional power in an age of organizations (Galbraith 1984). Its privileged position in a market economy provides it with a triple advantage compared to other social groups (Lindblom 1977). It is not limited by universal sufforage, but can readily express the intensity of its political preferences through collective action (Hirschman 1982). Moreover it has a privileged position in terms of organizing to promote its collective interests (Olsen 1965). And, although votes count in elections, other resources decide which policies governments pursue (Rokkan 1966).

SAF's activities demonstrate a clear strategy for changing the rules of the game in area after area and a long-term perspective for achieving their goals. SAF spelt out its strategy for changing Swedish opinion in 1971. The guidelines decided upon then are still valid today. During most of the 1970s it was a defensive strategy, but by the end of the decade it became more offensive. SAF now has the initiative in most economic, social and political questions in Sweden, as the above presentation shows.

It took ten years to decentralize Swedish industrial relations, but as Laurin stated last year 'the Swedish model is dead'. It took almost a decade to bring corporatism to an end in Sweden, but SAF recently announced its decision to leave the lay boards of public administrative bodies, leaving a vacuum behind them that is hard, if not impossible, to fill. SAF sponsors the adoption of a new constitution for Sweden, one which is a bastion of neo-liberalism. This project has been underway less than five years and cannot be expected to bear fruit yet. SAF has a timetable to privatize Sweden by the turn of the century. The list could go on and on.

The government, on the other hand, has by definition a much shorter time perspective, i.e., it must win the next election. At best the government's perspective stretches three years, at worst three months. In contrast, SAF and private business act according to a long-term strategy in question after question. The government must react to many proposals stemming from private business, or merely try to win time.

Numerous campaigns orchestrated by Swedish business interests illustrate the importance of public discourse in an age of organizations. Swedish business interests have several organs for pursuing their campaign and discourse objectives. They have spent a considerable sum each year for the last twenty years to put issues of importance on the public agenda. In many, if not most cases they aspire to de-institutionalize the negotiated economy, thus bringing about institutional change by elimination. They have a long-term strategy for achieving their objectives.

In contrast, labour does not appear to have a counter-strategy to meet these challenges, nor does it devote many resources to protect or promote its interests in the public discourse. Its participation is at best meagre and sporadic compared to that of private business. There does not appear to be any semblence of symmetric resources between capital and labour in the Swedish public discourse at present. Whether this reflects historical traditions and/or a future trend remains to be seen.

What stance labour will take to its loss of power is still unknown. Labour appears to be in a state of confusion and disarray at present. Each new day under the new government brings additional burdens to already worn and taxed movements. Sharply reduced public subsidies to co-determination education, two quarantine days for sick leave, increasing members' contributions to union unemployment insurance schemes six-fold in the near future, reforming labor law against the wishes of the trade unions, etc.; these are some of the proposals of the new bourgeois government. The Swedish labour movement may well prove to be a crisis branch in the 1990s. They lack both the analysis, strategy and resources to play a more active role in the contemporary public discourse in Sweden. Not being in a position to defend the institutions of the negotiated economy, labor must passively watch as they are criticized and dismantled.

The negotiated economy and concertational practices face numerous problems in Sweden as well as other Nordic countries. These problems concern centralization, institutionalization of concerted practices and the negotiated economy, the role of trade unions and business interest organizations in the economic and social policies of these countries, as well as internationalization and European integration of their economies. Reorganization and restructuring of concerted practices and the negotiated economy may entail rejuvenation in one country, yet it may spell-out demise in another. Decentralization and deinstitutionalization are of course a matter of degree. The internationalization and integration of the national economies appear to be a decisive factor in determining the thrust and direction of this reorganization and restructuring. This in turn depends upon the role and importance of various large economic actors, in particular that of multi-national firms and BIAs.

Sweden is normally in the forefront of social and political developments due to its centralized collective bargaining, strong unions, active labour market policy, and well-articulated welfare state. However, in the l990s she may well lead the retreat from concertational practices and the negotiated economy. Not much systematic attention has been given to Swedish business, its numerous multi-national firms and its unique business interest associations. This lack of attention perhaps made sense during the long period of Social Democratic hegemony, when concertational practices thrived and the negotiated economy took root. But today, at the beginning of the l990s we are witnessing a new era in which the politics of compromise are being replaced by the politics of confrontation. In Sweden the reorganization and restructuring of concertational practices and the negotiated economy do not imply a rejuvenation, rather they demonstrate the demise of such practices and patterns and a return to the market.

This process can go much further and proceed more rapidly in Sweden than in the neighboring Nordic countries, due to the importance of Swedish multi-national firms. Swedish trade unions and the governing Social Democrats appear to be at a loss in terms of their analysis of the current situation, in terms of their stance toward the reorganization and restructuring of concerted practices and the negotiated economy, and most important, in terms of developing a strategy and providing adequate resources to promote their own preferences on these matters. Thus, it might not be far fetched to suggest that Swedish employers appear to be inspired by their American counterparts. They are actively striving for 'an organization free environment' and a 'trade union-free environment' by the turn of the century; and they may well be in a position to achieve it.

Bibliography

Aldrich, H. & R. Stern (1983) 'Resource Mobilization and the Creation of US Producer Cooperatives, 1835—1935', *Economic and industrial Democracy*, 4 (4), 371—406.

Aldrich, H. & U. Staber (1984) 'The Creation and Persistance of Business Interest Associations: an Ecological Approach' Chapel Hill: University of North Carolina, unpublished paper.

Beckamn, Å., et al. (1991) 'Från löneförhandling till EG—propaganda', Stockholm: Department of Journalism, student paper.

Berrefjord, O. (1982) *Rafnes—saken: forhandlings— okonomien i aksjon*,

Stockholm: Department of Journalism, student paper.
Berrefjord, O. (1982) *Rafnes—saken: forhandlings— okonomien i aksjon*, Oslo: Universitetsforlaget.
Berrefjord, O. (1989) 'Ökonomimotiverte beslutninger eller beslustmotiverte kalkyler?' in K. Nielsen and O.K. Pedersen, eds., *Forhandlingsökonomi i Norden*, Copenhagen: Jurist— og Ökonomforbundets Forlag.
Berrefjord, O. (1990) 'Semi—Public Projects and Corporate Behavior: A Negotiated Economy in Norway', Washington, D.C.: SASE Conference.
Berrefjord, O. et al. (1982) 'Ökonomiske maktgrupperinger' in *Maktutredningen Slutrapport*, Oslo: NGU l982, vol. 3.
Berrefjord, O. and G. Hernes (1989) 'Storforetak, marked og byråkrati' in K. Nielsen and O.K. Pedersen, eds., *Forhandlingsökonomi i Norden*, Copenhagen: Jurist— og Ökonomforbundets Forlag.
Bresky, T. et al. (1981) *Med SAF vid rodret — Granskning av en kamporganisation*, Stockholm: LiberForlag.
Crouch, C. (1990) 'Generalized Political Exchange in Industrial Relations in Europe During the Twentieth Century' in B. Marin, ed., *Governance and Generalized Exchange — Self—Organized Networks in Action*, Frankfurt: Campus.
Dagens Nyheter, 12.01.1991 and 21.02.1991.
Dahl, R. (1957) 'The Concept of Power', *Behavioral Sciences*, v (2), 201—205.
De Geer, H. (1986) *SAF i förhandlinqar*, Stockholm: SAF.
De Geer, H. (1989) *I vänstervind och högervåg, SAF under 1970—talet*, Stockholm: Allämnna förlaget.
Elvander, N. (1989) 'Inkomstpolitik i Norden' in K. Nielsen and O.K. Pedersen, eds., *Forhandlingsökonomi i Norden*, Copenhagen: Jurist— og Ökonomforbundets Forlag.
Engeleau, P. (1988) 'Interview' in *Folket i Bild* (Stockholm).
Galbraith, J.K. (1984) *The Anatomy of Power*, Boston: Houghton Miffin.
Hansson, S. O. (1984) *SAF i politiken*, Stockholm: Tidens förlag.
Hansson, S.O. and Lodenius, A.-L. (1988) *Operation högervridning*, Stockholm: Tidens förlag.
Hernes, G. (1978) *Forhandlingsökonomi og blandnings— administrasion*, Oslo: Universitetsforlaget.
Heckscher, G. (1946 and 1951) *Staten och organisationerna*, Stockholm: KFs förlag.

Hirschman, A. (1982) *Shifting Involvements — Private Interests and Public Action*, Princeton: Princeton University Press.

Jessop, B., Nielsen, K., and Pedersen, O.K. (1990) 'Structural Competitiveness and Strategic Capacities' (reprinted in this volume).

Katzenstein, P. (1985) *Small States in World Markets*, Ithaca: Cornell University Press.

Key, V.O. (1942 and 1958) *Politics, Parties and Pressure Groups*, New York: Cromwell Co..

Key, V.O. (1964) *Public Opinion and American Democracy*, New York: Alfred Knopf.

Korpi, W. (1978) *The Working Class in Welfare Capitalism*, London: Routledge and Kegan Paul.

Korpi, W. (1981) *Den demokratiska klasskampen — Svensk Politik i jämförnade perspektiv*, Stockholm: Tidens förlag.

Lagerkrantz, O. (1986) 'Interview', *Tiden*, no. 1.

Lindblom, C. (1977) *Politics and Markets — The World's Political Economic Systems*, New York: Basic Books.

Linder, P.J.A. and Grönstedt, A. (1990) *Bra för Sverige*, Stockholm: Sellin.

Lundberg, F. (1989) *The Myth of Democracy*, New York: Carol Publishing.

Marin, B. (1985 and 1990) 'Generalized Political Exchange' in idem, ed., *Generalized Political Exchange*, Frankfurt: Campus.

MOU (1988) 'En ny grundlag — ett förslag', Stockholm: Timbro (Report 1988/1).

MOU (1989) 'Sänkt skatt för alla — ett förslag till nytt skattesystem', Stockholm: Timbro (Report 1989/1).

Micheletti, M. (1991) 'Swedish Corporatism at a Crossroads: the Impact of New Politics and New Social Movements', in *West European Politics*, 14 (1), 144—65.

Nielsen, K. and Pedersen, O.K. (1988) 'The Negotiated Economy: Ideal and History', *Scandinavian Political Studies*, 11 (2) 79—101.

Nielsen, K. and Pedersen, O.K. (1989) 'Forhandlingsökonomi i Norden en inledning' in idem, eds., *Forhandlingsökonomi i Norden*, Copenhagen: Jurist— og Ökonomforbundets Forlag.

Nielsen, K. and Pedersen, O.K. (1990) 'From the Mixed Economy to the Negotiated Economy in the Scandinavian Countries', paper presented at SASE conference, Washington DC.

NOU (1978) 'Om konsentrasionn og marknadsmakt', Oslo: NOU (Report 1978/33).

NOU (1982) *Maktutredninqen — Slutrapport*, Oslo: NOU (final report).

Offe, C. & Wiesenthal, H. (1980) 'Two Logics of Collective Action. Theoretical Notes of Social Class and Organizational Form' in *Political Power and Social Theory 1*, 76-115.

Olson, M. (1965) *The Logic of Collective Action*, Cambridge, MA: Harvard University Press.

Olson, M. (1982) *The Rise and Decline of Nations*, New Haven: Yale University Press.

Olson, M. (1991) *How Bright the Northern Lights? — Some Ouestions about Sweden*, Lund: Student literatur.

Pedersen, O.K. (1989) 'Läreprocesser og forhandlingsspil, om löndannelse og forhandlingsökonomi i Danmark' in K. Nielsen and idem, ed., *Forhandlingsökonomi i Norden*, Copenhagen: Jurist— og Ökonomforbundets Forlag.

Pedersen, O.K. (1990) 'Learning Processes and the Game of Negotiation. Wage Formation and Negotiated Economy in Denmark', paper presented at SASE conference, Washington, DC.

Pestoff, V. (1984a) 'The Swedish Organizational Community and its Participation in Public Policy—Making: an Introductory Overview', Stockholm: Department of Political Science, AASBI RR No. 6.

Pestoff, V. (1984b) 'Konsumentinflytande och konsument— organisering — den svenska modellen', Stockholm: Finansdepartment, Ds Fi 1984:15.

Pestoff, V. (1987) 'The Effect of State Institutions on Associative Action in the Food Processing Industry', in W. Grant, ed., *Business Interests, Organizational Development and Private Interest Government*, Berlin: W. de Gruyter.

Pestoff, V. (1988a) 'Exit, Voice and Collective Action in Swedish Consumer Policy', *Journal of Consumer Policy*, 11 (1), 1—27.

Pestoff, V. (1988b) 'The Politics of Private Business, Co—operatives and Public Enterprise in a Corporate Democracy — the Case of Sweden', Florence: European University Institute.

Pestoff, V. (1988c) 'Näringslivets strategiska marknadsföring av värderingar' (The Strategic Marketing of Values by Business) in *Kooperativ årsbok*, Stockholm: Föreningen kooperativa studier.

Pestoff, V. (1989a) 'Organisationernas medverkan och forhandlingar i svensk konsumentpolitik', *Tidskrift för Rättssociologi*, 6 (3/4), 1—45.

Pestoff, V. (1989b) *Näringslivsorganisationerna och politiken i Sverige*, Stockholm: TCO.

Pestoff, V. (l990a) 'Organizing Consumers in a Negotiated Economy — Swedish Consumer Policy', paper presented at SASE conference, Washington, DC.

Pestoff, V. (l990b) 'Joint Regulation, Meso—Games and Political Exchange in Swedish Industrial Relations', in B. Marin, ed., *Governance and Generalized Exchange*, Frankfurt: Campus.

Pestoff, V. (l991a) *Between Markets and Politics — Co—operatives in Sweden*, Frankfurt: Campus.

Pestoff, V. (l991b) 'From the Market to Negotiations and Back Again? The Negotiated Economy in Sweden' in J. Hausner, B. Jessop, and K. Nielsen, eds., *Markets, Politics and the Negotiated Economy — Scandinavia and Post— Socialist Perspectives*, Cracow: Academy of Economics.

Pestoff, V. (1992) 'The Decline of the Swedish Model', in T. Treu, ed., *Participation in Public Policy—Making. The Role of Trade Unions and Employers Organizations*, Berlin: de Gruyter.

Pestoff, V. and Ronit, K. (1990) 'Changing Environments and European Integration: Accommodation by Organized Business in Denmark and Sweden', conference paper, Reykjavik.

Pettersson, O., et al. (1990) 'Demokrati och Makt i Sveriqe — Maktutrednings huvudrapport', Stockholm: Statsrådsberedningen (report SOU 1990/44).

Pizzorno, A. (1983) 'Political Exchange and Collective Identity in Industrial Conflicts', in C. Crouch and A. Pizzorno eds., *The Resurgence of Class Conflict in Western Europe Since* 1968, London: Macmillian.

Porter, M. (1990) *The Competitive Advantage of Nations*, London: Macmillan.

Porter, M. et al. (1991) *Advantage Sweden*, Stockholm: Noedstedt.

Rokkan, S. (1966) 'Numerical Democracy and Corporate Pluralism', in R. Dahl ed., *Political Oppositions in Western Democracies*, New Haven: Yale University Press.

Ruin, O. (1991) 'Three Swedish Prime Ministers', *West European Politics*, 14, 58—82.

SAF's letter to the Prime Minister, 10.02.1991.

SAF tidningen (1991) 'Ett nytt SAF haller på ta form', open letter in *SAF tidningen*, 16.05.1990 and 01.02.1991.

SOU (1985) 'Hushållninq för välfärd — Den framtida konsumentPolitikens inriktning', Stockholm: Finansdepartment (report SOU 1985/33).

Sailsbury, R. (1984) 'Interest Representation: the Dominance of Institutions', *American Political Science Review*, 78 (1), 64-76.

Sainsbury, D. (1991) 'Swedish Social Democracy in Transition', *West European Politics*, 14, 31-57.

Schmitter, P. and Streeck, W. (1990) 'Organized Interests and the Europe of 1992', Florence: European University Institute Discussion Paper.

Schneiberg, M. and Hollingsworth, J.R. (1991) 'Can Transactions Costs Explain Trade Associations?' in R.Czada and A. Windhoff-Heritier, eds., *Political Choice: Institutions Rules and the Limits of Rationality*, Frankfurt: Campus.

Söderpalm, S.A. (1976) *Direktörsklubben*, Stockholm: Raben & Sjögren, tema Teori 12.

Söderpalm, S.A. (1980) *Arbetsqivarna och Saltsjöbads—Politiken*, Stockholm: SAF.

Streeck, W. (1989) 'The Social Dimension of the European Firm', Florence: European University Institute Discussion Paper.

Streeck, W. (l991a) 'Interest Heterogenity and Organizing Capacity: Two Logics of Collective Action?' in R. Czada and A. Windhoff—Heritier, eds., *Political Choice: Institutions Rules and the Limits of Rationality*, Frankfurt:Campus.

Streeck, W. (l991b) 'The Impact of European Economic and Political Change on Industrial Relations', Bari: IIRA key-note speach and conference paper.

Svenska Dagbladet, 20 & 21.09.1983, 21 & 23.02.1986, 01.03.1986, 05.11.1990.

Traxler, F. (1991) 'Two Logics of Collective Action in Industrial Relations', SASE conference, Stockholm.

Treu, T. (1992) 'An Introduction', in idem, ed., *Participation in Public Policy—Making. The Role of Trade Unions and Employers' Organizations*, Berlin: de Gruyter.

Vogel, D. (1989) *Fluctuating Fortunes: the Political Power of Business in America*, New York: Basic Books.

Vogel, J. (1991) 'Ovetenskaplig opinionsmätning', *Dagens Nyheter*, 12th Jan.

Weber, M. (1969) *The Theory of Social and Economic Organization*, New York: Free Press.

8 The institutional history of the Danish polity: From a market and mixed to a negotiated economy

Ove K. Pedersen

1. Introduction

While Denmark is often characterized in economic terms as a mixed economy, in political terms it is probably better seen as exemplifying a country with a highly structurally differentiated and functionally very complex institutional structure.

Danish political history is marked by several distinctive traits: a small and open economy; a stable political system; a high proportion of organized wage earners; a political culture marked by social partnership; and a long tradition of institutionalized class cooperation (on the latter see Pedersen 1985, 1989). Due to this long political history the institutional structure is 'impure' in the sense that the cooperative links among social partners (state, capital and labour) have developed into a multi-layered institutional structure. This contradicts most principles of how a liberal market oriented economy ought to be institutionalized. Institutions stemming from a market economy are blended with institutions from both a mixed and a negotiated economy (Nielsen and Pedersen 1991). Market power and state authority are mixed in cooperative bodies, decentralized state organs, private and semi-public institutions. Public authority is delegated to a large number of private and semi-public institutions and decisions are taken in negotiations among mutually autonomous and collectively organized partners. The various links between social partners have become institutionalized; institutions have clustered; and clusters have been ordered to form a system of generalized political cooperation.

In this chapter I identify several types of institutional structures in order to show how three institutional structures are mixed - structures pertaining respectively to a market economy, a mixed economy, and a negotiated economy. I also identify key aspects of institutionalization, of clustering and of systemic relations between social partners in a composite political order. Three levels of analysis will be presented: those of single institutions, institutional clusters, and clusters ordered to form a system. Thus special emphasis is given to how institutional preconditions for a market, a mixed and a negotiated economy have been created. The final section describes how a complex and variable set of clusters is articulated through new techniques of coordination creating possibilities for a negotiated economy. In this way I hope to show how the institutional preconditions for a negotiated economy are connected to the generation of a contingent and emergent system of generalized political cooperation between labour, capital and the state.

2 Institutional history: market economy

This and the next section describe the institutional histories of the wage relation and the welfare state. The purpose is not only to describe the distinctive institutionalization of the two policy fields, but also to see how this had led to a mixture of institutions pertaining to a market and a mixed economy.

Since the 1970s it has proved hard to draw a distinct line between direct state intervention in wage negotiations and indirect guidance and control of wage formation. Peculiar institutional arrangements on the labour market have enabled governments and peak organizations acting in concert to manage the wage formation by consensus mobilization, bi- and tri-partite negotiations, and external as well as internal control of members (Pedersen 1989; 1991b). Indirect guidance and control of wage formation rather than discretionary intervention by the government has increasingly been used to adjust nominal wages to ever-changing macro-economic conditions.

The flexibility secured through this lack of any clear-cut distinction between state intervention and self-regulation originates in the established Danish tradition for mixing collective with individual wage agreements. This tradition goes back to the turn of the century and has been characterized by ever-increasing problems of co-ordination.

In institutional terms labour market relations in Denmark were established by the individualization of workers and capital-owners as legal subjects and by the constitution of a certain government-centered order of autonomy between labour, capital and the state. We shall examine how the individualization and the creation of a government-centered structural order became linked.

During nearly three hundred years of struggle (from the late sixteenth century to the beginning of the twentieth century) four institutional features came to characterize labour market relations in Denmark:

(1) Juridification. The making of the 'Danish working class' occurred through legal and administrative means. Even if many and varied economic and political struggles paved the way for the individual freedom 'to possess and to alienate the capacity of labour', absolutist kings just as democratic parliaments were always able to set the pace and the direction for the deregulation of customary rules bestowing guilds, towns, nobles, masters and husbands with the right to decide the use of the capacities of labour in their possession. The individual right for 'all and everyone' exclusively to possess labour was constituted by formal acts according to general principles of constitutional law. The constitution of market relations came to be government-centered. During absolutist as well as democratic regimes, the right to possess labour was enacted by generally accepted rules for policy-making (Pedersen 1991c).

(2) Universalism. The making of the 'Danish working class' followed different timetables. While restrictions in accordance with social status and property were deregulated from the mid-nineteenth century, regulations about residence (town or countryside) were removed from late-nineteenth century. Yet, it was not before the beginning of the twentieth century that restrictions according to sex, age and matrimonial status were eased. Skilled men were the first to be entitled, married women the last. Economic individualism became universal from the mid-twentieth century (Pedersen 1991c).

(3) Economic Individualism. The exclusive right to possess the capacity of labour was assigned to individuals both as a personal right (the right to enter - or refuse to enter - a labour contract according to one's own free will) and as an economic right (the right to enter a labour contract at conditions agreed upon). The capacity of labour became the monopoly of individuals and not of guilds, towns, nobles, masters or husbands. In terms of competence and conduct, individuals were assigned the right of

self-regulation or the freedom to enter (or to refuse to enter) self-interested relations with other individuals. The individual became the nexus of economic relations and economic individualism the constituent element of the labour market.

(4) Commodification. Labour-power was commodified. Economic individualism created opportunities for a commodity exchange of labour. The legal interpellation of individuals made it possible for them to possess, alienate and use their capacity to labour as 'a thing'. This capacity was nonetheless seen as a very peculiar commodity. In legal terms it can be possessed, alienated and used, but always within limits defined by maxims of law. The personal right, stricto jure excludes any indefinite, unlimited or unlawful alienation of the capacity to labour (Larsen 1857-58; Lassen 1882; Gram and Vogt 1887-88).

Accordingly, economic individualism came to assume a particular form of state. While individuals were endowed with autonomy (exclusive rights of capacity to labour) by the state, the authority to protect this autonomy and defining how far and with what purpose the self-regulation can be used were centered in the government. A government-centered form of state was constituted.

This government-centered form of state was never fully universalized before the first element of structural transformation was introduced. A long list of restrictions were still attached to the right to possess the capacity to labour (especially for married women, young people, criminals and social clients), when workers and employers alike in the late nineteenth century began to organize in collective entities. Unions were organized as early as the 1870s and 1880s but were twice destroyed when the state judged them to be subversive (socialist) organizations. They were also resisted by employers refusing to enter into legal agreements with organizations on behalf of individuals. From 1870 to the turn of the century the Danish labour movement then fought two interrelated battles: one for the right to organize in economic and political associations; and one for the right as a union to enter into legally binding collective agreements with employers. Both struggles were finally settled in 1899-1900.

From 1890 the state lifted its ban on unions and socialist parties alike. From 1896 to 1898 employees and employers were both organized in nationwide peak organizations, and in 1899 the two peak organizations signed the so-called 'September Agreement'. This agreement laid down procedural rules concerning industrial action. It also paved the way for the Parliament to accept the right of workers to associate in economic organizations.

Figure 7.3.1 GOVERNMENT-CENTERED FORM OF STATE

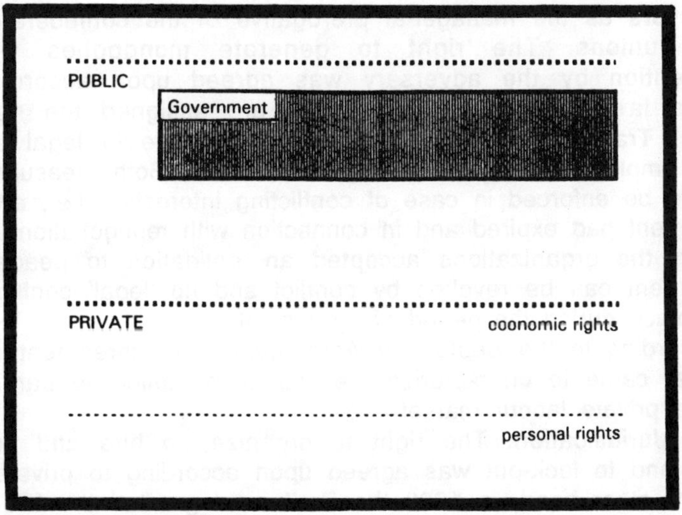

GOVERNMENT-CENTERED FORM OF STATE. The institutional boundary between state and market was defined by maxims of law. Constitutional law stricto jure prevented (and prevents) the State from invalidating personal rights (Haarløv 1958; Zahle 1986). The individual was assigned exclusive control of his own capacities. In market relations, though, this autonomy came to be relative. The state was permitted to intervene in economic law - setting conditions and limits for what can be agreed upon. State and market, accordingly, became formally separated but also interdependent. Economic individualism was both delegated and protected. The autonomy was both absolute and relative. State and market came to be two distinct yet mutually dependent institutional arrangements constituting a particular order of autonomy.

The September Agreement still applies today and embodies the legal relations between employers and employees. This is done in three ways.

Firstly, the two organizations mutually accept each other as equal and free legal subjects according to private law. The right of the workers to unionize was recognized by the confederation of employers as the managerial prerogative of the confederation of trade unions. The right to generate monopolies without intervention by the adversary was agreed upon according to private law. Secondly, organizations are assigned the right of action. Trade unions have the right to engage in legal strikes while employers obtained the right to lockout. Both measures are only to be enforced in case of conflicting interests - i.e., after an agreement had expired and in connection with renegotiations. And, thirdly, the organizations accepted an 'obligation to peace'. No agreement can be revoked by conflict and no 'legal' conflict can take place during the period of agreement.

According to the September Agreement, then, three features of interest came to characterize the system of collective bargaining on the private labour market:

(a) Juridification. The right to organize, to hire and fire, to strike and to lock-out was agreed upon according to private law. On the other hand, in 1900 the Parliament granted the two peak organizations autonomy to generate a position of monopoly on the labour market and to negotiate working conditions according to rules agreed upon in the September Agreement.

(b) Institutionalization. In the period 1890 to 1910 private and semi-public institutions were developed on the labour market. Private bi-partite institutions were erected to negotiate wages and working conditions and to arbitrate conflicting interests. Semi-public tripartite institutions were established by public law granting the organizations the authority to sanction illegal conflicts in the 'Industrial Court' (Arbejdsretten) and to settle interest disputes in 'The Board of Concilation' (Forligsinstitutionen). Organizations were granted authority to conciliate and to sanction conflicts. Organizations were delegated 'public authority' to control their members by external institutional means.

(c) Centralization. Collective bargaining became centralized during the 1920s at the sectoral level and in the 1950s and 1960s at the peak level. In contrast, conflict initiation and control stayed at the sectoral level. An internal hierarchy, then, was erected between the organizations. Peak organizations could negotiate general agreements, while sub-organizations could negotiate specific agreements in a 'hierarchy of functions'. Internal means of control were generated.

The Basic Agreement, then, had a number of radical consequences for the relation between labour and capital as well as for the overall structure of the Danish form of state:

(1) The organizations were assigned independent rights and obligations. Hence, the relationships between the organization and its members, or between the legal subject (the organization) and the legal person (the member), became divided. Labour agreements came to have two subjects: the collective and the individual. A particular mixture of collective and individual rights and obligations was established (Hasselbalch 1979). Over the years the organizations were increasingly made competent and responsible in relation to economic rights, while the individual stayed competent and responsible in relation to personal rights:

- The individual still had the right to enter (or to refuse to enter) a wage agreement. Neither the State nor his organization could (or can) force him to work.
- The individual, too, had the right to enter an agreement bringing him conditions better than those agreed upon by collective agreement. His personal right to search for better conditions was (and is) retained.
- Finally, wages and other disbursements are his personal property. Neither the State nor his organization could (or can) confiscate his payments without authority granted by public law.

Thus, the first significant consequence of the Basic Agreement was the constitution of a specific organizational structure. The structure came to be based on a distinction between the organization as an independent legal subject with authority to sign and enforce collective agreements and the member as an independent legal person with autonomy to enter (or refuse to enter) any agreement. This distinction has since constituted the basis for the development of an internal hierarchy within organizations between leadership and members, whose respective rights and obligations are regulated by organizational statutes.

(2) The industrial class conflict was institutionally isolated. An industrial arena was established delimited by the statutory regulations embedded in the Basic Agreement. Hence, another important consequence of the Basic Agreement was the constitution of a certain social system. This system came to be based on the separation of the industrial from the political arena. An independent arena pertaining to labour legislation was generated for how to enter, terminate, and maintain agreements just as for how to distinguish between industrial (legal) and political (illegal) conflicts.

(3) Finally, authority was delegated from the State to the labour market organizations.

Figure 7.3.2 THE DUAL FORM OF STATE

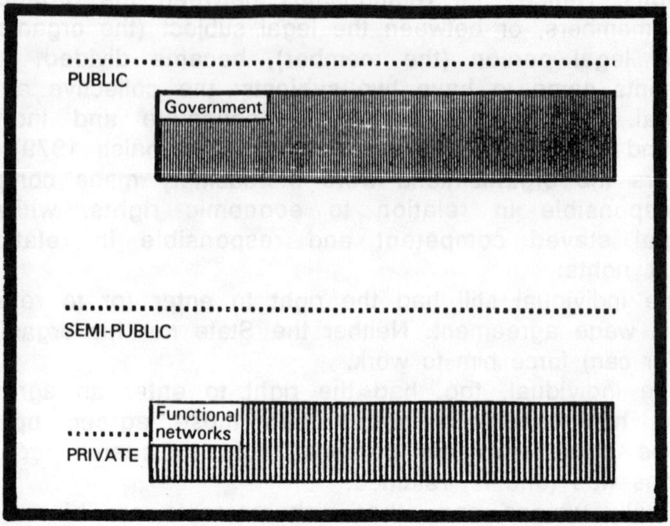

DUAL FORM OF STATE: Individual autonomy was bifurcated: autonomy pertaining to personal rights remained in the hands of the individual, that pertaining to economic rights (for members) was delegated to the organization. Individuals could (and still can) decide on their own well-being, while organizations could (and still can) regulate market relations by collective agreements. This regulation, however, was depoliticized. Collective actions with political purposes were deemed illegal according to agreements between the peak organizations. A division of labour between organizations and the political system was institutionalized. Organizations could (and can) regulate wages and working conditions, the State could (and still can) intervene when possible in political terms. The labour market came to establish not merely a single authoritative decision-making centre, but a dual structure within which mutually autonomous (individual and organizational) actors as well as mutually autonomous (industrial and political) institutions could function.

Through Parliament's acceptance of the organizations as autonomous parties, the State delegated parts of its sovereignty to regulate, judge and to sanction the relations between employers and employees. A third significant consequence of the Basic Agreement, then, was the constitution of a new form of state. A dual form of state was constituted. Besides transforming the structure of the Danish form of state, The Basic Agreement also transformed the relation between labour and capital. This relation became institutionalized and institutions became clustered in a functional network (FuncNet). Mutually autonomous organizations as well as mutually autonomous industrial and political institutions were coordinated by non-authoritative, negotiated principles commonly agreed upon. Cooperative institutions negotiated, conciliated, mediated and sanctioned private agreements and did so from different positions of competence in an interinstitutional division of labour among private, semi-public and public bi- and tripartite institutions.

However, it was not before the end of the fifties that the unintended consequences of this institutional cocktail of individual and collective arrangements and of industrial and political institutions became evident. From then on and for more than thirty-five years, two interrelated yet seemingly irreconcilable and still more accentuated problems of coordination came to play a decisive role in macro-economic policy making.

The first was articulated in the 1950s and came to be formulated as follows: organizations are unable to control members and sub-organizations, as long as the latter are free to enter agreements bringing them better conditions than agreed upon in collective agreements (Blueprint 154 1956). The second problem was first voiced in the 1970s and was finally formulated in the 1980s: organizations have gained too much authority restricting the freedom of members and sub-organizations to prefer their own well-being to that of others (Pedersen 1991b).

During the seventies, then, it became increasingly clear that the problem of coordination had changed from too little to too much collective authority and from too much to too little individual self-reliance. It became evident that the organization of industrial relations was somehow unable, simultaneously, to control the formation of wages and to secure individual mobility and flexibility. However, it was not before the late seventies that more subtle guidance and control of wages was introduced in a search for a more balanced mix of individual incentives and collective solidarity and control. From 1985 interventions by the State were deemed inefficient as were centralized negotiations between peak organizations. From 1987 decentralized bargaining became mixed with mechanisms for centralized coordination. Finally, from 1989 there was an attempt to blend local as well as individual agreements with wage steering mechanisms in the hands of the organizations (Pedersen 1991b).

This search for a finely tuned mixture of individual autonomy and collective solidarity and control has so far (from 1987 to 1991) probably led to the most effective control of the entire wage formation ever seen in Denmark (Sønderriis 1990).

Yet, despite the successful application of wage policy measures, severe macro-economic problems remained. Reports from the Government and OECD during the 1980s show that Denmark has increasingly become specialized in international markets in goods with low technology content and that productivity both in absolute and relative terms has continued to fall in the same period (Finansministeriet 1986). Accordingly, the flexibility of the labour force has been severely hampered by the successful application of the wage policy.

3. Institutional history: mixed economy

Having discussed the development of institutions of wage formation, we now turn to the organization of the welfare state. The organization of welfare state policies took place between 1950 and 1975 through gradual compromises between the social-liberal, conservative and social democratic parties. The welfare state was never developed on the basis of a comprehensive plan. It developed through an on-going pragmatic policy process of negotiations, deals and eventually compromises between political parties, private interests and social and economic experts. Five significant features came to characterize the organization of the Welfare State:

(1) Co-optation of private interests. Private interest organizations - mainly those representing the two parties on the labour market as well as the welfare professions - were granted a monopoly by the government to influence or directly to participate in decision making processes in the public administration. A vast number of normally tripartite policy- and decision-making bodies (councils, boards, and commissions) were established inside the public administration. Thus private interests were co-opted in public administration and an 'open administration' in contrast to a 'closed bureaucracy' was established.

(2) Delegation of policy authority. The administration - together with tripartite boards and councils - was empowered to make discretionary decisions, and to develop standards for state

interventions through administrative rule-making. The relationship between the legislative and the executive power was reformulated. The Parliament was increasingly in charge of staking out overriding objectives, whereas the administration was assigned the task of implementing these through compromises between multiple interests in cooperative bodies. A 'political administration' in contrast to a 'neutral bureaucracy' was thus established.

(3) Segmentation in policy fields. The overall administration and control was handled by policy segments. Five important segments were developed: the labour market, agriculture, education, social policy, and health care. These were only gradually generated as policy segments as representatives from political parties, interest organizations, public administration and municipalities - from different positions in a hierarchy of competences - came to formulate public policies and make decisions through negotiations and agreements. A 'segmented' in contrast to a 'unitary' administration was thus developed.

(4) Decentralization of welfare tasks. Welfare functions were transferred from the central state to either the municipalities or the organizations. Welfare programmes were pursued under broad statutory statements of general purpose decided by Parliament, and implemented through the delegation of policy-making and discretionary decision-making powers to the municipalities or the organizations. The majority of welfare state functions became financed and handled by municipalities. Thus a 'local' in contrast to a 'centralized' Welfare State was established.

(5) Coordination of dispersed authority. From mid-1970s attempts were made to coordinate this comprehensive dispersion of public authority to tripartite bodies, municipalities and organizations. Cross-boundary institutions were formed to coordinate and control public expenditures, thereby integrating multiple public and private organizations. The municipalities became permanent partners in implementing a public expenditure policy represented by their own private interest organizations KL (National Association of Municipalities) and AR (National Association of Counties). A 'negotiated' in contrast to a 'hierarchic' coordination of budget and expenditures was attempted.

Important differences came to characterize these segments. Institutions were clustered differently, establishing different types of segments. In Hierarchical Segments (HieraSegs) institutions were ordered in a hierarchy of competences with the minister (i.e., the government) 'at the top' in a delicate interplay with formally competent but non-autonomous tripartite bodies. In Horizontal Segments (HoriSegs), on the other hand, institutions

Figure 7.3.3 POLYCENTRIC FORM OF STATE

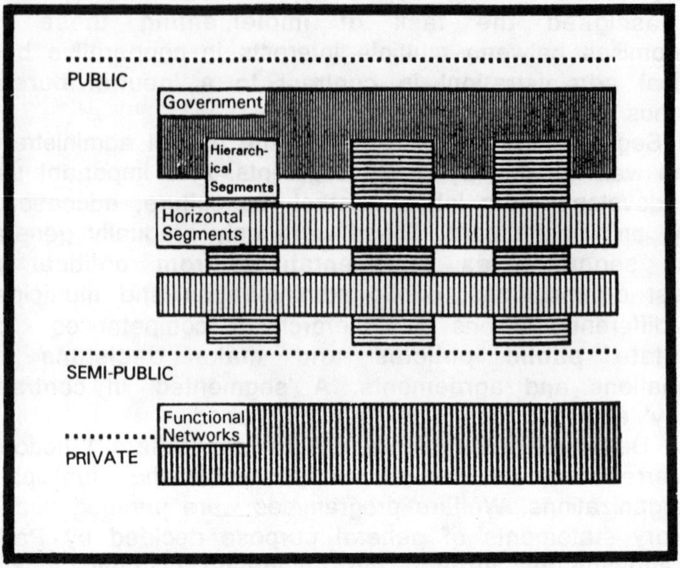

POLYCENTRIC FORM OF STATE. The state-form changed again - this time from a dual to a polycentric distribution of autonomy. Organizations were co-opted and they delegated public authority to formulate, decide and in some cases even to implement public policies. Universal social (welfare) rights were distributed to individuals while tripartite bodies and municipalities were granted authority to perfect and to elaborate these through discretionary decision-making. Hierarchical and horizontal segments were generated to co-ordinate dispersed public authority by concerted actions between multiple actors and institutions. Thus a polycentric structure of authority and autonomy was established within which mutually autonomous (individual and organizational) actors, as well as mutually autonomous (central and local) institutions and mutually autonomous (hierarchical and horizontal) segments could function.

were ordered by a horizontal distribution of autonomies between mutually autonomous hierarchical segments and central and local governments within an overall hierarchy with the central government 'at the top'. Thus a polycentric form of state was constituted.

However, it was not before the beginning of the 1970s that the unintended consequences of the uncontrolled development of welfare state policies and the organization of an open, political, local and segmented welfare state administration became evident. The reason for this can be seen in the following data. Whereas Danish public expenditures were lower in 1960 relative to GNP than the average level within the OECD countries (DK: 24.6 per cent, OECD: 26.0 per cent), the picture had changed dramatically by 1982 (DK: 60.2 per cent, OECD: 48.5 per cent). This trend had quite specific political effects during the mid-seventies. For the need to curtail internal cost and external demand was transformed into a policy for public expenditures which had still not had much impact even in 1982. Denmark had an enormous public finance deficit (10 per cent of GNP) in that year. Four years later this had been transformed into a surplus (3 per cent of GNP) (Nielsen 1988).

4. In search of new instruments

Thus, in the period from 1982 to 1991 both wage policy and public expenditure policy began to demonstrate effectiveness in coordinating the functional network (the FuncNet) and the segments (HieraSegs and HoriSegs). Objectives were met as far as wages and public expenditures were concerned.

However, severe macro-economic imbalances remained. The growth of the competitive industrial sector was never sufficient to finance imports and growing welfare expenses. Consequently, from 1963 to 1989, Denmark had a permanent deficit on the balance of payments, just as from the 1960s and onwards it accumulated a foreign debt (almost 40 per cent of GNP in 1988). Austerity measures created a high and stable level of unemployment (1980: 7.0 per cent; 1983: 10.5 per cent; 1986: 7.9 per cent; 1988: 8.7 per cent). New and growing pressures were put on welfare state services (public expenditures in per cent of GDP: 1980: 56.9 per cent; 1983: 62.0 per cent; 1988: 59.8 per cent). The tax burden was constantly rising. Productivity continued to fall (average annual growth rate: 1973-79: 1.19 per cent; 1979-89: 0.92 per cent).

Thus new means were needed if the government was to be able to repair the macro-economic imbalances. This need was further strengthened by a growing awareness that the days of 'fine-tuning' stabilization policy were over and that the mechanisms for gradual adjustments of industrial relations and public expenditures had been pushed towards their limits. The relative importance of a structural policy and supply-side measures was increased and the need for a change in the toolbox of macro-economic instruments was formulated.

This change in the toolbox of instruments took place between 1976 and 1986. Measures for a structural policy (Nielsen and Pedersen 1989) were created in two ways: through the development of an active industrial policy, on the one hand, and, on the other, from a reformulation of macro-economic problems and objectives for the country as such.

By the end of the 1970s a new set of macro-economic problems and instruments were initiated by a shift in the understanding of international competitiveness. New socio-economic objectives were highlighted and the need for new means was recognized. A structural policy was formulated which emphasized supply-side measures such as technological renewal and industrial restructuring. These changes in the collective views about the nature and imperatives of international competitiveness indicated a genuine capacity to formulate macro-strategies for a national economy as such.

In the following I shall describe how this strategic capacity was generated through a very complex institutional transformation in bi-, tri- and even quadripartite cooperation and consultation. The emphasis will be on how social partners have contributed to the formulation and implementation of national strategy through changes in collective orientations and in the existing set-up of institutions.

To understand how it has been possible to formulate and even propagate a national strategy (the structural policy) in a polycentric form of state, we have to distinguish at least three different policy-making processes in the 1980s: (1) A structural policy has been formulated and all the major political actors have been mobilized around a mutual understanding of structural competitiveness as the primary objective of societal changes and adjustments. (2) A stalemate between political parties, organizations and municipalities, however, has blocked a coordinated and controlled participation of the state in the implementation of a structural policy. (3) However, single policies have been formulated and implemented according to guidelines for a structural policy.

These three policy processes have unfolded within newly established institutions and clusters thereof as well as within pre-existing institutions and institutional clusters. In combination with the inherited distribution of autonomy, a new form of state has been generated creating possibilities for a systemic ordering of the actual institutional arrangements in a polycentric state-form.

5. Changes in cooperative institutions

Having provided an overall picture of the institutional history and background to the labour market, I now provide a more detailed study of how new institutions and clusters of institutions have been established following the shift from demand to supply-side measures in macro-economic policy making. So this and the next section describe the institutional history of the structural policy and its patchwork implementation. This involves introducing two new institutional clusters and showing how they came to be coordinated through a generalized system for political cooperation. It will be shown that a systemic order has been created for the coordination of a polycentric form of state and that this has taken place through the formulation and implementation of a national strategy for structural change.

To begin with, I will describe how multi-partite communicative actions from the mid-seventies have developed into a Communicative Arena (ComArena). The formation of the arena is closely connected to the generation of a socio-economic ideology. The latter was originally formulated by a tripartite 'Labour-Market Commission' (1949-57). Later it was developed into communicative actions among social partners circumscribed by a socio-economic ideology defining the field of policy intervention and the range of proper policies. A whole series of institutions were created in on-going processes of institutionalization and policy constitution (Pedersen 1985, 1989).

One of the single most important institutions in this regard was appointed in 1955. The purpose was to study if and how macro-economic imbalances could be explained by the lack of coordination between economic and social organizations and institutions. In 1956 the committee submitted Blueprint 154, describing for the first time not only the need to coordinate the formation of wages with socio-economic objectives, but also suggesting the establishment of the Economic Council ('Det Økonomiske Råd').

The purpose of the Economic Council was clear. By law it was obliged to 'contribute to the coordination of economic interests' by identifying socio-economic problems and developing macro-economic policy-measures capable of achieving broad acceptance among the major interests on the labour market and throughout the political system. The Council has done precisely this for nigh on thirty years. In a little less than one hundred reports it has identified ever-changing socio-economic problems and solutions and thereby (over the years) transformed what were originally some very broad socio-economic ideals into an ever more wide-ranging socio-economic ideology reshaping the fundamental conceptual grasp of reality on the part of the general public and policy-makers alike.

Yet, in spite of the Council's contribution to the formulation and propagation of the socio-economic ideology (Pedersen 1985, 1991b), it is much more important to point to the fact that the role of the Economic Council has been copied in other areas. In particular, from the early 1970s onwards, policy institutions began to note that welfare-state expenditures had grown out of control (Perspektivplan I and II, 1971, 1973). Later on institutions were established within the Treasury to transform this warning signal not only into a public expenditure discourse but also to integrate this with the socio-economic ideology propagated by the Economic Council. A conceptual link was established between public expenditures and socio-economic objectives and imbalances (Nielsen and Pedersen 1989).

In a first phase (1960-75) a socio-economic ideology was formulated and propagated. Wage and expenditure policy measures became dominant in a demand-side oriented socio-economic ideology.

From 1973 a shift in the socio-economic ideology was undertaken. A new institution - TR ('The Technology Board') - was assigned the task of monitoring technical and industrial development, and to take or guide action in order to promote technological development. TR was expected to formulate and propagate a new technology policy, to design new institutions and to conduct experimental implementation. The long term objective was to modernize the Danish economy and to eliminate the macro-economic imbalances through promotion of technological progress.

A vital step was taken 1983, when a 'Programme for Technological Development' was proposed by the Technology Board and endorsed by Parliament. The programme laid the ground for an active industrial policy and for a break with nearly 30 years of demand-side oriented macro-economic policy measures. It covered promotion, development and internationalization of technology, financial support for R&D and technological service.

One of the reasons for this political consensus in 1983 was the simultaneous reformulation of socio-economic problems and objectives for the country as a whole. A long lasting debate among various institutions and organizations started around 1980 about the content of the concept of international competitiveness.

In the 1960s and 1970s international competitiveness was generally perceived as equivalent to the relative unit costs of labour. The dominant perceptions stressed the exclusive importance of relative prices. International competitiveness was understood as wage competitiveness managed by demand-side policies (i.e. wage, incomes and public expenditures policies).

Already in the early 1980s a revised version of this formulation was applied by The Economic Council. Competitiveness were now measured by a composite index including relative unit cost of labour, capital costs, productivity and exchange-rate development. In 1984-86 a broad political consensus was established around an extended version of this formulation. The dominant perception stressed the importance of a national economy's productive structure, the technology content, the marketing of its products, and the degree of flexibility on its labour markets and in its industrial organization.

International competitiveness came to be understood as structural competitiveness. Product innovation and productivity, technology content, marketing and flexibility on the labour market were made part of the concept. This reformulation was primarily promoted by the Technology Board and the Industrial Council of the Labour Movement ('Arbejderbevaegelsens Erhvervsråd'). They both successfully pointed to the fact that technological development and industrial restructuring could have an important impact on the competitiveness of Danish industry.

The decisive formulation of the new consensus, however, was produced by the Ministry of Finance in 1986 (Finansministeriet 1986). Employing a broad conception of competitiveness it called attention to the fact that Denmark suffered from the following structural problems: export products had an insufficient content of technology and Danish export markets had declining shares of International demand. The conclusion was clear: a structural policy had to be applied to increase the level of technology, education and research, and to change the composition of exports as far as products and markets were concerned. In 1976-86 the content of the socio-economic ideology was changed. Active industry- and labour markets policies became dominant in a supply-side oriented socio-economic ideology. Nonetheless, even if the above-mentioned institutions came to contribute both to the propagation of a socio-economic ideology and to a shift in its content it is much more important - once again - to point to the fact that their role too was copied.

Institutions with the task of participating in the formulation and propagation of the socio-economic ideology (i.e. campaign institutions) were established by the government, the municipalities, the Central Bank, the interest organizations and even the large banks and insurance companies.

None of these second-generation campaign institutions became tripartite bodies - like the Economic Council. They were established as economic secretariats for trade unions, employers organizations, municipalities and central governmental agencies. There are many examples of such campaign institutions. However, rather than discussing examples, it is more important to underline the existence of a certain form of communicative action (a verbalized 'multi-partite dialogue') among capital, labour, municipalities and government through the roles played by campaign institutions.

To identify communicative actions as a type of social partnership is no doubt rare. However, in defending my thesis, I want to emphasize at least three facts: (a) all the institutions mentioned actually were (and still are) formulating social and economic problems in the terms of the prevailing socio-economic ideology - they are 'talking' within the same discourse, making common outlooks possible; (b) the institutions do participate in communicative actions where they comment on and criticize the models, data, formulated problems, and proposed solutions proposed by the other participants - they 'talk' to each other in an ongoing debate, creating common knowledge and making common understandings of problems and solutions possible; and (c) the institutions have shown they can pass this debate onto the social partners in particular, and to the public in general - they have mobilized the majority of the Danish population to form an opinion on these positions, permitting a popular consensus around national problems and solutions (Petersen et al., 1989).

Accordingly, my understanding of a ComArena (or of multi-partite consultation and coordination through communication) is as follows. A ComArena exists when the social partners, through a series of institutions have constructed a common ideology and in ongoing communicative actions among their campaign institutions, formulate common knowledge, common outlooks and common understandings of problems and solutions.

In this way the social partners in Denmark have proved capable of verbalizing experiences and constructing perceptions of changing macro-economic situations. Also, they have proved themselves capable of formulating a strategy for structural change and technological renewal and of achieving broad acceptance of this among the major interests on the labour market and in the political system.

Since 1987 politics in Denmark have encountered two paradoxes:

Firstly, a national strategy has been formulated. A structural policy has been initiated. All social partners have, moreover, come to identify international competitiveness with structural competitiveness. Yet, paradoxically, only a patchwork implementation of the strategy has been possible. Consistent, overall and coordinated implementation has been blocked by political stalemate.

Secondly, opinion polls show a clear acceptance in the population of the socio-economic ideology; they show a prevailing agreement on the gravity of the national debt problem, and even a readiness to make 'great sacrifices (decreases in real wages, etc.) to take the nation out of the crisis' (Petersen et al. 1989). Yet this popular consensus has not resulted in electoral support for a stable party system which would enable a majority in Parliament to agree upon economic policy measures governed by the guidelines of a structural policy.

Underlying both paradoxes is the fact that, after 1973, a situation of extreme minority parliamentarism dominated every corner of Danish politics. Extreme minority parliamentarism (EMP) is characterized by at least four different features (Rasmussen, 1989): (a) minority governments without permanent majority coalitions; (b) shifting majorities behind economic policies; (c) no guarantee of a majority to support the yearly Budget Bill; and (d) no guarantee that a minority government will step down when outvoted by a majority in Parliament.

Denmark has undergone two periods of EMP. The first was 1973-83. The second started in 1987. The lack of a majority behind a stable economic policy 1987 forced the bourgeois government into consultations and negotiations with various actors. A MegaArena was created with political parties, municipalities and organizations in ongoing consultations and negotiations across the boundaries between politics in Parliament and bi- or tripartite cooperation in segments and networks. In such an arena social partners coordinate policies through 'grand bargains', 'political pacts' or 'political packages' combining aspects of different policy fields - that is wage, expenditure, industry, labour market, tax and social policies. They do so with a given purpose: to implement a given and commonly accepted strategy.

A MegaArena has existed in Denmark for many years. Examples of grand bargaining across the boundaries between politics in Parliament and bi- and tri-partite cooperation can be found since the 1930s especially in times of economic crisis. However, prior to the 1980s it was not possible to coordinate a poly-centered form of state through negotiations in a MegaArena circumscribed by a commonly accepted macro-economic strategy.

In autumn 1987 the prime minister for the first time invited LO (the association of trade unions) and DA (the federation of employers associations) to join the government in tripartite consultations. A common rubric for consultations soon came to be 'Structural Problems in the Labour Market'. But even if the headline stayed the same during the following three years a number of different sub-topics were negotiated. Every single sub-topic, however, stemmed from failed negotiations in HieraSegs or FuncNets. Unsolved problems spilled over into the MegaArena, and became mixed with questions related either to wage formation or to public expenditures and revenues.

During four years of continuous negotiations policy adjustments and changes in the labour market structure have been agreed upon by quadripartite bodies in the MegaArena. The prime results are: a common agreement that the labour force has to be re-structured through pre- and on job training programs; that employment programs have to be used accordingly (Larsen, 1989; Carlsen, 1990); and a decision to implement two programs for restructuring the labour force.

Today three clusters of institutions for policy-making are in operation: segments inside the bureaucracy; networks outside direct political influence, and the arenas integrating a new set of actors in a new set of functions (ComArena and MegaArena). A Center-Drifting Form of State has been constituted.

6. Conclusion: negotiated economy

I maintain that a national strategy (the structural policy) has been formulated. I also maintain that profound changes in attitudes have occurred (structural competitiveness), and that new policy instruments and institutions have been created. These achievements, however, ought not to divert attention from the problems and ambiguities. The emergence of a structural policy is a very new phenomenon and severe questions remain as to implementation. Only a patchwork quilt of policies has been implemented.

The most decisive factor in explaining how Denmark during the last ten to fifteen years has coped with problems of adaptation and development is to answer how social partners have been able to govern national changes through joint policy-making in a world of multiple actors and institutions. We have to look at how a system for generalized political cooperation has been developed enabling social partners to formulate and implement a change in national strategy.

Figure 7.3.4 CENTRE-DRIFTING FORM OF STATE

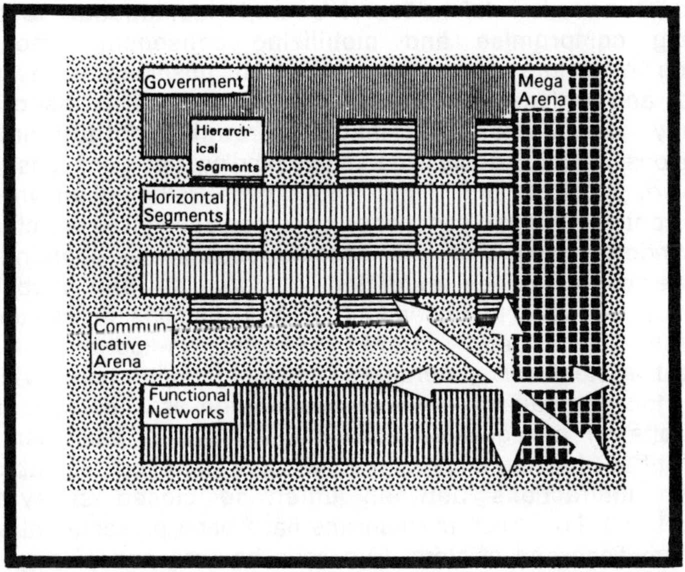

CENTRE-DRIFTING FORM OF STATE. The form of state was changed for the fourth time. This time from a polycentric to a center-drifting form of state. Decision-making in three clusters was compounded within the ad hoc defined limits of the MegaArena. Policy processes could drift from one cluster to another, from one center of authority to another. Possibilities were created for synchronized and temporally timed actions within clusters but also across boundaries. The plurality of different clusters each of which performs crucial functions and none of which can claim unchallenged supremacy over the others, were coordinated by quadripartite negotiations and inter-associational communicative actions. A contingent and emergent system for generalized political cooperation was established.

In doing so I will use elements from the theory of negotiated coonomy (see Nielsen and Pedersen in this volume). In the ideal-type negotiated economy allocation of resources Is neilher determined by individual agents adapting to market changes, nor through autonomous decision-making by public authorities. Instead an essential characteristic of a negotiated economy is the interconnection of discursive and institutional features enforcing compromise and mobilizing consensus among a multitude of actors acting from different positions in a multi-layered and polycentric institutional setting. In a negotiated economy decisions are made through institutionalized negotiations among agents who reach binding decisions based on discursive, political and moral imperatives rather than through formal contracts, legal sanctions, or organizational hierarchies.

To understand how it has become possible to coordinate a multitude of actors by enforcing compromise and mobilizing consensus we have to understand how institutions or clusters of institutions have been ordered to form an contingent and emergent system for generalized political cooperation. While a system for generalized political cooperation is the institutional prerequisite for a negotiated economy, the system itself can only be identified by identifying mechanisms and bodies able to establish interactions between otherwise closed subsystems (Jessop 1987). Four such mechanisms have been presented above:

(1) Institutions and clusters alike have become part of a general field of communication. They are innovators of the ComArena and participants in its common orientations. As participants they are bound to accept the logic of argumentation (Pedersen 1989; Nielsen and Pedersen 1991). This logic, then, provides the first mechanism linking otherwise closed subsystems together in a system for generalized political cooperation.

(2) Institutions and clusters alike have been equipped with internal discursive structures representing the socio-economic ideology as such. The construction of a series of discursive subfields (wage, expenditure, industry and labour market discourses) and the gradual integration of these into the overall ideology of socio-economics provides the second mechanism coupling subsystems with their environment. This mechanism permits subsystems to reflect on the identity of the system and their proper role and function in its reproduction.

(3) Policy- and decision-making processes in institutions and clusters alike have been interlocked by the synchronization of events. The MegaArena provides means for the timing of policy processes and for the temporal ordering of choice and opportunities. Events in institutions can spill-over into clusters

just as events in clusters can spill-over into the MegaArena. The synchronization of events, then, provides the third mechanism for coupling subsystems to their environment. This mechanism permits agents to reflect on how to coordinate short-term incentives with long-term calculations, and to subordinate their ego-preferences to the possible outcome at the systemic level (Pizzorno 1978; Marin 1985; March and Olsen 1989).

(4) Direct linkages between institutions and clusters have been secured through single agents (persons and organizations alike) with roles in several clusters and arenas. There are only a small number of organizations and of persons representing these in negotiations at the top-level, across boundaries and in the MegaArena. They provide the fourth mechanism for bridging otherwise closed subsystems and contributing to the possibilities of systemic cooperation.

These and other mechanisms will have to be studied further. Only additional research can provide a full description of the system for generalized political cooperation. A full identification, however, will have to take into consideration how these four mechanisms have been institutionalized in a special set of bodies.

In the theory of a negotiated economy five such complementary bodies have been described:

(a) Policy bodies aim at formulating economic and social problems and at identifying political measures necessary to solve them. They are usually erected by the government or the Parliament. 'The Technology Board' mentioned earlier is an example.

(b) Campaign bodies aim at describing societal problems in socio-economic terms, while at the same time transforming the socio-economic ideology into a rationale capable of achieving broad acceptance throughout the political system and by the entire population. The 'Economic Council' is an example.

(c) Discourse bodies aim at transforming the dominant perceptions of socio-economic problems into systematically structured, analytically justified, internally coherent and externally verifiable language codes. An example is the role played by Departments of Economics at the universities in developing socio-economic theories reflecting the dominant perceptions of the socio-economic ideology between social partners.

(d) Negotiating bodies draw up timetables and outline frameworks for forthcoming negotiations. They negotiate rules for conjoining and voting, mediate specific and general demands, and sign agreements. Examples are bipartite round table negotiations between peak organizations on the labour market.

(e) Conciliating and sanctioning bodies are normally semi-public, i.e., created by law but governed by bi- or tripartite representatives with the purpose of conciliating and sanctioning where agreements have been breached. Examples are the 'Industrial Court' and the 'Board of Conciliation'.

The system for generalized political cooperation is much more than an instrument for decision-making and coordination of a multi-layered and poly-centered set of institutions. The overall system of generalized political cooperation can be seen as the institutional prerequisite for a negotiated economy.

Bibliography

Berrefjord, O., Nielsen, K., and Pedersen, O.K. (1989) 'Forhandlingsøkonomi i Norden - en indledning', in K. Nielsen and O.K. Pedersen, eds., *Forhandlingsøkonomi i Norden*, Copenhagen: JøF.

Blueprint 154 (1956) 'Samsarbejdsproblemer i den danske oekonomiske politik', Copenhagen.

Eggert, Petersen, et al. (1989) *De krisebevidste og offervillige danskere. Den politisk-psykologisk udvikling 1982-86-88*, Psykologisk Institut, Aarhus Universitet.

Eggert, Petersen, et al. (1991) *De trivsomme og arbejdsomme danskere. Krisen og den politisk-psykologisk udvikling 1982-90*, Psykologisk Institut, Aarhus Universitet.

Finansministeriet (1986) *Finansredegörelsen 1987*, Copenhagen.

Gram, G.W. og Vogt, H.H. (1887-88) *Den Nordiske Obligationsret: almindelig del. Nordisk Retsencyklopedaedi II*, Copenhagen.

Haarløv, T. (1958) 'Retten til arbejde - og pligten', in E.A. Abitz, et al., eds., *Festskrift til Poul Andersen*, Copenhagen.

Hasselbalch, O. (1979) *Arbejdsretlige Funktioner*, Copenhagen.

Jessop, B. (1987) 'Economy, state and law in autopoietic theory', *Essex Papers in Politics and Government*, no 42, Essex University.

Katzenstein, P.J. (1985) *Small states in world markets. Industrial policy in Europe*, Ithaca: Cornell University Press.

Larsen, J.E. (1857-58) *Samlede Skrifter*, vol. 1-2, Copenhagen.

Lassen, J. (1882) *Danske Obligationsrets Almindelig Del*, Copenhagen.

March, J.G. and Olsen, J.P. (1989) *Rediscovering Institutions: the organizational basis of politics*, New York.

Marin, B. (1985) 'Generalized political exchange: preliminary considerations', *EUI Working Paper*, no 85/190, Florence.

Meier Carlsen, E. (1990) 'En kegle ad gangen', *Det Fri Aktuelt*, 15.10.

Nielsen, K. (1988) 'Den borgerlige regerings styring af den offentlige sektors økonomi', in K.H. Bentzon, ed., *Fra vaekst til omstilling - Modernisering af den offentlige sektor*, Copenhagen.

Nielsen, K. and Pedersen, O.K. (1989) 'Is small still beautiful?', *Scandinavian Political Studies*, 4.

Nielsen, K. and Pedersen, O.K. (1991) 'From the Mixed Economy to the Negotiated Economy - the Scandinavian Countries', in Coughlin, R.M., ed., *Morality, Rationality, and Efficiency: new perspectives in socio-economics*, New York: M.E. Sharpe.

Pedersen, O.K. (1985) *Institutionel Historie*, Roskilde: RUC.

Pedersen, O.K. (1986) 'Forhaldingsøkonomi og samfundsøkonomi', in *Scandinavian Political Studies*, 3.

Pedersen, O.K. (1989) 'Laereprocesser og Forhandlingsspil. Om låndannelse og forhandlingsøkonomi i Danmark', in K. Nielsen and O.K. Pedersen, eds., *Forhandlingsøkonomi i Norden*, Copenhagen: JøF.

Pedersen, O.K. (1991a) 'At first they were two, then three and now four. Generalized political cooperation in modern Danish political history', in E.M. Kassalow, ed., *Tripartite Consultation and Cooperation in Making National Economic and Social Policy*, Geneva: ILO-report.

Pedersen, O.K. (1991) 'För, nu ... og derefter. Om stabilitet og forandrning i aftalesystemet på det private arbejdsmarked', in J. Hoff and F. Mikkelsen, eds., *Faglige Organisationers modernisering i den offentlige sektor*, Copenhagen.

Pedersen, O.K. (1991c) *Arbejdets institutionelle historie. Økonomisk individualisme i Danmark 1550-1800.*

Perspektivplan I and II (1971 and 1973) Copenhagen: Budget ministry.

Pizzorno, A. (1978) 'Political exchange and collective identity in industrial conflict', in C. Crouch and A. Pizzorno, eds., *The Resurgence of Class Conflict in Western Europe since 1968*, vol 2, London: Macmillan.

Rasmussen, E. (1989) 'Partiernes adfaerd ved den endelige afstemning om finansloven', *Politica*, 2.

Skov Larsen, L. (1989) 'Det gråhåarede skal redde dansk økonomi', in *Weekendavisen*, 13.10.1989.

Sönderriis, E. (1990) 'Industriens Arbejdsgivere: vores lånstyring redder landet', *Information*, 29.11.1990.

Zahle, H. (1986) *Dansk Forfatningstet. Menneskerettigheder*, vol. 5, Copenhagen.

9 Private industrial policy in the Danish negotiated economy

Niels Åkerstrøm Andersen and Peter Kjær

1. Industrial policy, negotiated economy, and strategic capacity

Like other small West European countries, Denmark has a very open economy in terms of foreign trade and exposure to international competition and is therefore quite vulnerable to the fluctuations and transformations of the global economy. Thus, the international recessions of the 1970s and 1980s had severe impacts on the Danish economy, resulting in both high unemployment and huge trade deficits. Two traits of the Danish economy constitute the specific national context for handling the consequences of openness and integration in the world economy: the predominance of small and medium-sized firms; and the strength of the agricultural sector, including the agricultural-industrial complex, traditionally organized in co-operative firms.

In economic policy discourse, the performance of the Danish economy in this particular context were traditionally linked to a notion of competitiveness focusing on prices, costs and exchange rates (See also Jessop, Nielsen and Pedersen in this volume). Thus, the function of economic policy making was to minimize the costs of industries exposed to international competition through wages and incomes policy, tax benefits and, in the context of industrial policy, various forms of direct and indirect economic aid to particular firms and industries to overcome the financial barriers to competitive performance on international markets.

However, during the last 10-15 years this interpretation of the role of economic policy in general and industrial policy in particular has been thoroughly transformed. While reminders of the traditional structures remain, the focus of industrial policy has changed in three important ways:

(a) From subsidies to *campaigns* as the predominant policy instrument;

(b) From individual firms to *industrial structure* as a whole as the chief target of the various policy measures; and

(c) From the state to *private policy communities* as the locus of policy formulation and implementation.

Thus in the early 1990s the traditional industrial policy structure has to a large degree been replaced by multiple private industrial policies both on the national and on the regional and local level.

This chapter attempts to characterize these emergent private industrial policies both in terms of the new institutional practices, roles and strategies constituted in the area of industrial policy, and in terms of the general structures in which this transformation and re-constitution of industrial policy has taken place. The empirical evidence in the following is to a large extent based on Pedersen et al., (1992).

On the level of practices and strategies, we will describe the institutional effects of private industrial policy making on private enterprise, while on a structural level we will interpret the changes in industrial policy as symptoms of a transformation of the organizing principles of the economy towards a negotiated economy.

We contend that these structural changes of the mode of economic governance cannot be interpreted meaningfully in terms of market or hierarchy or even as a mix of these two principles. Rather we wish to emphasize the centrality of communication as a mechanism of co-ordination in the economy. This in turn entails the establishment of a particular institutional system, a negotiated economy, to ensure the communicative co-ordination of economic action.

1.1. Market, mixed, and negotiated economy

The negotiated economy may be seen as the result of a sequence of structural transformations of the Danish economy from the constitution of the market economy through the development of the mixed economy.

The market economy was legally constituted in the middle of the nineteenth century; the economy became an autonomous sphere of action consisting of private individuals and firms, formally separated from the state. Individuals and firms acquired economic, political and legal rights, i.e., property rights which could be realized in market relations. The role of the state was that of creating a formal space of enterprise action, enabling the realization of individual rights in the market through the potential enforcement of contracts.

From around the turn of the century, the rationality of the liberal market economy was seriously questioned. A number of social and political movements demanded compensation for the social side-effects of the operation of the market, and the political correction of different market failures. A 'mixed' economy was constituted, in which the fundamental distinction between state and market was maintained while the boundary between the two spheres was perforated by political interventions into the mechanisms of the market.

Beginning in the 1950s the rationality of both political and economic institutions was challenged from the perspective of the national economy as a whole. This gradually led to the constitution of a negotiated economy.

Problems of co-ordination were formulated across the boundaries between private and public, i.e., the problem of how to secure the efficient performance of the economy on a macro level through concerted action by the multiplicity of formal organizations and institutions involved in the mixed economy. These problems were seen as problems of reaching a mutual understanding or consensus about the state of the economy. Public institutions, private firms and other institutions of the economy were to relate themselves to a shared economic world-view and take responsibility for realization of the common interest in maintaining an efficient macro-economic performance when maximizing individual utility.

New institutions were established to formulate common images of the state of the economy, and to propagate these images or conceptions through policy campaigns and counselling. Bargaining institutions were established to coalesce firms and other institutions in communicative processes within the economic frame of meaning in order to establish common coordinated strategies.

Whereas co-ordination in the market and mixed economy was based on the principles of contract or hierarchy as institutionalized in market, firms and state, co-ordination in the negotiated economy takes place through the communication of ideals, norms and world-views within a shared conception of the state of the economy.

1.2. Towards second order strategies

One important institutional effect of the development of a negotiated economy is the transformation of the preconditions of strategic action in firms, public institutions, financial institutions etc., We shall interpret this as a shift from first order strategy to second order strategy (see Pedersen 1990; Jessop 1987; Teubner 1989).

We define *first order strategy* as co-ordination of preferences between a set of actors through compromising about common short-term goals. Any kind of bargaining about contracts and dealing on the market reflects first order strategy. Strategic action in this context concerns the selection and manipulation of markets, the establishment of strategic alliances and the securing of relations of trust. We define *second order strategy* as co-ordination of preferences between a set of actors through consensus-building in order to fulfil shared long-term goals. As opposed to compromise, consensus-building implies that one reaches a mutual understanding and shared cognition of the situation of the present and the future, i.e., a common space of experience and a common horizon of expectation (cf. Koselleck 1985).

Thus industrial policy strategies of the second order entail the production of common representations of the future of the national industrial structure, i.e., a shared understanding of the economic necessity of supporting entrepreneurs, labour-training etc. Such common representations and norms make it rational for private firms and institutional investors to invest in technological service institutions, industrial parks, networks, educational centres etc., with no expectation of a normal rate of profit, but with the intention of securing the future potentials of the industrial structure.

Strategic action in this context implies attempts to influence the conceptualization of the economy, i.e., the creation of norms and images of the future of the industrial structure, the status of certain institutions as socially responsible actors, and the goals and institutional conditions of the various private industrial policies.

The change from first order strategy to second order strategy occurs in a parallel process where private firms and financial institutions link their internal economic performance with the long-term development of the national economy and recognize that the state of the economy and their own future success depend on the co-ordination of preferences and strategies in relations to what is seen as socially responsible.

It is the purpose of the following argument to show how the capacity of second order strategy emerges in private industrial policies, and how firms, in these private policies, are governed or coordinated not by market mechanisms or organizational hierarchies but rather by their integration in communities of communication which produce shared notions of economic and social responsibility.

We shall do so by describing the changes in the discursive and institutional structures of industrial policy in the last 10-15 years leading to the emergence of private industrial policies in three arenas: local and regional industrial policy, the capital market, and national industrial policy. For each of these arenas we shall present examples of private industrial policy campaigns to show how private industrial policy-making entails the emergence of second order strategies and a particular set of institutional roles which, taken together, constitute a negotiated economy.

2. The emergence of private industrial policies

Until the late 1970s Danish industrial policy was basically a matter of providing direct financial aid to private firms under various headings: investment guarantees, export subsidies, aid for technological development, aid for the relocation of production to less developed parts of the country, etc..

Since the 1920s a complex industrial subvention structure had evolved incrementally, with virtually no central co-ordination. One common denominator of this segmented industrial policy was the justification of financial aid by reference to various market failures: firms fail to develop primarily due to either weak market signals or other financial constraints or barriers. Industrial policy was to re-establish or compensate for these weak signals, while retaining a fundamental respect for the autonomy of private enterprise.

Thus prior to 1980 Danish industrial policy did not really question the rationality and potential of private enterprise. The area of industrial policy maintained its segmented character and continued to be very weakly coordinated with no precise general objectives and hardly any ambitions of more interventionist measures.

From the mid 1970s several important policy actors started to question the Danish industrial policy. Initially, the efficiency and consistency of the aid structure was questioned, but soon the entire role of industrial policy in economic policy as such became a political issue. With the abandoning of demand-side macroeconomic policies in favour of supply-side economics in the late 1970s, industrial policy was situated as a key economic policy instrument within the discursive framework of the socioeconomic frame of meaning. However, these considerations tended to conflict with the traditional low-key industrial policy that usually did not question the belief that 'industry knows better'.

In 1983 the Technological Development Programme of the Ministry of Industry became the test case of a new industrial policy paradigm, which had evolved in the technology policy segment around the Danish Technology Board, the main policy institution of Danish technology policy. The Programme offered large scale economic support to technological development projects in industry, especially in the area of information technology. It involved not only economic support but also an awareness campaign targetted at small and medium sized firms.

The programme differed from previous technology policy efforts not only in scale and policy instruments. It explicitly questioned the economic rationality of Danish firms in the area of technological innovation and consciously selected one specific key area of technology for support. This in turn implied a redefinition of the traditional cost-oriented notion of competitiveness in favour of one that linked competitiveness with technological innovation and economic flexibility.

Later, in 1986-87, an ambitious attempt was made to install this new industrial policy paradigm as a central policy objective. The Ministry of Industry and three other ministries outlined a structural policy which was to coordinate industrial policy, science policy, labour market policy, and educational policy within an overarching economic frame of meaning. As an immediate effect the whole area of industrial policy was reorganized and a number of subsidy programmes were terminated.

However, this reform initiative failed to gain the necessary political support both within the bourgeois government and in parliament. Instead, in 1989 the Ministry of Industry suffered serious budget cuts and was forced to relinquish many of its former ambitions of a centrally coordinated structural policy. Part of this failure can be ascribed to the extreme minority parliamentarism with weak minority governments which has plagued the Danish political system since the early 1970s resulting in parliamentary stalemate in numerous policy areas. This combined with the highly segmented character of the state had created a situation where the government was unable to function as a centre of policy formulation and economic coordination. Rather the government was forced to relinquish its privileged status and simply become primus inter pares in the arenas of economic policy making.

As a more or less conscious reaction to this paralysis of central government, private industrial policies have emerged in at least three different institutional contexts: local areas or regions, the capital market, and even in the context of national industrial policy.

2.1. Local and regional industrial policies

At the municipal level local varieties of the macro-economic conception evolved. From the late 1970s there was a growing tendency to view regions and local communities as aggregate economic units. Private firms, local governments, regional technological service centres and banks began to connect their own problems with what was now conceived as the 'local economy'.

High unemployment rates place serious strains on budgets of municipalities but municipal governments have only very limited competence in the area of local economic policies, such as industrial policy, and is thus often restrained from taking more substantial initiatives. This places the responsibility for the development of the local economy in the hands of the private actors of the local community. Often they have accepted this responsibility.

An increasing number of local industrial councils have emerged from the late 1970s. These councils compound private firms, municipal governments, technological service centres, and banks in private policy making processes in which strategies for local economic development were formulated. Until the mid 1980s these strategies focused on the problems of small firms and entrepreneurs whose function in the local economies was politicized, and whose management skills and potentials of development were questioned. A wide array of institutions were established to guide, train and in other ways support small firms and entrepreneurs in their processes of technological, organizational or strategic development: industrial counsellors, regional technology service centres, regional technology councillors, industrial parks, research parks and entrepreneur centres.

After 1985 many local actors started to realize that it was not enough to support, train and advise the individual firms. It was considered necessary to reorganize and co-ordinate the entire local industrial structure from the perspective of the local economy. As a consequence several regions and local communities formulated regional and local structural policies which mobilized a multitude of economic and political actors and involved substantial economic and institutional resources in the pursuit of a structural transformation of the economy. The main tool for these structural policies was the strategic establishment of network cooperation between firms, where local and regional policy and service institutions actively engaged in the mediation and creation of inter-firm networks through campaigns, seminars and counselling procedures.

Thus the development of private industrial policies in the local and regional context has resulted in the emergence of a complex institutional system, a private policy community comprising numerous actors and institutions engaged in policy formulation and implementation. This institutional system of private policy making has developed a capacity for second order strategic action: i.e., the general notion of local economy is translated into a particular industrial policy strategy which entails the production of shared conceptions of local economic responsibility that redefines the roles and strategic capacities of actors and institutions of the local economy. We shall illustrate this by describing the policy campaign for strengthening entrepreneurship in the local and regional sphere.

2.1.1. Producing producers: the entrepreneur campaign

The image of 'the entrepreneur' surfaced for the first time in the debate about local industrial policy around 1978. The question was how to improve the performance of the local economy through a steady influx of viable new enterprises.

First the problem of entrepreneurship was understood as a problem of financing and physically facilitating the entrepreneurs. But a large campaign from 1983 has totally changed the formulation of the problem.

Many actors participated in the campaign: municipal governments, the Research Institute of Counties and Municipalities, the Danish Federation of Small and Medium Sized Enterprises, local banks, accountants, technological information centres and private local industrial councils.

The campaign pointed out that the entrepreneurs did not simply suffer from financial problems or the lack of a proper material infrastructure, i.e., premises for production. Rather they seemed to be constrained by a lack of rationality and knowledge in many areas: law, economic management, accounting, finance, marketing and sales, project development and, not least, strategic management.

This was understood as a problem of institutionalizing local capacity to hatch new enterprises through counselling, mediation and generation of ideas. A lot of local institutions such as entrepreneur centres and courses in marketing, sales, etc.,, personal counselling, local entrepreneurial committees, 'senior entrepreneur contact fora', and discussion groups and product development centres for entrepreneurs were to develop and shape the entrepreneurs. One important feature of many of these concrete entrepreneur initiatives was that they were not merely viewed as a helping hand to new entrepreneurs but also as a way of separating the 'bad' entrepreneur projects from the good in an early stage, and advising some entrepreneurs to discontinue such projects which were not considered viable. In some instances the question of viability was linked to particular ideals of the composition of the local industrial structure.

All these activities attempted to interpellate the entrepreneurs. They were now constituted as local economic actors with responsibility of the local economy. They were offered counselling by local industrial counsellors, and they were expected to let their ideas and concepts be evaluated and shaped in counselling processes. The strategy of the single entrepreneur was no longer a private matter but a matter of all the local industrial policy institutions. Further the local responsibility was sanctioned. The possibility to get financial credit from the bank was connected to the ability and willingness of the entrepreneurs to receive advice from the local institutions.

Thus in the period from 1980 to 1985 the role of the entrepreneur in the local economy was defined. This role embodied demands to entrepreneurs of engaging in counselling processes. The entrepreneur campaign of the early 1980s seemed to have a double function: on the one hand to make individuals into entrepreneurs in a specific way, and on the other hand to make municipalities, industrial councils, financial institutions and accountants accept the local economic responsibility towards the entrepreneurs.

2.2. *Industrial policies in the capital market*

At the national level, the large institutional investors (pension funds, wage earner funds, insurance companies, etc.,) became deeply involved in industrial policy making during the 1980s.

The background of this involvement was the emergence of a discourse linking the investment strategies of the institutional investors with the socio-economic frame of meaning. This began in the late 1970s with a critique of the so-called 'institutionalized money illusion', connoting that securities such as bonds with high yield-rates but no basis in production do not refer to any real value. It was argued that one had to differentiate between yield-rate and real value, and that pension funds and insurance companies, who had a long term survival interest needed to emphasize real value. Real value on the other hand implies production capital. Only investments in production could be the foundation of the economy of the future. Instead of buying bonds, institutional investors ought to buy stocks in future-oriented firms engaged in production.

Accordingly the institutional investors began to practise active ownership via venture capital enterprises; the supply of risk-capital was accompanied by management support in order to improve the strategic basis of firms.

However, the supply of risk-capital was larger than the demand for it. Future-oriented firms do not grow on trees. Instead of being a matter of picking the firms of the future and supporting them with management, the question of security was now seen as a question of how to secure the supply of new investment projects. This led to an interest in strategies of economic restructuring. The institutional investors realized that they were only able to reorganize the industrial structure through concerted investment strategies and the mobilization of willingness from the firms themselves. They gradually developed procedures of collaboration and in 1988 they created a common policy and campaign institution: the Forum for Industrial Development.

The explicit goal of this institution was to produce knowledge about the industrial structure, to mediate a dialogue between institutional investors, private and public managers and trade union leaders, and to investigate how the institutional investors could take part the creation of an internationally competitive industry. The Forum for Industrial Development included representatives from institutional investors, the public sector, private firms, trade unions and political parties.

Through the Forum for Industrial Development the institutional investors began to represent themselves as 'financial architects, who invest in and restructure the Danish industry'. The Forum became one of the most central and enterprising actors in several restructuring projects, among others the creation a food-industry complex.

2.2.1. The industrial locomotive of the food industry

In the campaign for the restructuring of Danish food industry one concept was particularly pervasive: the image of the so-called 'industrial locomotives'. This image conditioned and to some extent reorganized or changed the terms of the debate about industrial strategy in relation to a number of industries.

The vision of Danish industrial locomotives marked a significant change of perspective in parts of the Danish industrial policy debate. A departure from the idea that 'small is beautiful'- and a general acceptanco of the idea that Denmark needed large internationally competitive industrial corporations. This change in attitude was primarily propagated by pension funds in collaboration with insurance companies.

The campaign of the Forum for Industrial Development for an industrial locomotive in the food industry started in 1988 and culminated in 1989, where it resulted (among other things) in the creation of the two large corporations MD Foods International and Tulip International.

The campaign may be divided into three phases In phase one the food industry was identified as a potential basis of the establishment of an industrial locomotive. In phase two the institutional investors prepared for the implementation of the strategy through the acquisition of shares in the food industry and the establishment of holding companies. In phase three a strategy of a food industry locomotive was formulated and the cooperative movement was discursively linked to this strategy.

The campaign had some important institutional effects besides the actual mergers and acquisitions of the institutional investors The organizations of the cooperative movement were 'forced' to engage in the discussion, to accept a dialogue with the institutional investors about their position in a strategy aimed at the establishment of a locomotive, and to acknowledge their own responsibility as actors in the strategy.

Phase one lasted from the foundation of the 'Forum' until November 1988. In May 1988 the Forum 'went public' and published a report (Forum for Industriel Udvikling 1988a) with the central message that Denmark needed to establish a number of large industrial locomotives. The proposal generated substantial public attention. In November 1988, a second report was published (Forum for Industriel Udvikling 1988b). Again the necessity of the establishment of industrial locomotives was emphasized. This time, however, the food industry was emphasized as the potential base for the construction of the most important industrial locomotives. The report was followed by a conference which also highlighted the role of the food industry.

Phase two: The publication of the two reports was followed by frenetic activity of (among others) the institutional investors in the stock market and in particular firms. In October 1988 the Danish Sugar Factories bought 16 per cent of the stock in the Danish Spirit Distilleries; an event followed by the January 1989 merger of these two companies and Danisco to form the corporation Danisco A/S. The two wage-earner funds, ATP and LD, a number of pension funds, and one insurance company owned a substantial part of the stock of this new large corporation. The new chairman of the board was a person closely associated with the Forum for Industrial Development.

Two months later it was revealed that the investment company SN-invest had secretly been acquiring shares in the Danish fertilizer corporation Superfos which was to serve as a spearhead in a scheme to take over the part of meat manufacturing controlled by the cooperative movement. In April 1989, the strategy was accepted by Superfos.

This chain of events may be seen as a partly coordinated attempt to create industrial locomotives in the food industry. Through acquisitions and shareholder agreements, a growing number of companies became parts of locomotive strategies. This by no means occurred without conflicts. Conflicts arose between former boards of directors and the institutional investors who in their strategies attempted to impose certain roles on the individual firms.

In *phase three*, the strategy of food locomotives was developed in more explicit and detailed terms. The cooperative form of enterprise was deemed problematic in relation to the strategy and the cooperative movement was more or less forced into a dialogue with the institutional investors. This dialogue led to a restructuring of the food industry according to the ideal of industrial locomotives.

The delegitimation of the cooperative form of enterprise started as early as November 1988 in the second Forum report on the future of Denmark as an industrial nation [see above]. If Denmark was to recapture and develop its position in the international food market. a liberalization of the property legislation in agriculture was necessary to enable the free acquisition of farms. Shareholder companies had to be allowed in the agricultural sector in order to provide it with better financial means. In April of 1989 the Planning Secretariat of the Ministry of Industry supported the conclusion of the Forum in a report titled 'Danish industry on the way to the internal market'.

The leadership of the cooperative movement rejected the notion of a locomotive as an engine of the food industry. The notion of agriculture as part of the national strategy in the manner envisioned by the Forum was deemed problematic. Similarly, the motives of the institutional investors were questioned. However, the most important critique based itself on the particular notion of security and rationality of the cooperative movement. This notion, which would be lost in a transition to shareholder companies was said to ensure that the food industry would remain under the control of Danish interests. Also the cooperative form of enterprise actually gave the cooperative companies access to the capital of individual farmers; a unique source of capital not available to other forms of enterprise.

While this rather hostile campaign was still going on, a dialogue was staged between the different institutional investors and a number of cooperative firms about concrete projects.

- In July of 1988 a round of negotiations started between the cooperative Danish Slaughterhouses, the wage earner fund LD, and the trade unions in order to find new forms of financing in the food processing industry. Two working committees were established to analyze the needs of new investments in the meat industry.

- In March of the following year a cooperative slaughterhouse in Jutland started to collaborate with the wage earner fund LD about the canned food factory DAK.

- The following month the cooperative enterprise Tulip announced that it was planning a seminar about the changes in the ownership- and capital structure of the corporation. The idea of separating parts of the enterprise, i.e., processing from the rest and creating a separate shareholder company for these activities was considered.

- In May 1989 a big slaughterhouse in Jutland, VS, and LD together with DAK presented a preliminary plan for a merger in meat processing. The idea was to separate the processing industry from the rest of the meat manufacturing industry, and to supply capital from the outside for processing.

- One of the working committees founded one year earlier published the report on 'the pork industry and the institutional investors'. The report focused on the problem of co-ordinating the initiatives of the cooperative movement with those of the institutional investors on the basis of a common acknowledgement of the fact that, if the meat industry were to be successful on the future growth markets, it was necessary to invest in research, product development and marketing on a much larger scale.

- In August of 1989 the third Forum report was published (Forum for Industriel Udvikling, 1989). The report, which was financed by the National Council of Agriculture, the Union of the Food Industry Workers, and the Ministry of Agriculture, analyzed the potentials of developing industrial locomotives in the food industry and proposed the establishment of one of the largest meat corporations in the world financed by pension funds and insurance companies. A major symposium with 150 participants from the food industry, the business community in general and politicians were held to discuss the report.

At this juncture the problem of industrial structure and the locomotive strategy in the food industry as originally proposed by the Forum were accepted by all the involved parties. At the same time there was a mutual recognition of the autonomy of the interested parties, and thus the rationality of the cooperative enterprise in production. The institutional investors were said to have 'specific capabilities' as they controlled large capital resources that may be invested in high risk projects on a long term basis.

There was a shared recognition of the fact that processing, product development and marketing were fields in which the cooperative form of enterprise was not optimal, as it could not mobilize the necessary risk capital. The risk capital was on the other hand exactly the 'capability' of institutional investors. Here was the obvious potential of cooperation.

This model of cooperation was realized in the creation of two large joint stock companies, MD Foods International and Tulip International. MD Foods International was to engage in the manufacturing and marketing of international dairy products. Tulip International was to take over the processing division of Tulip. The initial stock value of each of the two corporations was approximately 1 billions DKr.

The locomotive campaign was not merely an attempt to change the focus of attention in the industry in a short term perspective. Rather it was a comprehensive and sophisticated attack on the cooperative form of enterprise. In the course of the campaign, the Forum and other actors attempted to destabilize the cooperative discourse by delegitimizing the cooperative form of enterprise and offering risk capital with a perspective of substantial economic development in the food industry. The transformation of the industry took place in a complex interplay of a vast number of private and public organizations, institutions and firms, which actively engaged in the formulation and implementation of a shared strategy of industrial restructuring.

The image of the locomotive mobilized numerous actors in the debate. It conditioned the discourse of industrial restructuring by offering a specific perspective on the restructuring and by outlining specific roles of participants in the process as parts of great locomotive of the food industry.

2.3. *The transformation of national industrial policy*

The failure to establish a coordinated structural policy also led to a re-orientation of national industrial policy. As announced in the 1989 annual Industrial Policy Statement from the Ministry of Industry, the primary ambition of the industrial policy of the state had become that of being a qualified participant in private policies. The state no longer played an autonomous role outside and above private policy. It was positioned in the private policies as first among equals. State agencies were to influence the private policies through campaigns, analyses of the industry, removal of formal barriers for private policy, and strategic financial support for selected actors in the private policies.

Although the 1989 statement may be seen as the first manifest articulation of this new role of the state, the transfer of economic and political responsibility to private economic institutions had actually been taking place since the early 1980s. The formulation of the problem of the rationality of private firms as the main structural problem of the economy entailed the articulation of new ideals of the competitive and responsible enterprise; ideals of flexible firms paying careful attention to technological Innovations, with substantial competence both in organization and management, and most important: with a willingness to cooperate with other firms. These ideals of responsible enterprise were propagated through campaigns, and through practical guidance and counselling in the system of private technological service institutions and in the agencies of the Ministry of Industry.

A interesting example is the national Network Programme which was launched in 1989 to stimulate the creation of networks between firms.

2.3.1. The critical juncture: the networking campaign

The concept of 'network' had its major break-through in industrial policy with the publication of the 'Action programme for network co-operation' which was presented in the 1989 Industrial Policy Statement as part of the government's 'Strategy 92' for internationalization of the Danish economy. The break-through occurred almost simultaneously in national, regional and local industrial policies alike.

The programme depicted networks as a rational form of enterprise organization for small and medium sized firms in the context of increasing international competition following the establishment of the EC Internal Market from 1993. Networking enterprises compensate for the lack of economies of scale through a flexible organization adapted to the specific preferences, needs and competitive situations of the individual firms.

The programme consisted of two parts. First, a number of direct measures to encourage private firms to form or join networks. These measures included information campaigns and (limited) financial aid to the establishment of networks. Second, an attempt to institutionalize the network strategy at the local level through the establishment of an educational programmeme which was to educate local financial institutions, R&D and technological service institutions, private consultants, and accountants as 'network brokers'.

After the publication of the network programmeme in the Spring of 1989 the Ministry of Industry (or rather its National Agency of Industry and Trade) and the Institute of Technology conducted an intense public campaign for the programme. Already by late 1990 a number of institutional effects of the campaign, i.e., massive response from industry and a successful dissemination of the network rhetoric to numerous industrial policy communities, could be observed.

The campaign propagated the image of networking to industry and other economic actors through numerous publications, meetings and seminars and through the educational programmeme focusing on network brokers. We shall briefly illustrate each of these activities:

- The Ministry of Industry and the Institute of Technology engaged in systematic publication of information about the network idea to be spread through the press, through the existing institutional network of industrial policy and through direct contacts with firms and industries. This started with the publication of the 'Action Programme' in which the idea of networking was coupled to the general economic context and presented as a viable strategy for small firms in a more hostile environment of international competition. It was followed by the publication of numerous pamphlets, newsletters and special editions of information newspapers by the institutions. In these publications the general idea of networking was presented and endorsed by leading figures from the national industrial policy community; often with reference to international experience, e.g., the Italian case of Emilia-Romagna industrial district, and the particular Danish preconditions for success in networking. Also the network concept was given an operational definition as: 'long-term contractually binding co-operation involving the establishment and operation of shared functions', i.e., production, R&D, and marketing. This specification of the concept was accompanied with interviews with existing 'network brokers' and case descriptions of selected existing Danish pilot networks which had 'already proven their viability and perspective' in 'strategically important areas'. Finally, the potential areas and recipients of public financial support to the process of network formation such as small and medium sized firms, banks, consultants, and accountants were defined.

- Only a few months after the publication of the 'Action Programme' a training programme for network brokers started with seminars and courses for representatives from financial institutions, consultants and accounting firms and other enterprise service institutions. The seminars and courses, which were to equip the participants with a state licensed status as network brokers were soon over-booked.

- Simultaneously, representatives from the Ministry of Industry and the Institute of Technology participated in seminars all over the country in technological service institutions, in regional service institutions and in local industrial policy institutions to spread information about the programme. At a number of official network conferences representatives of three pilot networks took part to 'inspire managers of firms to consider network cooperation and to communicate practical experiences which may be of great value in the early stages of a network'.

These central points in the network campaign illustrate how the campaign has focused on teaching firms and 'brokers' what networking means, why networks are necessary and how they work in practice. Thus the pilot networks played an important role as practical exemplary models. The emphasis was constantly on the communication of attitudes and experiences, whereas the element of subsidization tended to be down-played[1].

The response to the network programme and the campaign was impressive. In March of 1990, after less than one year approximately 1500 firms had applied for financial support to the construction of approximately 260 networks. In August 1990, the Ministry of Industry announced that so far 2000 firms had applied, out of which 1200 had received support.

Apart from the large number of applicants the campaign had a number of other institutional effects from the early start of the process. First, it attracted substantial public attention, primarily in the local debates on industrial policies. Second, a number of private actors, e.g. banks, initiated series of meetings, seminars and conferences on networks. Third, the Danish business newspaper 'Erhvervsbladet' gave the programme extensive and continuous coverage and it established a 'network exchange'; a column for mediation of networks much like the 'personals' of daily newspapers. And fourth, it has become common to designate firm consultants as 'network brokers', disregarding the question of whether or not they had been officially licensed.

This seems to reflect the double function of the campaign: on the one hand to make firms realize that joining networks is both sensible and responsible and, on the other hand, to make advisers of private firms think of themselves as 'network brokers' and view the firms that they engage with from this perspective.

4. The negotiated economy of industrial policy

Private industrial policies develop both at local and national level. These private policies politicize private enterprise and seek to integrate firms, banks, service institutions etc., in local and national strategies.

The industrial policy campaigns that result from formulation of these local and national strategies share a number of important traits:

- They all seem to be organized around a single central image or metaphor (entrepreneur, locomotive and network) around which a specific language code is constructed to mobilize and condition the targetted actors and institutions of the campaigns.
- They all entail the production of particular positions and roles of the different actors and institutions by placing them in particular cognitive and normative contexts and endowing them with specific problems and certain idealized preferences and interests.
- In this production of roles, world-views and norms all of the campaigns rely heavily on the existence of a number of institutional roles forming an institutional environment of economic agency to continuously produce and reproduce the common representations of the state of the economy, the situation of actors and institutions in it, and the necessity of coordinating short term preferences with long term interests.

This institutional environment is formed by at least the following institutional role types:

- *Policy roles* oriented towards the building of consensus around socio-economic strategies. Policy roles were institutionalized both at national level in institutions such as the Forum for Industrial Development and at the regional and local level in numerous industrial councils.
- *Discourse roles* aimed at the role of industrial policy in the socio-economic frame of meaning. They were institutionalized at national level in universities, interest organizations, public and semi-public institutions. At the local level these roles are relatively weakly institutionalized. However, some degree of institutionalization may be found in banks, regional labour market councils and in some municipal governments.
- *Campaign roles* aimed at mobilizing attention around specific economic problems, making firms and other institutions recognize themselves as responsible actors in a shared economic context. Campaign roles were institutionalized both at the national level in pension funds, and wage-earner funds, the Forum for Industrial Development, the National Agency for Industry and

Trade, etc.,, and at the local level (in local industrial councils, regional technology centres, banks and industrial associations.

- *Therapeutic roles* oriented at propagating particular economic ideals to individual firms by consultancy, giving advice, and serving as 'sparring partner' in processes of change. Therapeutic roles were institutionalized at the national level in institutions such as the Institute of Technology and the Academy of the Technical Sciences, and at the local level in venture investment companies, training centres, regional technology centres, 'export houses', local industrial councils, research parks, industrial associations, entrepreneur centres, etc.,
- *Networking roles* aimed at transforming socio-economic ideals into network strategies for selected firms, organizing the networking processes, and helping firms to handle conflicts and practical problems. Networking roles were mainly institutionalized at local level in banks, regional technology centres and private consultancy firms.

The linking of economic actors with this institutional environment through campaigns, counselling processes or other forms of institutionalized communication secures the continuous coordination of preferences and interests of numerous actors and institutions with the requirements of the national, regional or local economy.

Thus the participants in these communicative processes acquire a strategic capacity not merely to weigh their own short term goals with their own long term interest, but also to influence and coordinate the formation of preferences of a large set of actors through consensus-building processes to fulfil shared long-term goals, i.e., a second order strategic capacity.

This second order strategic capacity turns industrial policy-making into continuous open ended social learning processes of a number of policy communities in which flexible responses to changing economic conditions are premised on the ability of the economic institutions to reflect on and communicate about the state of the economy, to formulate and propagate interests and roles within strategies of economic restructuring, and to condition other actors and institutions to the particular set of values and norms implied in the emergent role structure of the strategies.

In this negotiated economy, the social production of economic world-views, norms and values, and the re-constitution of economic practices in continuous discursive processes in private policy communities, based on second order strategic capacities, not only perforates boundaries between public and private. It also tends to dissolve the very boundaries of the business firm by questioning its identity and status as a sovereign and autonomous economic institution and institutionally integrating it in these discursive processes. Thus, there is a tendency in tho negotiated economy towards the creation of de-centred economic subjects or de-centered firms[2], endowed with second order strategic capacities, whose economic practices are coordinated not through market interaction or existing organizational hierarchies but rather through their involvement in continuous institutional learning processes, discursively defining their identities, preferences, interests and the range of legitimate and rational actions at their disposal.

Notes

[1] The subsidies are usually relatively modest; often no more than 50,000 Danish crowns per network for the different stages in the networking process.

[2] for a more extensive development of the concept of the de-centered firm see Pedersen, Andersen, and Kjær (1992).

Bibliography

Forum for Industriel Udvikling (1988a) *Foranalyse*, Copenhagen: Forum for Industriel Udvikling.

Forum for Industriel Udvikling (1988b) *Har Danmark en fremtid som industrination?*, Copenhagen: Forum for Industriel Udvikling.

Forum for Industriel Udvikling (1989) *Hvad skal födevareindustrien i Danmark leve af?*, Copenhagen: Forum for Industriel Udvikling.

Jessop, B. (1987) 'Economy, State and Law in Autopoietic Theory', *Essex Papers in Politics and Government*, no. 42. Colchester: University of Essex.

Koselleck, R. (1985) *Futures Past*, Cambridge, MA: MIT Press.

Pedersen, O.K. (1990) 'Short Notes on Second Order Strategies' (memo), Copenhagen: Centre for Public Organization and Management, Copenhagen Business School.

Pedersen, O.K., Andersen, N.Å. and Kjaer, P. (1992) 'Private Policies and the Autonomy of Enterprise: Danish Local and National Ondustrial Policy', *Journal of Economic Issues*, (in press).

Pedersen, O.K., Elberg, J., Andersen, N.Å. and Kjaer, P. (1992) *Privat politik*, Copenhagen: Samfundslitteratur.

Teubner, G. (1991) *Recht als Autopoietisches System*, Frankfurt: Suhrkamp.

Part 3

POST-SOCIALIST PERSPECTIVES: THE POLISH CASE

10 Trends and perspectives in the development of a system of interest representation in post-socialist societies

Jerzy Hausner and Andrzej Wojtyna

1. System of interest representation: general remarks

In every social system the realization of group interests depends upon the system of power. The social features of the power system define its 'frequency range' or 'strategic selectivity': its receptiveness to certain interests and its disregard for others. Only by creating an appropriate mechanism of interest articulation can a social group ensure that its aspirations are taken into account. The structure and character of the system of power determines which mechanisms of interest articulation are effective. They are not merely a passive medium. They perform the function of actively selecting and aggregating group interests. During the process of articulation these interests are appropriately defined (given a symbolic code) and addressed. The interrelationship between group interests and the system of power does not only consist in the responsiveness of the system to changing relations between groups. In addition the system of power influences the interplay of group interests, because the relationship between the awareness and expression of interests is reciprocal. Group consciousness is shaped by the ways in which these interests are expressed. By activating certain mechanisms of articulation, the system of power influences this consciousness. The process of articulating group interests is therefore also a mechanism for controlling social behaviour.

By making decisions affecting the interests of various social groups and conflicts between them, power elites aim above all to preserve the social conditions for the process of reproduction, so as to prolong the basic types and forms of the division of labour. One should also bear in mind that, while performing this basic function in the name of the economically dominant class, power elites also express (in varying degrees) the interests of the state administration through which they implement their policy. The greater the independence of the administration, the more its interests will influence the behaviour of power elites. Thus one should not assume that there is a simple relationship between the social division of labour, the conflict of interests, and the behaviour of power elites. The relationship between these areas (dimensions) of social life is complex, and power elites play the role of an active agent.

The relations between interest groups and power elites are made more complex as a result of the establishment by these groups of organizations intended to defend and promote their interests. Usually social groups exert influence over power elites through such organizations. As a result, the complexity of the structure of interests is reflected in the complexity of the organizations which articulate them. These organizations are not merely passive agents mediating between interest groups and the authorities. Their existence modifies the structure of group interests, and also creates new interests. This is caused by the members of these organizations becoming groups in themselves and forming their own internal hierarchies. Although the purpose of these organizations is ostensibly to represent and promote the interests of a given group, they in fact 'break free' and start to represent the interests of either their members or the leaderships which govern them (Ossowski 1982: 81-4). Therefore, not only those groups which create the given organizations, but the organizations themselves should be regarded as interest groups (Kolarska and Rychard 1980: 166).

In studying the impact of group interests on power elites through or-ganizations created by these groups, one should acknowledge the existence of an inverse relationship. Power elites can themselves both establish organizations whose purpose it is to promote the interests of a given group, and licence the grass-roots creation of organizations. Even if we disregard the active role of power elites in shaping the relations between social organizations, their influence on the workings of these organizations cannot be overlooked. Organizations affect power elites, but equally they are to some extent affected and controlled by these elites. Therefore, those sociologists who claim that there is a close connection between the workings of these organizations and social order (broadly understood) are right. Social divisions and the fundamental principles of social development are reflected in the functioning of these organizations (Pankow 1989: 206-7).

The operation of groups and social organizations generates conflicts of interest, which in turn lead to processes of integration and disintegration in society, and thus become a basic factor in the development of the social system. The role of the system of power is to ensure a state of dynamic social equilibrium, i.e., a sufficient degree of society's long-term integration. This system establishes appropriate mechanisms regulating the conflict and coordination of interests, and the mechanisms become an instrument for regulating the behaviour of opposing parties.

Following Dahrendorf one can distinguish three basic types of reaction to situations of conflict on the part of the system of power: resolution, suppression and regulation. Resolution, which eliminates conflict by removing its causes, is rarely possible, thus practically limiting the choice to either suppression, i.e., stopping any action that the sides might take, or regulation, i.e., influencing the course of a given conflict (Dahrendorf 1969: 327-31).

The general capacity of the system of power to absorb social conflict becomes a basis for guaranteeing the rational functioning and development of a given society. In this area we are dealing with a very complex system of inter-dependencies: the more receptive the system of power is to the articulation of group interests, the more effectively it must absorb social conflict and be sensitive to changing inter-group relationships. If the system of power is not flexible enough, then receptiveness to the articulation of differing interests may cause its disintegration and loss of operational cohesion. On the other hand, if the system of power is unreceptive to group aspirations, then it may lose the capability to influence and control social behaviour. Furthermore, even if groups cannot make use of mechanisms of articulation that transmit their interests to the system of power, they do not abandon the realization of their interests. They also make use of mechanisms of articulation outside the bounds of the system, and turn to such expediencies in the interplay of group interests that allow them to realize their aims independently of the system of power. This means that they break free from the course of social development imposed by the system. The groups whose interests are not recognized by the system of power try to create certain areas of 'negative power', in which their behaviour cannot be effectively controlled by the system. This enables them to prevent the implementation of decisions that might damage their interests. Hence, the lack of group interest representation in the system of power causes disintegration in society due to the centrifugal tendencies of groups whose members do not identify their needs with those of society as a whole.

If one looks at the system of power from the viewpoint of its reaction to the incompatibility and conflict of interests, then one can distinguish two types of policy:

1. the distribution of socially desirable goods and values - performing the distributional function of power;

2. the establishment of rules of cooperation between people in the realization of their common aims - performing the coordinating function of power.

The effectiveness of the system of power undoubtedly depends on the maintenance of a relative balance between these two functions of power. This balance in turn depends on the structure of the system adapting to the differing interests of social groups and conflicts arising between them. Figure 1 attempts to convey this relationship.

The figure consists of three areas. The case in which the structure of the power system reflects existing social differentiation falls within the area representing the dominance of the coordinating function of power. As a result, the representation of various group interests is very weak in such a system. Nevertheless, the distributional function of power remains and becomes dominated almost exclusively by the interests of the group in power. The area where the distributional function of power dominates represents the case in which the differentiation of social groups and their conflict of interest is relatively pronounced, and where the representation of these interests in the system of power is strong.

The dominance of power's coordinating function generates inefficiency in the operation of the system of power ; this occurs because of opposition by social groups whose interests are not sufficiently recognized by this system. The dominance of the distributional function of power, on the other hand, makes the system of power less able to coordinate the activities of various social groups. The wide representation of very different interests disintegrates the system of power and causes its policies to become too unstable. Between these two extreme cases one finds an area of relative balance between the two functions of power. Two vectors delineate this area: one, the relatively low differentiation and conflict of social group interests, and two, their relatively broad representation in the structure of power.

Systemic solutions that fall within this area create conditions that enable the system of power to function effectively.

The existence of a hierarchical structure in the system of power and the role of political power in this system introduces a hierarchical structure into the interplay of interests. It is a mistake to consider all group interests on the same level. Their social importance depends on what is at stake in a given conflict, and by extension on what level of the system of power this conflict is resolved. At the same time, solutions affecting more general interests create the framework for solutions affecting more particular interests.

To conclude we would like to distinguish the following relationships in the structure of group interests and the workings of the system of power: (a) the system of power selects and legitimates group interests; (b) the workings of the system of power lead to solutions, but also to the creation of conflicts between social groups; (c) the workings of the system of power are one of the factors differentiating the status of groups in society; and (d) the articulation of group interests by power elites is one of the factors that shapes their consciousness and controls their behaviour.

In defining in general terms the relationship between interest groups and the organs of power as representatives of these interests, we are led to the notion of 'the system of interest representation', which we will take to mean the structure of organizations and institutions expressing the interests of various groups and putting pressure in their name on the organs of power. Thus defined, the system of interest representation is created above all 'from below' in the course of thedevelopment of social groups and the establishment by them of organizations to realize and defend their interests. The role of the organs of power in the creation of this system is never passive. Hence, influence 'from above', in particular the impact of the organs of state, is also reflected in the system of interest representation. This influence is stronger when the power of the state and the scope of its intervention in social life, and above all in the economy, is greater. Taking this into account, Schmitter distinguished the following kinds of systems of interest representation in contemporary societies (Schmitter 1979a: 63-4):[1]

1. Pluralism can be defined as a system of interest intermediation in which the constituent units are organized into an unspecified number of multiple, voluntary, competitive, nonhierarchically ordered, and self-determined (as to type or scope of interest) categories that are not specifically licensed, recognized, subsidized, created, or otherwise controlled in leadership election or interest articulation by the state and that

do not exercise a monopoly of representational activity within their respective categories.

Figure 1.1 Dependence of the system of power on the set of group interests

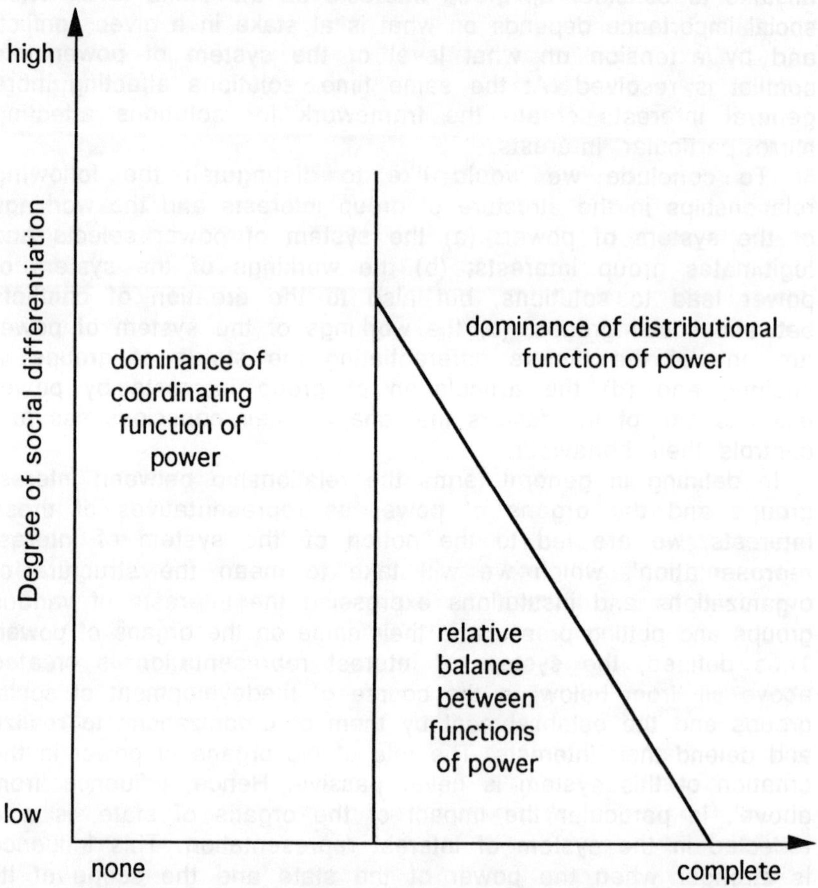

2. Corporatism can be defined as a system of interest intermediation in which the constituent units are organized into a limited number of singular, compulsory, noncompetitive, hierarchically ordered, and functionally differentiated categories, recognized or licensed (if not created) by the state and granted a deliberate representational monopoly within their respective categories in exchange for observing certain controls

on their selection of leaders and articulation of demands and supports.

3. Syndicalism can be defined as a system of interest intermediation in which the constituent units are an unlimited number of singular, voluntary, noncompetitive (or better hived-off) categories, not hierarchically ordered or functionally specialized, neither recognized, created, nor licensed by state or party, not controlled in their leadership selection or interest articulation by state or party, not exercising a representional monopoly but resolving their conflicts and 'authoritatively allocating their values' autonomously, without the interference of the state (Schmitter 1979a).

4. Monism can be defined as a system of interest representation in which the constituent units are organized into a fixed number of singular, ideologically selective, noncompetitive, functionally differentiated and hierarchically ordered categories, created, subsidized and licensed by a single party and granted a representational role within that party and vis-a-vis the state in exchange for observing certain controls on their selection of leaders, articulation of demands and mobilization of support (Schmitter 1969b: 16).

There can be no doubt that Schmitter's classification does not take into account all aspects of the system of interest representation. In particular, while stressing the relationship between the state and interest articulating organizations, he overlooks the relationships between social groups and the function of interest representation by organizations. He also overlooks the question of internal mechanisms governing the workings of these organizations (Nedelman and Meier 1969, 102). Nevertheless, this classification should be regarded as a very valuable starting point for analysis and empirical research. The author himself points out the need to distinguish between two different versions of pluralism, corporatism and syndicalism - societal, developing 'from below', and statist, developing 'from above'.[2] This distinction brings the models of representation systems closer to reality, and gives them a more dynamic character. For example, this allows one to distinguish between totalitarian corporatism in fascist Italy and democratic corporatism in Sweden (Pestoff 1983, 13).

The development of contemporary systems of interest representation is undoubtedly linked to the increase in the number of functions performed by the state and its intervention into public life, leading to the institutionalization of representation and conflicts of interest. As a result, the network of organizations mediating between social groups and the organs of state is expanding. Only 5 per cent of Sweden's national economic organizations had come into being by 1900, a further 15 per cent by World War I, and a subsequent 16 per cent by 1930. However, the remaining two thirds were established after the Great Depression, when the government embarked upon a policy of active intervention into economic affairs (Pestoff 1983, 65).

As a result of this process - and many other factors - contemporary systems of interest representation have a highly extensive structure, in which one can distinguish four types of subjects: a) social groups and individuals, b) various types of interest articulating organizations, c) self-government, d) the State and its organs.

An analysis of the system of interest representation must take into account, apart from its structural (organizational) dimensions, the dimension of consciousness and the way it functions. A thorough investigation of this last dimension is particularly important, considering the fact that besides the formal aspect of the relationship between various subjects in the system of interest representation, there also exists an informal, frequently concealed, aspect to this relationship. To illustrate the complexity of the mechanism of the system of interest representation we once again turn to the Swedish experience. Commenting on this, Pestoff distinguished the following spheres where interest organizations and political decision-makers interact (Pestoff 1983, 44):

- participation in extraordinary parliamentary commissions and re-presentation as consultants on the boards of various central state agencies;
- consultation with the government and opposition parties before fundamental economic policy decisions are made;
- preliminary consultation on draft laws before they are formally submitted to parliament;
- various individual contacts with MPs, permanent parliamentary commissions, political parties, directors of central state agencies.

To take into account the complex internal structure of interest art-iculating organizations would further complicate the description of the functioning of the representation system.

2. Development tendencies of interest representation in post-socialist society

We will take the well-known phenomenon of strong inconsistency in people's views and expectations as the starting point for a discussion of the subject mentioned in the title. Without doubt the views on social order harboured by various social groups are never perfectly consistent and never fully reflect a group's consciousness of its own interests relative to those of other groups. Nevertheless, in the case of post-socialist societies the degree of this inconsistency and disorientation seems to be particularly large. To some extent this is the result of the transformation currently under way, but its roots can also be found in the mechanisms of social integration and interest representation characteristic of the former system. These mechanisms determine how people behave in new situations, and also the extent to which they are able to adapt to the current situation.

Considering the fundamental characteristics of the socialist economy in its fully developed and decadent stage (Poland during the 1970s and 1980s), two mechanisms of integration shape the consciousness and the economic behaviour of individuals and economic groups in a fundamental way: (a) the corporatist system of production and distribution (Hausner 1987; Hausner 1988; Hausner, Wojtyna 1991); (b) a redistribution system based on family and friendship connections (Hryniewicz 1990; Zukowski 1989). The corporatist structure was the basis of the system of interest representation, whilst family and friendship ties thrived on the bureaucratic system of goods and services allocation which constituted the core of the corporatist system.

The thesis that the system of interest representation in socialist society assumes the form of a corporatist system becomes convincing in the light of the definition of corporatism proposed by Schmitter. Organizations which articulate interests possess in this system all the characteristics of corporatist structures mentioned in the definition. In particular, they are characterized by:

- functional specificity related to the sector of the economy which they represent;
- a monopoly within the bounds of this sector, i.e., lack of competition in their function of representing interests;
- compulsory membership understood in the sense that being outside the organization or leaving it has serious consequences for the individual concerned;
- a hierarchical structure, which means that only the organization can represent the given sector in its relation to the state; there is no direct dependence between its members and its internal organizational units on the one hand, and the state on the other.

By being members of branch corporations and having family connections, the majority of society was able to satisfy most of its material needs, played the role of both producer and consumer, articulated, defended and realized its economic interests. Obviously, besides these two fundamental mechanisms for the defence and articulation of interests, there were also others, for example those connected with the representation of regional and ethnic interests. However, their significance was either marginal, or they were incorporated into the functioning of the corporatist system, and therefore had a dependent and secondary nature.

Without embarking here upon a wider discussion of the functioning of both these mechanisms of integration, we would like to underline only those characteristics, which have a strong bearing on the consciousness and economic behaviour of members of society in a period of systemic transformation:

- for various reasons, participation in both these types of mechanisms impeded the possibility of social self-organization. In the case of branch corporations this was directly linked to bureaucratic control over the functioning of almost the entire economy, while groups dependent on family and friendship connections had to function in self-isolation so as to effectively satisfy the needs of their members, which in consequence led to the atomization of society (Hryniewicz 1990: 64);
- the ability of branch corporations and groups based on family connections to satisfy the needs of their members depended mainly on bureaucratic and informal bargaining on the macro, meso (branch corporations) and micro (family connections) level, in which they tried to influence the allocation of goods advantageous to themselves;
- as a result, corporations and groups based on family connections both entered an economic game, which was usually zero-sum. By taking part in bureaucratic bargaining they indirectly competed with other parallel structures, while having no direct contact with them. The existence of parallel structures was seen by them as a major threat;
- there was very little discourse and dialogue in the relations between branch corporations and groups based on family connections on the one hand, and bureaucratic structures and other similar, competing groups on the other. Communication in both directions was impeded and manipulated;
- because of the mechanisms governing goods allocation, short term aims were dominant in the functioning of branch corporations and groups based on family ties; they aimed at the immediate acquisition of the maximum possible quota of goods;
- the functioning of branch corporations and groups based on family and friendship connections never overstepped the limits imposed by the system. Any actions falling outside the system would harm the short term interests of their members. Although the functioning of these groups eventually led to the erosion of

the system, in the short term it legitimated and sustained the system;

- consciousness, articulation and representation of interests within both these mechanisms consisted in upholding the groups' narrowly conceived material interests in the face of the party-state bureaucracy.

If sociologists researching social consciousness find that people are increasingly assuming the attitude of defensiveness and conservatism, and are putting demands to the authorities, then this is obviously not a result of the current transformation, though it does engender uncertainty and for many groups entails a fall in their standard of living. The root of these attitudes is above all the mechanism of social integration and interest representation characteristic of the former system. The fact that people have rejected communism and communist government does not necessarily mean that they have abandoned the corporatist way of thinking, or that they can express and defend their interests in other ways.

The weakness and inadequacy of the system of interest representation is a permanent structural cause of the combination of passive expectation and anarchic defensive behaviour that characterizes post-socialist society. Unless appropriate institutional change occurs, this type of attitude could in time become semi-permanent, because of its stimulation and exploitation by populist parties for political reasons. Should these parties and their leaders gain a strong position within the political system, the road to democratic order and the market economy would be permanently blocked. The inclination to 'escape from freedom', which can be discerned in the behaviour of individuals and groups, would then be reflected in the system of power and the structure of the political system.

Gardawski's research confirms the reality of such a danger. Firstly, he found out that 68.7 per cent of workers were of the opinion that their interests were not represented on the national level in any way. 'Solidarity', which scored best in this research, was mentioned by only 12.6 per cent of respondents (Gardawski 1991, 22). At the same time a significant proportion of respondents rejected all forms of mediation by organizations and political institutions, expecting that before taking important decisions the government would be in direct consultation with society (ibid, 19). The 'legitimation crisis' experienced by both representative and self-governing organs of power, as well as by parties and political associations, is an important symptom of the fact that many years of state corporatism and the existence of groups based on family connections created, on the one hand, a powerful hindrance in the development of civil society, and, on the other, a demand for antagonizing ideologies and a breeding ground of autocratic- populist leadership (Hryniewicz 1990, 68-72).

We may generalize the analysis by saying that the process of org-anizational formation and development of the system of interest representation appropriate to the new conditions is progressing very slowly. This is caused to a large degree by the consolidation of the mechanisms of integration in groups based on family and friendship connections and their adaptation to the new conditions. The increasing danger of material impoverishment enhances the influence of this mechanism, despite the fact that the problem of consumer goods shortages has been overcome. This not only hinders the creation of various forms of civil society, but also strengthens the preference for those forms of economic activity which sustain the system of family connections (Hryniewicz 1990, 71-2). One should also see this as a cause of the increasing importance of the black economy with its cliques, speculation and profiteering. Marx's remark perfectly illustrates the Polish situation. He stated that there are such periods in the economic life of modern nations when everybody is enveloped in a madness of trying to secure gains without producing anything. This condition of speculation which recurs periodically reveals the real character of competition, which seeks to avoid the need for industrial rivalry (Marx 1976, 191).

The second cause (but also the effect) of the slow development of the organizational structure in question is the weakness of political parties as intermediaries between particular groups, organizations and power elites. Parties on the Polish political scene are characterized amongst other things by (Labedz 1992):

- an unwillingness to undertake actions oriented to long term aims and a concentration on short term political aims due mainly to the instability of the political system;
- the greater importance attached to emotional and personal ties compared to programs;
- the tendency to define the party's identity in terms of its relation to the past;
- a reliance on very general conceptions of social order, and, in consequence, a concentration on the theoretical, rather than practical, interests of various groups.

As a result, the ties between particular groups, organizations and political parties are very weak and they are only gradually beginning to communicate with each other.

The difficulties experienced by 'Solidarity' in adapting to the new conditions constitutes a fundamental barrier to the development of the system of interest representation. Surdej is right in claiming that the dilemma facing the union cannot be unambiguously resolved by choosing either wage claims or co-government, the unionist or the political course of action. The crux of the matter lies not so much in the union's choice of strategy, as in the institutionalization of its position in the political system understood in the broad sense. If the union's functions are institutionalized in a particular way, then it will be able (to a greater or lesser degree) to fulfil (in one way or another) people's diverse and often contradictory expectations. Otherwise, union leaders will be forced into short term expediency measures to alleviate tension arising from the dilemmas mentioned above (Surdej 1991, 18-21).

The phenomena we have described reveal a basic contradiction in the development of 'Solidarity' which came into being as a movement of social protest against economic ineptitude, social injustice and the autocratic nature of the former system. The movement was born in large state-owned factories and the core of its membership were employees in those factories. In bringing about the downfall of the communist system of power, the movement created the possibility for profound structural reform. But now the inescapable consequence of this reform must be the elimination of the socialist state sector and the mechanisms on which it is based. The costs of this process are born primarily by the employees of state-owned companies, and therefore precisely those people who gave the nascent 'Solidarity' movement its power (Modzelewski 1990, 101-2).

The doctrines and strategies of neo-liberalism applied to post-socialist conditions constitute yet another barrier to the formation of a system of interest representation. Lacking a strong base of public support, the ruling liberals, by stimulating the growth of the 'middle class' , want to quickly create such a base.

In order to accelerate the fulfilment of their strategic aims, the liberals seem to be prepared to weaken or even eliminate all those institutions and social organizations, which will slow down this process. In particular, this is true of all forms of self-government and worker participation. This implies the elimination of a significant part of the infrastructure of public activism. This must lead to the limitation of the already weak institutional mechanisms of grass-roots influence and civic control over central and local decision-making bodies, which in turn will block the process of creating and developing civil society.

3. Perspectives for the development of the system of interest representation in post-socialist society

To reiterate our previous conclusion, the representation of interests in classical socialist society resembles most closely the model of 'state corporatism'. In such a system, the state eliminates the possibility for society's self organization through political-legal and administrative-economic means. The articulation and representation of interests occurs exclusively through officially licensed and bureaucratically controlled social and economic organizations. The real possibility for the defense of interests not subject to bureaucratic control is only open to groups based on family and friendship connections, which function in an outstandingly parasitical way, precipitating the dynamic development of the 'black economy'. The state-corporatist system of interest representation affords, it is true, the possibility for the stabilization of political power, but at the same time hinders economic development, and, as a further consequence, erodes the whole social system.

The outcome of the corporatist system was that political divisions did not correspond to economic divisions. Political rights and interests were tied mainly to membership of and active participation (or the lack of it) in officially licensed social and political organizations, whilst economic interests were connected to employment in the former corporatist structure. As a result, the links between particular economic and political preferences were very weak (Kolarska and Rychard 1983: 443-53). The growth of social forces and political groupings around comprehensive programmes for the building of a new social order is hindered by the absence of functional links between economic and political interests. Should this state become permanent, the development of horizontal social structures along the cooperation-competition axis, would be blocked. Moreover, the continuing preponderance of the vertical structures along the subordination-domination axis would be strengthened.

Abandoning state corporatism is one of the basic conditions for the transformation of the socialist system. The question is, how this system of interest representation will be replaced, and by what. As is usual in such dilemmas, the solution lies somewhere between 'the desired' and 'the possible'. Government elites' thinking is very limited due to the fact that they employ (in part consciously) a very simplified, mechanical picture of the market economy. Discussions over interest representation are not the outcome of imaginative thinking or of strategic analyses, but rather of reactions to short-term tensions and conflicts, which usually take governing elites by surprise. Moreover, they are side-issues in political disputes and they testify to the instrumental treatment of various groups and organizations in the political struggle.

Consequently, the mechanisms of interest representation develop in a spontaneous and uncontrolled manner, with a heavy leaning towards traditional corporatist structures. This is becoming more and more of a fundamental barrier to further change and brings with it the danger that society may question the current reforms. It is also becoming more certain that the continuation of reforms will not be possible if the vision of the social order on the part of both the governing and the governed is limited to a doctrinal negation of socialism and anti-communist faith. There is a need for ideas, conceptions and actions which will bolster the reform process, as well as encourage and enable public activism.

We are of the opinion that in the sphere of interest representation the direction of change ought to be determined by the model of 'societal corporatism', in which social integration is a result of the process of interaction and adjustment through negotiation of particular interests, and various social groups are free to self-organize.[3] The implementation of the model of social corporatism is very difficult, and yet, in our situation, it seems much more realistic than the neo-liberal model of pluralistic balance between various groups regulated by the market. What the liberals are offering is to some extent a utopian idea, in the sense that it is not reflected in western societies. What is more, it is not realizable in practice, considering the post-socialist reality. The pluralistic model of interest representation is most often criticized in the following three ways (O'Sullivan 1988):

- in reality, only a few large groups compete, rather than many small ones, and though formally voluntary, membership of them is compulsory for economic reasons;
- the role of the state in its interactions with interest groups is not merely passive; in reality, it actively influences the formation of these groups and the shaping of their interests;
- public and private domains overlap in practice, and the delineation of their boundaries is impossible.

The resolution of a few fundamental problems would seem to be par-ticularly important as far as the formation of a neo-corporatist (socio-corporatist) system of interest representation is concerned (Gorniak, Jerschina 1991). They are as follows:

1. The difficulty of finding a solution to the entire problem of real property rights, without administrative bias in favour of any one kind of privatization programme.

The policies undertaken so far by the governments of post-socialist countries are marked by a very simplified view of privatization. They concern almost exclusively the transfer of state-owned means of production into private hands. Other elements of property rights, relating to the utilization of the means of production, are not given due attention. Consequently, governments implement privatization programmes without prior legal preparation, e.g., in the area of anti-monopoly legislation, or labour market and environmental protection legislation. They fail to see that even the most liberal states (governments) develop governance regimes appropriate to their own economies precisely through the creation of property rights (Campbell 1991).

2. The difficulty of clarifying the functions performed by the instruments of state control over the economy, given that the state should pursue an active industrial and social policy without attempting to comprehensively organize the economy.

In fact, what we observe in the transition from a socialist to a market economy is, on the one hand, the significant limitation of the state's role in the economy, and, on the other, the parallel centralization of this role. This creates a noticeable deficiency in governance regimes (Lash 1991). Taxi service in large cities provides a good example. The state (public authorities) has ceased to interfere in this market in any way, whilst professional associations of taxi drivers have proved too weak to create legal governance regimes. Within a short time the market came to be controlled by mafias, ruthlessly eliminating all competition so as to wholly subordinate the interests of the client to the interests of the taxi driver. The government reacts to open criticism primarily through taking punitive measures, rather than through the development of appropriate governance regimes. This example demonstrates clearly that the role of the state in the economy must be considered in relation to the particular character of the given market(s) and the efficacy of the governance regimes functioning within it (or them), rather than in relation to some doctrinal model.

3. A real de-politicization of administration at all levels and its professional and organizational preparation to the fulfilment of its functions and tasks entailed by the determination of the state's role in the economy.

This issue is strongly connected with the problem of institutionalizing the position of employers' and employees' organizations. This institutionalization - considering the post-socialist reality (the weakness of both the political and economic systems) - should be conducted in such a way that the mechanisms of negotiation will separate the arena of employees' disputes from the arena of political disputes as much as possible. In other words, particular conflicts should be negotiated upon and resolved where they occur, rather than be automatically shifted to the central structures of the political system. This demands the strengthening and not the weakening of the position of employees' representation at the factory and micro-regional levels, as well as the strengthening of their counterparts' position. If employees' organizations could acquaint themselves with the experiences of western trade unions in shaping the supply side of the economy, then this would undoubtedly facilitate this process (ibid.).

4. The weakness of regional state structures and local self-government, particularly in the economy, and the undue importance of branch structures of industry.

Although it may create local tensions and clashes of competence, the simultaneous strengthening of regional state structures and local self-government is a necessity, considering the threats posed by the development of the market economy. Regional imbalance, and inter-regional competition for foreign capital, will become unavoidable. In such a situation - as J. Campbell has aptly remarked - local authorities which have gained full autonomy would relinquish any prerogatives in relation to ownership rights so as to make their regions maximally attractive to the influx of foreign capital. In a short space of time this would lead to a loss of control over the economy on the national level (Campbell 1991). In thinking about the mechanisms of regional politics it is also worth taking into account Toffler's predictions on the shifting of centres of power in contemporary societies. Toffler - in contrast to prevalent attitudes - claims that local communities and regions will diverge in the course of future development, rather than become uniform (Toffler 1990).

5. The need for effective de-monopolization of the economy and the prevention of branch corporations from becoming monopolists.

As shown by our analysis of the role of branch corporations in the socialist economy, these aims have a fundamental importance. The Scandinavian experience also testifies to the significant influence of large companies (corporations) on the development of the system of interest representation, as stressed by Pestoff among others. Pestoff points out that the collapse of the Swedish model was brought about primarily by multinational corporations, whose role in the Swedish economy was relatively large in comparison to other west European countries, and for whom the EC, not the Swedish or

Scandinavian markets, provided the greatest opportunity for development (Pestoff in this volume). This perspective casts even greater doubt on the Polish government's policy of carrying out privatization sector by sector, which actually shows that the government still thinks in terms of branches of industry. This policy can hinder the process of de-monopolization, and at the same time preserve the traditional position of corporatist structures in the Polish economy.

6. The need to secure media independence.

7. The need to establish and give support to independent arbitration tribunals and professional advisory bodies.

The Scandinavian experience in the development of a negotiated economy makes the importance of the aims mentioned in points (6) and (7) particularly obvious. Nielsen and Pedersen, who have analyzed these experiences, lay particular stress on the role of the mass media in the formation of both the ideological superstructure and institutional structures in this type of economy. This is reflected in their model of a negotiated economy. They put institutions engaged in the formulation of ideas, in conducting (discursive) debates, and in shaping public opinion, side by side with institutions engaged in policy-making, in conducting negotiations and arbitration, and in applying legal sanctions (Nielsen and Pedersen 1991). In this approach, in accordance with historical experience, the negotiated economy is not understood as a procedure within a given system, but also as interactive policy, which leads to the formation and transformation of the system. It is precisely because of this that, in our opinion, the Scandinavian experience, though inimitable, is so interesting and important as far as sketching the future development of the system of interest representation in post-socialist societies is concerned.

The realization of these aims will secure the institutional and material conditions for public discourse over socio-economic problems, and the development of opportunities for dialogue and negotiation. Only then can one expect a change in the interests of major social groups, the way these interests are defined, and a weakening of attitudes dominated by revindication and a desire to preserve the status quo.

Notes

[1]In his analysis the author uses the term 'system of interest intermediation', because 'interest representation' - the term he used formerly - could be understood, namely by suggesting that the organizations representing interests faithfully articulate the needs and preferences of thei members or, even worse, are representative in the statistical sense, and that the representation of interests is the

main and only function of these organizations. To our mind, the notion of 'interest intermediation' does not eliminate the concern mentioned above.

2 One should stress that although the distinction between societal and state corporatism seems to be clear in itself, the definition of corporatism proposed by Schmitter contradicts this distinction. It applies to the case of state corporatism, but to a far lesser degree to the case of societal corporatism (for more on this sucject cf. Cox 1988).

3 A similar transition from state corporatism to societal corporatism took place in Spain after the demise of Franco's regime (Martinez-Alier, Roca 1988).

Bibliography

Campbell, J.L. (1991) 'Property Rights and Economic Governance: U.S. Implications for Post-Socialist Societies', in J. Hausner, B. Jessop, and K. Nielsen (eds.) *Markets, Politics, and the Negotiated Economy - Scandinavian and Post-Socialist Perspectives*, Cracow: Cracow Academy of Economics.

Cox, A. (1988) 'Neo-corporatism versus the Corporate State', in A. Cox, N. O'Sullivan (eds.), *The Corporate State. Corporatism and the State Tradition in Western Europe*, Aldershot: Edward Elgar.

Dahrendorf, R. (1960) *Class and Class conflict in an Industrial Society*, London: Routledge and Kegan Paul.

Gardawski, J. (1991) *Pracownicy o polityce i gospardarce (wstepne omowienie wynikow badan)*, Warsaw: Friedrich Ebert Stiftung.

Gorniak, J. and Jerschina, J. (1991) 'Out of Corporatism towards Neo-Corporatism?', paper presented at the joint IAREP/SASE conference, Stockhold (modified version reprinted in this volume).

Hausner, J. (1987) *Branzowe grupy intersu w gospardarce socjialistycznej*, Cracow: Cracow Academy of Economics.

Hausner, J. and Wojtyna, A. (1991) 'Evolution of the Interest Representation in Poland', in J. Hausner, B. Jessop, and K. Nielsen (eds.) *Markets, Politics, and the Negotiated Economy - Scandinavian and Post-Socialist Perspectives*, Cracow: Cracow Academy of Economics.

Hyrniewicz, J.T. (1990) 'Procesy aktywnosci publicznej w miejskich spolecznosciach lokalnych. Struktualizacja spoleczna, zmiana spoleczna a ksztalt instytucji publicznych', *Stuida Socjologizcne*, no. 3-4.

Kolarska, L. and Richard, A. (1980) 'Wplyw organizacji przemysolowych na strukture spoleczenstwa socjialistycznego', *Studia socjologiczne*, no 2.

Kolarska, L. and Richard, A. (1983) 'Intersy politiyczne i ekonomizcne', in W. Morawski (ed.) *Demokracja i gospodarka*, Warsaw: Warsaw University Press.

Labedz, K. (1991) 'Partie polityczne w Polsce - niektore aspekty reprezentacji interesow', in J. Hausner (ed.) *Studia nad systemem reprezentacji interesow*, Cracow: Cracow Academy of Economics.

Lash, S. (1991) 'Disorganizing Socialism?', in J. Hausner, B. Jessop, and K. Nielsen (eds.) *Markets, Politics, and the Negotiated Economy - Scandinavian and Post-Socialist Perspectives*, Cracow: Cracow Academy of Economics.

Martinez-Alier, J. and Roca, J. (1988) 'Spain after Franco: from corporatist ideology to corporatist reality', in A. Cox and N. O'Sullivan (eds.), *The Corporate State. Corporatism and the State Tradition in Western Europe*, Aldershot: Edward Elgar.

Marx, K. (1976) *The Poverty of Philosophy*, in idem and F. Engels, *Collected Works*, vol. 6, London: Lawrence and Wishart.

Modzelewski, W. (1990) 'Lad demokratyczny a formy walki', in W. Nieciunski and T. Zukowski (eds.), *Studia nad ladem spoleccznym*, vol 2., Warsaw: Warsaw University Press.

Nedelman, B. and Maier, K.G. (1969) 'Theories of Contemporary Corporatism - Static or Dynamic?', in G. Lehmbruch and P.C. Schmitter (eds.) *Trends towards Corporatist Intermediation*, London: SAGE.

Nielsen, K. and Pedersen, O.K. (1991) 'The Negotiated Economy - the Structure, the Processes and the Instruments', in J. Hausner, B. Jessop, and K. Nielsen (eds.) *Markets, Politics, and the Negotiated Economy - Scandinavian and Post-Socialist Perspectives*, Cracow: Cracow Academy of Economics.

Ossowski, S. (1982) *O strukturze spolecznej*, Warsaw: PWN.

O'Sullivan, N. (1988) 'The Political Theory of Neo-Corporatism', in A. Cox and N. O'Sullivan (eds.), *The Corporate State. Corporatism and the State Tradition in Western Europe*, Aldershot: Edward Elgar.

Pankow, W. (1980) 'Lad utylitarny w przedsiebiorstwie jako element ladu spolecznego', in W. Nieciunski and T. Zukowski (eds.), *Studia nad ladem spolecznym*, vol 2., Warsaw: Warsaw University Press.

Pestoff, V.A. (1983) *The Politics of Private Business, Cooperatives and Public Enterprise in a Corporate Democracy - The case of Sweden*' in J. Hausner, B. Jessop, and K. Nielsen (eds.) *Markets, Politics, and the Negotiated Economy - Scandinavian and Post-Socialist Perspectives*, Cracow: Cracow Academy of Economics.

Schmitter, P.C. (1989a) 'Modes of Interest Intermediation and Models of Societal Change in Western Europe', in G. Lehmbruch and P.C. Schmitter (eds.) *Trends towards Corporatist Intermediation*, London: SAGE.

Schmitter, P.C. (1989b) 'Still the Century of Corporatism?', in G. Lehmbruch and P.C. Schmitter (eds.) *Trends towards Corporatist Intermediation*, London: SAGE.

Surdej, A. (n.d.) 'Trade Unions in a Period of Democratization and Restructuring' (typescript).

Toffler, A. (1990) *Powr Shift*, New York: Bantam Books.

Zukowski, T. (1989) 'Wzlot i upadek ladu administracyjneo', in W. Nieciunski and T. Zukowski (eds.), *Studia nad ladem spoleccznym*, vol 2., Warsaw: Warsaw University Press.

11 Out of corporatism towards..... neo-corporatism?

Jaroslaw Gorniak and Jan Jerschina

1. The functioning of the economic system in 'real socialism'

1.1. Economy of shortage

We can list three interrelated elements of the economic system which existed under 'real socialism': permanent shortage, allocation of resources based on the political power of branch corporations, and the maintenance of power based on the distribution of resources and privileges in return for social peace.

Shortage in the economy means that some factor crucial to the fulfillment of a presumed task is missing (Kornai 1980). Temporary shortages caused by various factors, including accidental factors, occur everywhere. In centrally planned economies, however, shortages became a permanent feature of the system and regulated it.

Shortage was always accompanied by a surplus of other resources which could not be used, however, because of the lack of yet other resources which caused bottlenecks. For example, some workers had nothing to do, because there was a shortage of certain raw materials or some other simple elements. Dismissing these workers would be a mistake (even if it were legally possible), however, since, after obtaining the necessary materials, the lack of workers might prove in turn to be a bottleneck.

One of the results of shortage was chronic inefficiency (though shortage was not the only cause). This inefficiency was a direct consequence of forced substitution, of changes in the structure of production, of excessive accumulation of resources 'just in case', etc.. Moreover, it resulted from the fact that permanent shortage of workers caused discipline to be relaxed and morale lowered. Shortages on the consumer market also weakened the work ethic. This made effective management very difficult and caused further shortages.

What were the reasons for the permanent shortage and for its consequences, i.e., domination of both producers and sellers over consumers, the waste of resources and time, the lowering of workers' morale, and a permanent search for labour power, especially low skilled workers. The main reason for this was that those who made investment decisions bore no responsibility for the economic risks they incurred. In the case of failure, the costs were paid by the state (read: society); in the case of success, rewards (money, prestige, and power) were given to those who promoted investments. The socialization of risk and the privatization of profit were very strong stimuli to expansion. This was connected with the structure of ownership and with the system of management in an economy in which decisions were often subordinated to other than economic criteria.

Another reason for permanent shortage was the combination of pressure to expand aggregate production at the same time that profit was neglected in both economic theory and practice. The characteristic feature of investment expansion under these circumstances was the preference for constructing new enterprises at the same time as production continued in the old ones, which made it possible to avoid production disturbances occasioned by modernization but also aggravated the consumption of capital and economic inefficiency.

1.2. Corporate allocation of resources

The mechanisms generating permanent shortage and the inflationary pressure on wages was connected to the system of allocating investments, capital, wages and privileges. The criterion for allocating such resources was not economic efficiency or satisfaction of social needs, but the political power of the participants in bargaining over resources.

Bargaining for resources, when both shortages and the centralized system of management existed, had created a specific institutional order that underlay the basis of the society's macrostructure. The basic feature of this order was the existence of interest-groups rooted in different economic sectors. These interest groups were branch corporations and their expansion was due to the branch management typical of the command economy system. Several levels of management in branch structures (up to ministries and departments of planning committees) served as the representatives of the central government and began to pass its directives and supervised their implementation. They also came to represent the interests of subordinated industries. These processes were generated by personal connections which resulted form the etatistic structure of promotions through branch channels (enterprise-federation-ministry) and also by the amalgamation of interests of different levels in branch structures. The responsibility of higher levels for the activities of the lower levels led to the former's involvement bargaining for resources for the latter.

A socialist economy was a huge fair, in which the performance level depended on the amount of assets obtained. However, bargaining was political in nature and oriented not toward efficiency, but toward maximal enhancement of one's bargaining position, because this very position was taken into account by the central authorities in their distribution of assets. Bargaining occurred on all levels and assumed corporatist form. A struggle for privileges (resources) for the whole corporation and then for their distribution within the corporation was taking place. The organizational ties within the corporation that ensured the relative stability of provision were also negotiated.

The bargaining power of corporations resulted from the orientation of the economy to sheer quantitative expansion. Corporations from the producer goods sector were certainly in a privileged position. The more basic the product of a corporation, and the more enterprises depended on its deliveries, the greater the potential for creating shortages a corporation had. Thus coal-mining, energy, metallurgy, construction, and some branches of metal and machine-building industries had an especially strong position. It was also very important that enterprises in these branches were usually big, they employed mostly men, and they were located in huge industrial centres. This increased their political power in the game for social peace as well as their bargaining power in the fight for resources and privileges. The role of branch corporations in a socialist economy was so important, that the level of investment, wages and subsidies depended on whether an enterprise did or did not belong to a given branch. Given this constraint, the level depended on the number of employees and the value of productive assets - economic efficiency and satisfaction of social consumption needs were disregarded (Hausner 1987).

1.3. The system of maintaining political power

The corporate institutional structure was functionally connected with the economic system characterized by permanent disequilibrium (shortage) and with a centralized and hierarchical political system, in which political authorities secured support for their policies because they exercised the right to distribute resources and privileges. This calls to mind feudal rela- tions (Elias 1977).

The inner pacification (social peace) of the whole state depended on pacification within its particular corporations (its vassals). The cost of obtaining social peace depended on the social power of the vassals, i.e., on the number of their employees (and the number of men), on their position in the material distribution chain of the whole economy, and on the degree of inner cohesion of interests. It was also influenced by the costs of obtaining inner peace within the corporations and the costs of maintaining relative stability of production. The factors that determined the relations between central authorities and corporations also determined those within corporations. The only difference was that the pacified subjects here were firms or companies in a given corporation. Particular firms face similar needs to social peace and to keep production at the level required by the plan; thus, analogous relations hold between the management and the productive units, and between the management and particular workers. Due to permanent shortage in the labour market, workers acquired specific power in the relations with their supervisors.

A 'fire fighting' principle governed this system; it consisted in mobilizing resources (always in short supply) in sectors in which the limits of tolerance had been reached (Kornai 1980). This was linked in turn with the postponement of supplies in other sectors in which the 'fire' has not yet started. This principle was chronically ineffective as a political mechanism. For the economy became a political subject and political power was strongly coupled to the structure and the functioning of the economy.

The above mechanism generated a spontaneous organizational concentration in the economy. This was particularly noticeable during the attempts to deconcentrate the Polish economy at the beginning of the 1980s. Concentration promoted the growth of bargaining power and the fight for privileges. It also diminished the uncertainty that followed from the inefficiency of the transactional forms of cooperation and of supplies in a shortage economy (it helped to avoid standstills in production and to diminish worker dissatisfaction). Thus we are dealing with a system of three elements connected by feedback.

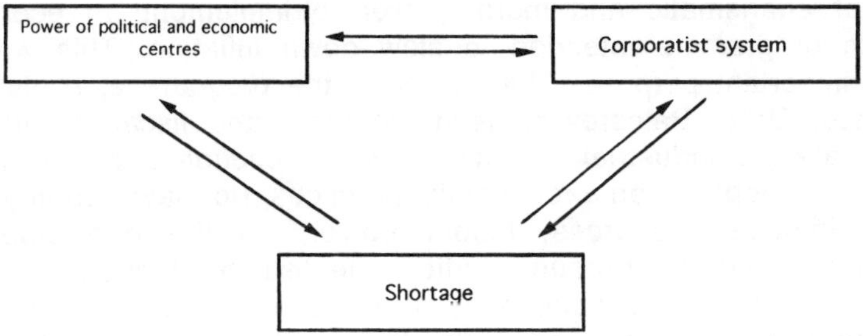

Figure 1.3.1: Feedback in the power system

2. The transition period - the old or the new corporatism?

The model described above did not end when NSZZ Solidarity assumed power. How would we regard the union in 1989, when it abolished the communist power elite, and what is it now?

We think that we may regard the union in the past as an alliance of corporate interests. These were groups of workers (from different branches) and middle rank technicians, clerks and others who decided to rebel against a communist power which could not control the economy and polity because it had lost its external protection - the protective power of the Soviet Union.

This alliance had a political character because its actions were directed against the centralized political structure. The most appropriate organizational structure in this situation was the territorial organization. NSSZ Solidarity had its headquarters in Gdansk and the huge regional organizations were controlled by leaderships located in big cities.

This organizational system has become dysfunctional for many reasons in the new situation, after power was assumed by the elite which emerged from Solidarity and the Church (another important political actor in Poland which also has a territorial structure).

The branch structure of industry, trade and services survived along with the dominance of state property in the economy (this will be continue to typify the Polish economy for many years). How could this system prove so durable?

The new power elite used its authority quite well - relying on a sort of charismatic and moral power to implement an economic reform programme intended to slow down inflation. This was its most important purpose. The author of the programme, Minister of Finance, Dr L. Balcerowiz, used monetary and fiscal instruments to create an industrial climate in which economic actors would have to adopt rational economic practices (to save energy and fuel, financial resources, labour power, on the one side, for example, and to pursue profit- oriented production, market-oriented planning, development of entrepreneurial activism, etc., on the other). Balcerowicz understood that they cannot afford to take one step back under the pressure of the big corporations, especially such as the coal or steel community.

However, the old structure defended itself. The first reaction of the system was an enormous and lasting drop in production, i.e., a recession. This, connected with the consequent centrally controlled policy of distribution of wages, caused a worsening of the living standard of all groups of people, especially in those branches where average wages were traditionally low. Balcerowicz neglected the structural aspect of reforms. He presented to the Sejm an attractive plan for privatizing the economy but took not even one step towards breaking the legal framework sustaining the corporations. Why did someone who used a charismatic and authoritarian political resources to implement his financial policy not want to sue legal means to liquidate the corporatist order in the economy?

It was not because Balcerowicz represented the interests of the technocracy which controlled and still controls the corporations. Although it is worth noting that only 20 per cent of the management was replaced and it is mostly communist nominees who still rule Polish industry, especially in heavy industry, fuel and energy production, and so on. Instead the reason was that the administrators, the new small group of rulers of the country had to use the old administrative apparatus and this could communicate only through the branch organization system. This structure could appear functional from the viewpoint of Balcerowicz and his people - they had to use authoritarian and centralized means to control the state-owned economy. This economy, let us repeat, a state-owned economy, could only be controlled centrally. Admittedly this control is now exercised indirectly, as opposed to direct control in the communist era: ministries today do not apply 'positive' means (such as through raw materials distribution or control over foreign currency for investments). But the government still continues its game with the managers of great corporations which brought about revival and survival of the corporatist system. This does mean, however, that the old structure survived intact and unchanged. Instead the technocracy was weakened through the imposition of new legal and fiscal constraints. They had to look for a new ally. And they found it.

Mazowiecki's government was abolished mainly because of increasing disappointment as people saw the same old individuals ruling their factories while their own standard of living was worsening. The authority of the government was melting away. Employees were looking for ways to articulate their interests and needed to organize in order to negotiate with the power elite.

Two factors contributed to people's belief to date that they could achieve their goals and just deserts only by talking to government. First, there was a long-lasting communist tradition that only by talking to the first party secretary could one be sure to have reached the real decision-maker. Second, the new order is centralized, perhaps less than it was, but it is still perceived as such. When government declines to intervene in the economy, people say that it is inefficient.

The manual workers and white collar employees employed in industry reorganized NSZZ Solidarity into branches. They adapted the union to the existing branch organization of economy. Thereby they gained an organization they could use on two levels of negotiations: the level of factories and branches and that of the central power and administration.

The unions soon became an important ally of the technocracy which controls the bureaucracy. During 1991 Balcerowicz and Prime Minister J.K. Bielecki fought a long war against coal miners who wanted their very inefficient branch to be subsidized. It was a very serious problem for the whole economy. The state budget plan could not be realized if the two politicians lost the fight - as they did because the technocrats were supported decisively by the unions.

The whole process was much more complicated than we can describe here. For instance, one of the most important mechanisms in the process was the generation of political and union elites. The old unionist apparatchiks left the union and now function as part of the political elite or hold posts in the administration and representative bodies. The new union leadership, grass roots people but of the new era, clearly less educated, endangered by the decreasing authority of Solidarity, endangered also by the OPZZ (old communist unions which play on workers' demands for better wages, hours, and working conditions), assumed the responsibility of voicing workers' interests - especially in the economic field. The most popular slogan during the last congress of NSZZ Solidarity was: 'we are not a political organization, we are a union which should look after the interests of workers'.

The alliance of the union elites and technocratic elite is structurally generated. It does not prevent conflicts. The unions are a career ladder for the new technocratic elite (the so-called 'new nomenklatura', or rather the middle ranking professionals who fought on the side of Solidarity in the past and who now strive for their piece of the action). Solidarity attacks both the old and new nomenklaturas, as does Walensa, but all this has now only a tactical significance. They do not like the old administration because workers never did. They do not like the new administration because workers have no love for any administration. But the directors do at least usually ally with unions when the new union apparatchiks fight for subsidies for coal mines, shipyards, steel mills, and so on.

In such cases one might ask how far unionists differ from those from the old communist days? In those times the alliance existed too. We believe there is a quite basic difference. The union apparatus at the time was only 'a transmission belt': first, of the party's will (from 1949-1956, i.e., in the Stalinist era), then of the administration (under Gomulka), and, finally, of the technocracy (in Gierek's era). Now the unions' apparatus is an autonomous politi- cal actor.

So where is Poland heading? From one corporatism based on state property towards another corporatism based on state property? Is it possible to create an alternative corporatism if state property survives? If not, are we return- ing to communism? The revival of corporatism results from mistakes made by the ruling elite. It was not understood clearly enough at the beginning of the reforms that it might be necessary to break the corporate order and that, in order to implement a new system, privatization must proceed faster. This has been understood too late. The new Prime Minister, J.K. Bielecki, presented a package of bills to the Sejm which should have accelerated the process of privatization. And at that moment it appeared that the old industrial elite also has allies among the new political elite - for months the Sejm kept the bills without pushing them through the legislative process. What is happening is best described as a political and economic stalemate.

The problem has to be solved and it will be solved. The economic system cannot produce efficiently and the recession will continue. The system cannot absorb foreign credits. The system is unable to improve and reform itself through its own forces and resources. The solution must be external; it must come from outside the economic system, and it has to be political.

The blockage of processes of change is also due to the weak development of the political infrastructure of the new Poland. The parliament is an old Parliament with 65 per cent of communist MPs and their collaborators from the past. The political parties have not yet gained experience nor consolidated real electoral support (there are at least 100 parties) and the most popular (Democratic Union and Alliance Centrum) have no more than 5-13 per cent of all electoral support. Thus the political articulation of interests is in the hands of unions and technocrats. This situation might change soon. For the political articulation of economic interests is a maller of both timo and opportunity. During the parliamentary campaign which is just beginning all the parties will have to fight in order to win support from the voters. The electors will get the opportunity to choose their representatives. The new Parliament and the new Government will have, from the first moment, to make a decision: continue the policy of defending the corporate system and collapse or else to break the old system and survive.

In order to survive the new Government will have to create a new system of negotiations and install the legal and institutional framework for it. There is much to do here. Poland, two years after the communist fall, has no new law on unions and their rights. Nobody respects the old law, neither the rulers nor the ruled. There are no customs, norms which would regulate the decisions of union leaders when they consider the question: to strike or not to strike? The territorial and factory units are not used to following and obeying internal union regulations and to respecting conclusions of negotiations. Populism dominates their behaviour.

3. Towards neo-corporatism?

The main indicator of the new stage reached in corporatist education is the negotiations between the representatives of the Government (including the Prime Minister himself) and union representatives. The talks are not easy. The two partners are discovering that there is too little mutual understanding of how they think, that they have different perspectives on the affairs of their common country, economy, people's problems. These are dramatic talks. The Prime Minister is a political child of

Solidarity and he has to fight other political children of Solidarity, for instance, coal miners' leader, Mr Petrzyk. Do all these differences simply reflect the different roles which they play?

Who really are the new politicians, ministers and their advisers, the former members of the opposition? Most often they are intellectuals. In the past they occupied rather high positions - university professors, doctors, engineers, lawyers, journalists, priests, artists, writers. Their language is abstract. Their perception of the world is dictated by doctrines they believe in.

Who are the leaders of unions? Quite often they are middle ranking profes- sionals, clerks, foremen, and the like. Even if they are professionals who could find a common language with politicians-intellectuals, they are under very strong pressure from the union rank-and-file.

Research conducted by the present authors in May 1991 for the Institute of Central European Market and Public Opinion Research revealed that educational attainment was a significant differentiating factor in Poles' attitudes towards the economic and political system and how it should be reformed.

Some examples should be quoted to illustrate this claim.

Our research shows that 45 per cent of Poles want most of the business in Poland to be run by private owners, and 49 per cent prefer them to be run by the state. This, however, is strongly related to age and education: among the youngest, those aged 18-29 years, 58 per cent are for private ownership and 37 per cent are for private ownership. Among people with elementary education, only 31 per cent are for private ownership and among those with full secondary education, 56 per cent, and with higher education - 61 per cent.

Results achieved with another question allow us to say more precisely that only 35 per cent of the population claims that they want unlimited privatization. Again, the highest percentage is among the youngest - 18-29 years old - 44 per cent, and among those with higher education.

And, finally, how many people in Poland really support the idea of privatization when we ask about their enterprise or firm, that for which they work? Only 17 per cent of respondents want their firms to be privatized, and 29 per cent said no. The largest proportion of respondents, 41 per cent replied that the question did not affect them because they work for a firm which cannot be privatized (or is in some cases already in the private sector) and 13 per cent did not answer. Thus the support for privatization among the electorate seems rather small. However three times as many want their firm to be privatized among those with higher education (23 per cent) as among those with elementary education (8 per cent).

The perception of important national problems also differs according to educational level. Unemployment was the most important problem according to 24 per cent of the people with elementary education and to only 5 per cent of those with higher education.

The standard of living was the most important problem for 18 per cent of the people with elementary education (20 per cent among workers) and 7 per cent of those with higher education although their salaries are quite often lower than the wages received by workers.

The opposite picture emerged when we asked about their views on economic reform. They were the most important problem facing Poland for 6 per cent of people with elementary education and 25 per cent of those with higher education.

These and other differences in the perception of the world determine how government communicates with different parts of society. The ruling elite speaks the language of the educated stratum of the society and wins some support from it but it is not understood by the less educated strata. People who work in the mass media belong to the same stratum of educated people and address their messages to them. Thus they speak to not more than 10 per cent of society.

This lack of communication was one of the factors that increased the tension between the new ruling elite and the wider society (especially workers and peasants). Both under Mazowiecki's government and now. It also caused the significant loss of prestige and confidence accorded to political institutions. Thus our research shows that the army, the Church and the police are trusted more often than the government, the Sejm, the Senate, the opposition group in the Sejm, the media, and so on.

However this is not only a problem of media and language. It is a problem of creating mechanisms of articulating and negotiating the interests of many different segments of society. As mentioned above, this is a problem of creating new legal regulations (union law), building institutions in which representatives could meet and talk, organizing research institutions to serve unions and government, developing the skills of media people, training politicians in the skills of negotiating, and so on. And finally this is the problem of getting rid of the old, autocratic and communist pattern according to which the power elite always knows best what is good for people and the country, and does not really care what people think and feel.

To conclude our discussion let us say briefly:

Poland is evolving from state corporatism towards a liberal neo-corporatism. There is still a long way to go. The most important step in this direction is economic reform which should liberate the state from being an employer and make entrepreneurs free actors in economic life. The different social segments and groups have to have the right conditions in which to articulate and negotiate their interests. The results of these negotiations should stabilize the system and help to develop a free market and democratic society.

Bibliography

Elias, N. (1978) *The Civilizing Process: vol. 2. State Formation*. Oxford: Blackwell.

Hausner, J. (1987) *Brankowe grupy interesu w gospardarce socjalistycznej* (Branch Pressure Groups within the Socialist Economy), Cracow: Cracow Academy of Economics.

Kornai, J. (1980) *Economics of shortage*, Amsterdam: North-Holland Publishing.

12 Social limitations for efficient allocation of resources in the post-socialist countries

Jan Czekaj and Stanislaw Owsiak

1. The direction of the changing economic system in post-socialist countries

The following two assumptions have been adopted in this paper: (a) the resource allocation mechanism constitutes the key element of any economic system; (b) resources are herewith defined as natural, material and labour resources - they do not include the money savings of businesses. Recognizing the resource allocation mechanism as the central element of an economic system, does not absolve us from carefully observing the whole system. This is particularly true for an economy under going systemic transition and seems to be very apposite today. Indeed, the more radical are the changes introduced into the economic system, the timelier is the above remark. Such a situation typifies post-socialist economies. Despite the relatively short period of time in which the reforms in post-socialist countries have been attempted, we can certainly distinguish the most important characteristics of the ongoing process: the radical market economy option, creating favourable conditions for the private sector, diminishing state control of industries, limitation of the state's regulating role towards businesses, and the tendency to economic integration with most developed countries.

The new economic doctrine now proposed in post-socialist countries seems considerably influenced by neo-liberal economic thought. The philosophy of the newly developed system is based on market and private ownership. This, so it is commonly believed, should ensure the exit of post-socialist economies from crisis and - in a relatively short period of time - guarantee them prosperity. It is worth considering, however, whether people's expectations about the market mechanism are too high and to what extent they are based on social and economic reality. The supporters of extreme free market concepts appear to minimize and downplay the economic difficulties facing those capitalist countries which have already introduced conservative economic doctrine. Yet it is obvious that the scale of those difficulties is incomparably smaller than in post-socialist economies. Moreover, even in the radical market economies, inefficiencies of market mechanisms are very often soothed by the conscious economic and social policy of state. It is true - and somehow characteristic - that people in post-socialist economies choose to refer only to the positive experience of those countries in which the market economy enjoyed visible success. Such an approach is quite understandable but we must not forget the many countries which, despite their longstanding market-based economies, are not as successful as other market-oriented systems. Consequently, we may put the question: why are certain market economies successful whereas others are not? What are the reasons for this? Should we identify them with the market mechanism itself or maybe with its deformations or perhaps there are other external, 'non market' reasons that might help answer our question?

Judging by the direction of changes in post-socialist economies and people's expectations about them, it is still difficult to define which model of market economy should be accepted. Although certain characteristics of the market economy are universal, there are many alternative models which differ considerably from one another. Among the variables distinguishing different models are the forms and extent of state involvement in the economy and the kind of social programme that is adopted.

The choice of a model should be made with regard to specific local conditions prevailing in each country. Yet the post-socialist countries are not entirely free to establish their own model of economy. For example, Poland, which is substantially indebted to the western countries, stands in a very difficult position. In order to solve its payment problems and receive foreign financial assistance Poland must accept certain conditions including the elimination of state control of industries, promotion of the private sector and extending the influence of market mechanism into areas whose social nature makes it hard to submit them to the tough laws of supply and demand. Among the latter areas are health care, housing, education and so forth. Such requirements are also imposed by international financial organizations, among them the World Bank and International Monetary Fund.

On the other hand, the reforms introduced by post-socialist economies cannot involve literal imitation of conservative economic ideas since this might prove as dangerous for those countries as the previously imposed system of centrally planned economy based on state ownership. Moreover, the fact that the suggested changes do not take account of all conditions and social barriers, may well jeopardize whatever form the implementation of economic reforms takes. We shall discuss these questions later.

2. Central planning mechanism as a resource allocation mechanism

In the socialist economy resource allocation was accomplished through the central planning mechanism. This attribute of the socialist economy was supposed to give advantages over a capitalist economy driven by unrestrained market laws.

In the centrally planned economy the market's role as an allocation mechanism was reduced to an instrument of minor importance. It still fulfilled some functions in the sphere of consumption but even in that area its effectiveness was considerably limited because prices and wages were actually set by bureaucratic institutions.

It is worth noting that the allocation of goods in the sphere of consumption was highly determined by decisions taken in the investment sphere. For instance, it was quite hard to buy cars because the domestic car industry was underdeveloped and the import policy run by the state was also unsatisfactory. Moreover, allocation of individual consumption goods was submitted to the general socialist consumption pattern so that substantial amounts of goods and services were allocated through the government. That automatically restricted the functioning of market mechanisms.

The necessity of expanding market allocation of a large amount of the national income seems to be crucially important for restructuring the economic system in post-socialist countries. Central planning has proved its unquestionable inefficiency as an allocation resource mechanism in the socialist economies. Furthermore, the longer it worked, the bigger were the developmental disproportions which appeared in the socialist economies and gradually slowed down the tempo of their growth. Then came the sharp crisis and socialist economies finally collapsed.

It is worth mentioning, however, that central planning was originally employed when the disadvantages of the market mechanism had nearly endangered the very existence of the capitalist economy. Those disadvantages were finally recognized by capitalist economists and politicians and - in the next years - gradually eliminated by state interventionism mainly with the help of the instruments of fiscal and monetary policy.

As emphasized above, state interventionism, an important component of the market economy, has not been properly understood by the post-socialist countries. The contemporary market economy is very often identified by post-socialist countries with a form of free competition system rather than with a market system in which the state intervenes into the economy.

3. Preconditions of effective resource allocation by the market mechanism

Before embarking on economic activity any business, whether it is a big enterprise or an individual producer, should answer the three following questions: (a) What to produce; (b) How to produce it; and (c) For whom to produce it. In a market economy the answers come from the market to the extent that consumer preferences meet producer preferences. All three answers are given by effective money demand and the supply of different goods expressed in prices. Under demand and supply laws, consumers' and producers' aspirations are matched. In a market economy it is the consumers who are in the privileged position. They have the right to choose between many goods which producers offer them.

The consumer market makes producers search for the best methods of production and best assortment of goods - in other words the consumer market make producers allocate resources effectively.

Long-term observation of the functioning of the market mechanism allows us to formulate certain conditions which should be fulfilled so that the mechanism might be determined as a substantially effective instrument of resource allocation in economy. They are as follows: (a) perfect competition, (b) the system of free prices, (c) domination of private sector in economy, (d) market-like labour resource allocation, (e) unconstrained transfer of goods and capital between countries

This list refers to the model of an ideal market which actually does not exist. Instead we must ask how far the contemporary market economy agrees with that ideal.

In practice there are different phenomena and processes preventing the market economy from appearing in a pure form, among them tendencies encouraging monopolization to acquire a monopoly profit or rent.

Principally, the main objective of any business is to obtain maximum profit. Unfortunately this goal is sometimes achieved at the expense of devastation of the natural environment and also produces other unfavorable side-effects affecting neighboring producers and the local population. Such a situation obliges the state to take rectifying measures towards market mechanism.

The market, as an anonymous mechanism, "ruthlessly" verifies all economic decisions taken by businesses. Market mechanlsms may thus determine people's income and settle it, for instance, at a level which is perceived as inadequate from the social justice viewpoint. Such income gaps need not be a fault of discrimination but can also stem from difficulties connected with people's finding a job.

The contemporary market economy requires state interventionism. This is because of two contradictory reasons. On the one hand, the state has to create conditions for the market economy to work (anti-monopolist law, commercial law enabling efficient transactions in the market etc.); and, on the other hand, the state has to soothe some negative effects of market mechanisms (redistribution of incomes, social programmes, struggle with unemployment).

The above discussion about contemporary market mechanisms leads us to the conclusion that an effective resource allocation mechanism should be based on market criteria and market laws. But this should also be rectified by the instruments of state interventionism.

4. Difficulties facing post-socialist economies when employing market mechanisms

In the capitalist countries it is the market that is the dominant regulator of resource allocation and thus the whole economy; whereas the economic system prevailing in the post-socialist countries is still very hard to define. Central planning, whose foundations and mechanisms have already been eliminated, was not replaced with a new clearly developed mechanism. It seems that in the foreseeable future the post-socialist economies will be in a state of transition, continuously introducing more changes whilo tho systom develops. That is why we are unable to provide a precise description of basic features of the economic mechanisms of post-socialist economies.

This state of affairs actually results from the lack of technical and social infrastructure for the market - infrastructure that must be built to let the market work efficiently. By technical infrastructure we mean the elements of a developed market mechanism, such as a banking system, capital market (stock exchange), business and anti-monopolist law, etc.. Social infrastructure is defined in terms of appropriate reactions on the part of producers and households to market stimuli. Removing technical and social barriers requires both time and resources. Some people believe, however, that a market economy could be built without difficulty and in a short period of time. These is wishful thinking. The number of problems connected with establishing the market economy is really large and the task is not easy.

We should emphasize that the most difficult problem to solve refers to eliminating social barriers. A centrally planned economy that operated for many years in the socialist countries had generated dramatic changes in social consciousness and created a very specific type of individual consciousness characteristic for socialist economy.

Any discussion about the problems involved in building a market economy in the post-socialist countries must put some essential questions concerning, for example, the possibilities of changing the patterns of economic behaviour of people whose attitudes developed under socialist economy. We must admit that current behaviour does not meet the needs of today's market economy and may even slow down the tempo of transition.

Both the theory and practice of the market economy are based on certain assumptions about the reactions of its various participants to market stimuli. Within the theory of consumer behaviour and the theory of enterprise, models were produced which help us to describe the functioning of the market economy and also to predict businesses' reactions to the changing conditions in which the economy operates.

Taking the above into account we should pose two crucial questions: firstly, whether the utility function of households in the post-socialist economies coincides with of that households operating within a market economy. In other words, could many decades of centrally planned economy have so changed the structure and the scale of household preferences in such a way that the analytical tools developed for studying and examining household behaviour in a market economy might prove useless?

This issue is of crucial importance, especially given the plans to establish a capital market, since the latter's efficient operation depends to a large extent on individual reactions - of a maximizing nature - to market stimuli (e.g., assuming rational investor's decisions). Secondly, the question must be put whether the models of businesses reactions produced under a centrally planned economy meet the needs of a market economy. To simplify the question we may ask if businesses in post-socialist economies will operate efficiently by basing their activity on the criterion of maximum profit.

It is difficult to give a definite answer to these questions but we can formulate some theses. As far as the first problem of household utility functions is concerned, we believe that the role and nature of this function is basically the same in both systems. Some manifestations of behaviour that might be found inconsistent with those typical for market economy household reactions are not so much a result of changes in the structure and scale of preferences as a product of the conditions in which those preferences were satisfied. Progress achieved in building a market economy should gradually lead to behaviour typical for market economy reactions.

As far as the problem of business behaviour is concerned it is ownership of the means of production that is believed to be a basic factor determining their behaviour. Without a dramatic transition of ownership structure in the economy, it is impossible to change businesses' reactions to those reforms. Enlarging the private sector should provoke new types of company reactions, suitable to the market economy, i.e., based on the criterion of maximum profit.

The factor which makes our efforts difficult whilst building a market economy is people's perception about private ownership. Their perception is actually vague and cautious. The reasons for this are complex. On the one hand, the post-socialist countries were submitted to strong indoctrination: private ownership was presented as an instrument of class exploitation. On the other hand, the governmental campaign to promote privatization is carried on very inefficiently. Because of negative perceptions towards the very notion of "privatization" we may expect huge difficulties when implementing the private economy. The word privatization does not reflect the character of changes because the aim towards which the economy is actually driving is that of socializing the national economy (people's capitalism).

In some post-socialist countries, such as Poland, there are strong workers' aspirations - generated by former reformists - to run the state-owned companies. This would complicate, if not hold back, the process of privatization, particularly as the unions as well as workers organized in their self-government bodies also seem to accept a similar attitudo. It is an interesting paradox we are observing now: company's property that has been nobody's until today becomes a subject of interest and care of workers employed in the same company. The reasons why workers are interested in participating in the company's property are obvious because privatization may threaten their own economic interests and may lead to lay-offs; the company may also be sold to a new owner at terms unfavorable for workers. People have become aware not only of the direct negative effects of privatization but also of the unequal distribution of benefits of that process. These potential obstacles to the process of privatization may threaten the introduction of the market economy and thus the improvement of the effectiveness of resource allocation.

The experience of the capitalist economy lets us conclude that private ownership is more flexible and has better abilities to adjust available resources to people's needs in changing market conditions.

The last thesis is less sharp for state-owned companies in western countries since they operate within a market economy and are continuously verified by market criteria. However, in the post-socialist economies, this thesis is fully justified because the competitive abilities of state-owned companies - as compared to private companies - and particularly those operating abroad, are dramatically smaller.

The problems we have discussed are strictly connected with the market allocation of labour resources, that is, with labour markets. This institution, which was unknown in centrally planned economies, is a basic element of the market mechanism. Allocation of labour resources accomplished according to market criteria constitutes a condition of its effective exploitation, i.e., flexibility of the labour force in adjusting to productive needs, labour force transfer between company's departments and regions, etc..

The market allocation of labour resources indicates the existence of competition in the labour market (the phenomenon of competition is mostly connected with the product market and with capital markets). The positive aspect of labour market competition is that labour has become a kind of a good. When carefully protected it boosts productivity. Another important use of labour markets is that they constitute a key factor which influences the income division between labour and capital.

There are also negative phenomena of labour markets, however, such as mass unemployment, in the post-socialist countries, a problem hitherto unknown. That phenomenon has appeared in

Poland along with introduction of market economy. For unemployment generates negative social effects and is perceived by many people as an element of the new economic system. Accordingly we may suppose it will hinder the reconstruction of post-socialist economies.

The situation is particularly difficult because the unemployment which the post-socialist countries are now facing will be structural, not cyclical in nature. The struggle with unemployment will be difficult. On the other hand it is inevitable if the post-socialist countries are going to go through the process of deep structural transitions, including closing down outdated industries, reconstructing agriculture, etc.. The latter refers especially to Poland and the Soviet Union. The appearance of unemployment has put the union movement in a very hard position for - as was the case in Poland - the unions were the powerful force that pushed Polish democratic changes ahead.

Anyway, we may expect labour unions - whose main duty is to defend workers' rights - to be a destructive factor, reluctant to introduce the structural changes necessary for building the market economy in the post-socialist countries.

The key element of the market mechanism is price. Therefore establishing a market economy in the post-socialist countries will require a radical retreat from the previous price policy that was based on the principle that prices were directly settled by the state.

The price policy of socialist countries was false because prices had nothing to do with real costs of production (hence the necessity for subsidies) and were also cut off from world prices. That phenomenon was accompanied by creating an artificial rate of exchange of foreign currencies, which by the way are also price indicators in a market economy.

Establishing the market requires dramatic change in the price level and price relations. There is no exaggeration in admitting we are facing a price revolution. The situation is even harder because this year the post-socialist countries are introducing new rules of settlement of mutual trade and capital accounts, basing them on hard currency.

All the circumstances we have talked about may cause a price shock within the society. This happened to Poland after the collapse of the communist regime despite the fact Polish society seemed to be prepared for price reforms by the former government. For it was running an active price policy aimed at introducing market mechanisms to create market price formation. If we want to indicate the most successful factors that helped establish the market economy in Poland we should put the price mechanism in the first place.

We must not forget that success would be impossible without the enormous confidence of Polish society in the government and strictly speaking the Solidarity Union, a major political power that provided nearly all of the cabinet from its most prominent members.

Now, it is hard to predict whether success is complete or not since there are some symptoms of society's disappointment.

The price policy actually resulted in the lowering of the standard of living of almost all people. Prospects, however, are rather pessimistic especially as a new wave of price increases is planned for early 1991 as a result of lifting of state guaranteed prices for energy.

If the new market system is built, state interventionism seems to be indispensable. That the state in Poland intervened unfortunately too late could have been a reason for social tensions. The contemporary market economy is to a large extent open to the inflow of goods and capital. This openness is an important factor of competition mechanism as well as enabling the most favourable use of resources in the domestic market and in foreign markets. The post-socialist countries were practically excluded from that process and what they are facing now is a hard task of building up international market relations based on capitalist patterns.

Similarly, as in the case of privatization the problems we may come across while establishing those links can be both technical and social in nature. The technical difficulties stem from differences in economic registration, different criteria of choice, maladjustment of the legal system that should facilitate a free flow of labour, goods and capital. Whereas the technical difficulties may be gradually overcome with the help of proper regulations, the social barriers are more dangerous when building a market economy. For example, the attitude of many groups of people to the question of foreign capital is still vague. Some groups express their strong resistance to an inflow of foreign capital to Poland (this is connected with the law according to which foreigners may buy Polish land and also with the very process of privatization).

The government receives many critical opinions and is accused of trying to sell Poland's national property to foreign capital. This - according to those groups of people - would certainly lead to wasteful exploitation of domestic resources of labour, real property and natural resources. The arguments raised by those groups of people are obviously anachronistic but they may sometimes find favourable conditions which could lead to autarkical tendencies in the economy or to a restrictive policy towards foreign capital or else encourage protectionism.

Generally speaking, it would slow down the process of building an efficient market mechanism.

Any economic process operates in conditions of risk and uncertainty. Those problems are especially intense in resource allocation and especially as far as long-term process is concerned. In the centrally planned system risk had basically a political and economic character and was linked to the guidelines and methods of economic policy run by the state. One of the specific characteristics of the centrally planned economy was that the negative consequences of wrong economic decisions were not revealed at the level of enterprise but were eventually disclosed at the top level of state administration. The government concentrated most of the economic decisions in its hand - especially those involving resource allocation. So, in the centrally planned economy the risk-oriented microeconomic mechanism, which is so important in taking economic decisions, did not work. The lack of experience and the lack of a risk-oriented mechanism might be major factors limiting the effectiveness of the resource allocation process in the economy. Transformations of ownership and the development of a capital market should none the less lead, however gradually, to establishing instruments and mechanisms that take account of risk.

5. The role of state in building a market economy

The state in the post-socialist countries is in a very difficult position. On the one hand, the state, by necessity, has inherited a most unfavorable economic situation from former governments and ever since has been responsible for every sphere of social, economic and cultural life. In practice, this would mean the state is to blame for anything, including crisis, collapse of the economic system, degradation of the material status of society, contamination of the natural environment, the undeveloped sphere of social services, and so forth. On the other hand, people, despite their critical attitude towards the state, seem to be very much attached to the social achievements the state has guaranteed them so far. Consequently people through their own organizations and unions address their - very often contradictory - wishes to the state. Some demand the introduction of market mechanisms while other social groups want their interest to be protected by the state (for instance farmers demand an extensive importation of machines and other means for agricultural production from abroad and at the same time declare that food imports should be reduced; other groups demand lower taxes and simultaneously higher budgetary expenditures).

Judging from the above discussion, it is very difficult to define the rolo of stato in the post-socialist economy. Since the system is in transition the situation is aggravated by the mistakes the state could make during the process of building market economy. Those mistakes are inevitable if we take into account the scale of reforms and the fact that the state must be a main inspirator of the process of building new economic order.

We should assume the state will be unable to get rid off its obligations towards society. Certainly the citizens treat many of their rights as firm and would resist any roll back.

The situation is additionally complicated by the fact that not all the elements of the market mechanism will be free of state control. For example, the salaries in the state-owned companies are regulated by the state whereas in the market economy they are regulated by market mechanisms. Salaries in state-owned companies will be freed at the moment when the process of privatization is much more advanced, i.e., when the owner of the company interested in maximizing profits rejects workers' demand for higher salaries. Of course, the state will not be released from the duty of being a mediator in conflicts between capital and labor nor from playing a more active role by setting a minimum wage, for instance. In the coming years the state will come under strong pressure from different lobbies, political parties, labour unions, industrial groups of interest, farmers etc. The circumstances in which the state will operate may considerably deform the mechanisms of state interventionism that are used by administrations of developed market economies. Consequently we may expect inefficient resource allocation caused either by deformation of price parameters or by the state's transgressing the scope of its appropriate interventionism.

Because the elites who rule the post-socialist countries have insufficient experience there is a dramatic need of thorough reconstruction of existing instruments (an anachronistic tax system in the first place) or create some others from the very beginning (network of commercial banks if we want to run an efficient monetary policy). Building the infrastructure that should enable us to conduct state economic policy may meet resistance because it will have negative consequences for some groups of people. This particularly refers to the problem of reconstruction of the tax system but we should also be aware of possible contradictory interests that may appear while building the new banking system (for instance liquidation of credit preferences for some debtors).

13 Impact of political changes in processes occurring in an enterprise

Stanislaw Rudolf

1. Introduction

An enterprise is an economic entity operating in concrete social, political and economic conditions. Taken together these conditions constitute a given socio-economic system with an internal logic. It means that there exist interrelationships or ties between particular elements of this system. The existence of such interrelationships or ties is best seen during the implementation of changes. Changes occurring within one of these elements exert a definite influence on elements connected with it, with the force of this influence depending upon the strength of their interrelationships. The following analysis focuses on the impact of political changes on the economy, and more specifically on the processes occurring within an enterprise. This topic has been extensively studied in the Western countries especially in Scandinavia. A far-reaching convergence can be observed, for example, between democratic changes in political life and democratization processes in an enterprise, at both management and shop-floor levels. The studies in question analyze the impact of political transformations on the processes in an enterprise and vice versa. Knowledge about such relationships has become increasingly more useful recently when implementing changes.

The interrelationships will be analyzed in Polish conditions using my earlier studies on structural changes in an enterprise and democratization processes occurring within it. The analysis encompasses the seventies, which were characterized by a relative political and economic stability, the second half of the eighties, when political and economic changes started, and the most recent period, which is witnessing a marked acceleration of these changes. We shall also discuss the results achieved till now in implementing the present research and development programme, which will serve as a background for an analysis of the already mentioned interrelationships.

2. Attempts at structural changes in enterprises in the 1970s and the 1980s

The postwar period in Poland was characterized by a centralized system of management and hierarchical organizational structure within enterprises. Decisions taken within this system at the central level were transmitted to enterprises in the form of detailed plans on how to realize them. They reached enterprises as a set of indices concerning, among other things, volume of production, its quality, variety, deadlines for implementation, allocation of industrial supplies, energy, and so on. The number of such indices would usually amount to several tens and in extreme cases it would even exceed one hundred. Their implementation could be ensured only by a hierarchical management structure. Consequently, it was a structure adapted to conditions prevailing in the then system.

Attempts made in the seventies to modify that structure proved to be a failure. An example might be the so-called autonomous groups, which were introduced in some enterprises at that time. The inspiration for setting them up was the Scandinavian experience, because they had won tremendous popularity in Scandinavia. They did not survive for very long, however, although they had produced favourable economic effects. Autonomous forms of work organization were completely irreconcilable with the hierarchical management structure in enterprises.

They represented an alien body in this system requiring constant care and attention. Whenever such care was missing or difficulties appeared, the existing system would reject them. Such would be the end of all attempts made in the seventies to adopt group forms in Polish enterprises (Jankowska 1984).

The period of martial law was not too favourable for expansion of autonomous solutions in an enterprise but they did win quite wide popularity in the second half of the eighties. Their development was inspired by the then supreme authorities, which accounts for their wide popularization in the mass media. In striving to popularize them the authorities hoped that they would pave the way for a 'bottom-up' restructuring of the existing economic system. However, enterprises did not display sufficient interest in such forms for this be accomplished, and hence they began to be popularized from outside, mainly through political pressure. Most active here were the communist party committees at different levels, which organized debates and meetings devoted to this subject, and tried to popularize successful experiments. Such pressures prompted numerous enterprises to adopt that system on a 'show-piece' basis, setting up one or a few groups to be able to report the expected information about group forms operating in these enterprises.

It was only in a few enterprises that group forms were introduced on a wider scale. Practically each of those enterprises enjoyed a privileged treatment by the state, which involved among other things suspension of certain prescriptions of the Labour Code, exerting influence on controlling institutions, etc.. Without these privileges it would have been impossible to use group forms of work organization on such a scale. At the same time, attempts at restructuring the economic system in that way proved impossible. Complying with suggestions of the top authorities, enterprises were setting up individual groups, which could hardly threaten the hierarchical management structure existing there.

The second half of the eighties should be evaluated, however, quite differently from the seventies. That period witnessed the beginnings of implementation of certain economic reforms releasing decentralization processes. A much smaller number of commands addressed to enterprises, changes in the system of planning or in the pricing policy created a novel situation, which was more favourable to solutions of this type. Thus the popularity of group forms resulted not only from political pressures but also from more favourable conditions for setting them up. These conditions were not favourable enough, however, to arouse an authentic interest among enterprises in such group forms (Rudolf and Piotrowski 1988; Rudolf 1989).

The above remarks confirm the thesis formulated earlier about the impact of political changes on the processes of economic and social changes occurring in an enterprise. Without earlier political changes it would hardly be possible to speak about such expansion of group forms. The constraints existing earlier on were eliminating any sign of autonomy and so there was practically no place for autonomous solutions. That does not mean that autonomous initiatives cannot appear in such conditions, but rather that possibilities of putting them into practice are very limited.

The question which may arise here is whether it was a one-way impact or whether it was a reverse impact as well. Something like a feedback mechanism does seem to have occurred in the eighties, because there is evidence that changes carried out in enterprises accelerated the processes of political changes. But there is also evidence to confirm a thesis that the changes were hampering such processes. Considering the first of these impacts it should be said that changes taking place in enterprises were creating a favourable atmosphere for further transformations in the political life and strengthening the position of those supporting such transformations. The changes offered them a strong argument in discussing the need for reforming political life in Poland.

The other impact mentioned here involves favourable changes in an enterprise as an argument for preserving the existing political system, on the grounds that profound political transformations are clearly not necessary. Thus, beneficial results obtained through adoption of autonomous organizational solutions weakened the position of those calling for political transformations as a key to real changes in the economy. Consequently, these changes were helping to strengthen the existing power structures and, hence, checking the political changes.

It is rather difficult to determine more precisely which of the two types of impacts played the most significant role here. A lot of evidence indicates that it might be the former. The changes occurring in enterprises were a result of earlier political changes - confirming simultaneously the correctness of such changes and indicating the need to continue the processes taking place.

3. Obstacles hampering structural changes in enterprises

The political transformation carried out in 1989 created new possibilities of changes for enterprises. Although they continue to be owned by the state, their autonomy is very wide. The state has practically resigned from direct intervention in their internal affairs and moved on to more indirect methods of control. So far it has not generated any major response in enterprises. Nor has it set into motion the processes of changes that might be expected. At the same time, one can notice some regress in the processes already under way which can be seen in, for example, the shrinking scope of application of autonomous organizational solutions.

It is quite puzzling why the management structure of the typical enterprise has not undergone any changes despite changes in the external conditions of its operation. The answer is not simple, because one single concrete reason cannot be identified. Let us start from most important reason, however, namely, nobody within an enterprise represents a sufficient force to effect such changes. The director role in state-owned enterprises is relatively weak, because decisions on all major affairs (and not just major ones) are taken by the employees' council. The council, in turn, generally displays conservative attitudes. It is a body composed mostly of workers not possessing any deeper knowledge about the problems of an enterprise and very wary about making major changes.

Quite an important role is played here by a long-standing conflict between the employees' council and the director of an enterprise. It sources should be sought in the existing division of powers in an enterprise (Rudolf, 1988; Rudolf, 1989 a). The present political changes aggravate this conflict due to the communist origins of directors and the Solidarity orientation of the employees' councils. Observations made in several enterprises indicate that today this conflict is more political than economic. The employees' council evaluates strictly negatively not only the director and the top management but also the middle-level management. Hence, it seeks improvement not in structural but personnel changes and concentrates all its energy and attention on the latter.

However, such reasons must often be sought in the management's conservative attitudes. Many directors, and especially those with a longer length of service, are probably unable to propose such changes - let alone to carry them out. Accustomed to execute external recommendations, they encounter big problems making independent decisions. They treat the present changes as only an experiment which should be patiently endured, because they are convinced that the economy will sooner or later return to its previous 'normal' state.

The above considerations show that neither the director nor the employees' council have any practical possibilities of carrying out such a reorientation of an enterprise. An additional impediment here is a deterioration in the economic condition of enterprises. Growing difficulties connected with selling their products have forced them to make substantial cuts in production (ranging from 30 to 50 per cent). This is accompanied by a continued high level of employment owing to the policy pursued by trade unions and to expectations of improved demand. All that gives rise in turn to serious financial problems faced by enterprises. Lack of financial resources constitutes an additional impediment to structural changes.

Slow structural changes can also be attributed to protection extended by the state to enterprises. The last few months have demonstrated that the State does not intend to allow its enterprises to go bankrupt (bankruptcy proceedings have been initiated in only a few cases). Consequently enterprises feel secure despite their very difficult financial situation and, instead of undertaking definite actions, they quietly await an improvement in the market situation.

Nor can such changes be a result of external decisions. Theoretically, the state as an economic owner of enterprises may advance an initiative of this kind. In practice, however, such an initiative would contradict the political changes already made, which guarantee a wide autonomy for enterprises. At the same time, changes carried out in this way would be doomed to failure, because they would not be making full allowance for the real conditions in which enterprises operate. One thing is indisputable, however, namely, that these changes must be prepared and carried out by enterprises themselves.

Sharing this opinion, let us consider now what these structural changes imply for an enterprise and how they may be carried out, as well as what forms of assistance may be extended to enterprises. As already noted, an enterprise's structure must be oriented to the requirements of the market today. It is no longer a central plan but the market which must provide information about what to produce, how to produce and for whom to produce. In the new conditions decisions determining the volume of production, its quality, variety, etc., must be subordinated to requirements of the market. Only production corresponding with demand permits an enterprise to survive on the market.

It should be realized that such a change of orientation is not easy in Polish conditions. Hitherto the entire effort of an enterprise was concentrated on implementing a plan, and more precisely on securing industrial supplies needed for this purpose. A normal consequence of this situation was excessively expanded procurement departments. A permanent superiority of supply over demand, which persisted throughout the whole postwar period meant that enterprises did not need to seek customers, they did not need to adapt themselves to customers needs and enjoyed fully all privileges offered by the seller's market. As a result, sales departments in these enterprises were relatively small and no marketing activities were undertaken in practice - at least as regards the domestic market.

Market orientation of enterprises should not be understood solely in terms of a reduction of procurement departments, expansion of sales departments, and setting up marketing units. Much deeper changes are desirable here in the direction of equipping particular organizational units of an enterprise (plants, departments, and so on) with much wider rights, creating an economic system of links among them, a different information system, etc.. However, these changes call, first of all, for a new way of thinking of an enterprise's entire personnel, and this is where, in my opinion, the processes of changes should be started. A lot of evidence shows that it is the most difficult task and that the greatest difficulties may appear in this field.

Speaking about a new way of thinking we mean, first of all, a liquidation of a deeply rooted division into those who make decisions and those who execute them. This division ensured that only the top management identified themselves with an enterprise's interests, while they do not mean anything for the remaining personnel so that, e.g., their wage claims proceed regardless of the economic situation of their enterprise. With such a division it is difficult to speak about the integration of personnel with an enterprise's interests, about their emotional ties with an enterprise, which are so pronounced in, for example, Japan.

Referring to the question posed earlier, let us consider now how such changes can be effected. It should be expected that the coming years will bring a further development of the market economy, which will be forcing out changes in the orientation of enterprises. Hence it can be expected that contradictions will intensify between conservative attitudes of the personnel of an enterprise and the necessity of carrying out desirable changes in it. Increasing contradictions and bankruptcies of some enterprises will ultimately lead to changes in the consciousness of the work force being a fundamental condition determining the success of such changes. Most likely it will be a long process encountering considerable resistance.

It is possible to point, at the same time, to some measures that might accelerate this process. This could be promoted, for example through special programmes realized with the assistance of external consultants. An example here is the programme being implemented in the Rubber Company 'Stomil' in Lodz. It aims at improving effectiveness and preserving jobs, but its long-term aim is to change the company's organizational structure and adapt it to the requirements of the market economy. The first phase of this programme is being executed at present, but observations to date permit us to present some of its initial results.

4. Programme of structural changes in the rubber company 'Stomil'

The difficult economic situation of this company and a set of advantageous circumstances were decisive factors in launching the programme. Its assumptions were largely based on the experience gained by the Western countries, mainly the United States and Norway. Utilizing this experience an original programme was prepared making allowances for the conditions in Poland. A three-level structure was proposed, consisting of the Council of Company Consensus, the advisory units, and 11 effectiveness groups.

The Consensus Council will be taking all the most important decisions concerning execution of the programme. It will be composed of the following persons: the company director, the chairman of the employees' council, and the chairmen of Trade Unions of Chemical Workers and 'Solidarity'. The members of the Council have signed an agreement called 'company consensus', in which they pledge to take joint coordinated activities aimed at improving effectiveness and preserving jobs. The Council of Company Consensus has appointed an advisory unit composed of company specialists in the field of costs of production, organization of work, technology of production, etc.,. Its main task was to assist effectiveness groups in accomplishing their tasks.

The name 'effectiveness groups' has been given to groups of employees consisting of three to five persons set up to stimulate rationalization processes and structural changes in the company. They are composed, first of all, of employees appointed by both trade unions, and one representative of the management in each group. Their areas of operation are particular departments, and only two of them are task groups, i.e., a group on work organization and one on marketing. The members of these groups have been delegated to do such work for a period of three months on a full-time basis.

In accordance with the company consensus, the object of activity of the groups remains practically unlimited. They have obtained full autonomy in making decisions about problems which they wish to solve and about ways of solving them. Their activity was to lead generally to a reduction of costs, improvement of quality, better use of working time, machines, raw materials, improvement of tools, organization on work, and so on. According to the accepted assumptions, they were to rely in their activity on all employees in a given department. The members of the groups were supposed, however, to win over employees for such activity, which proved to be a relatively difficult task.

In the course of preparations of this programme, the author invited researchers from Cornell University in the United States and the Work Research Institute in Norway to cooperate, and today the programme is being executed jointly with these centres. It began in mid-September 1990 with a few days' training for the members of the effectiveness groups, in which representatives of the above centres took part. These were generally training courses of different kinds, whose aim was to specify tasks for these groups in greater detail, and show them the ways of identifying problems and analyzing them, and ultimately solving them. The training programme also included information about the company's financial system, ways of calculating costs, new forms of work organization, etc.. The training was continued during execution of the programme, with usually one day a week being devoted for this purpose.

After completing their several days' training the groups proceeded to execute their tasks. Each of them obtained its own room with a telephone and other indispensable equipment. They started their work by identifying problems. To do that they conducted talks and organized meetings with all employees or groups of employees, in this also meetings with all employees of a given department. The groups also held talks with the management of different departments. Some of them gathered several tens of problems or symptoms of problems. Next, they proceeded to their selection choosing those whose solution they decided to treat as a first priority.

At this stage of their activity, the groups were meeting considerable difficulties with identifying problems. Very often symptoms were mistaken for the real problems, which would make it impossible to find a solution. That difficulty was overcome through appropriate training in particular groups. Another major difficulty was the analysis of problems. It often happened that those notifying the groups about a problem would also suggest how to solve it. The effectiveness groups believed that it would suffice to formulate a problem in writing and pass it to the Council of Company Consensus which would take a decision about its solution. As already mentioned it was a task of the groups to analyze problems in detail and find a solution or variant solutions for each of them. They should be submitted on a form prepared for this purpose containing such points as: formulation of a problem, description of its solution, costs of its practical introduction, time of introduction and effect that could be obtained within a year.

The first proposals for solutions appeared after two weeks' work. It was also then the problem emerged of how best to devise an effective mechanism of their practical implementation. While preparing the programme assumptions it seemed that decisions about such practical implementation would be taken by the Council of Company Consensus. However, already in the course of training of the effectiveness groups, the need to establish an additional level in the programme structure had been noted - and this was to be represented by the implementation unit or units. The latter were to be composed of company specialists in the field of investments, production technology, finance, and so on. After discussion, the Council of Company Consensus set up one implementation unit.

With the programme structure supplemented in such a way, the following method of execution was agreed. After identifying a problem the effectiveness group would proceed to its analysis obtaining assistance from the advisory unit. Then a group would work out its solution and pass it up on the form described above. A proposal coming from a group was then examined by the adviser unit and together with its opinion it was next passed to the implementation unit preparing decisions on a given issue to be made financed by the Council of Company Consensus. Such decisions were to be carry out by issuing proper instructions.

That procedure proved too time-consuming. While summing up the first part of the programme's execution it appeared that, from among around 50 proposals submitted by the groups, only seven were accepted for implementation, and implementation had begun on only three. A vast majority of proposals were held up at the intermediate levels, thereby not reaching the Council. Delays were due, among other factors, to difficulties connected with gathering particular units to evaluate or pass opinions on submitted proposals. A destructive role was played here by the negative or passive attitudes of a large part of the middle-level management.

The above difficulties seem to indicate the emergence of a contradiction between the hierarchical management structure still present in the company and the autonomous character of the effectiveness groups. The hierarchical structure clearly hampers a direct implementation of proposals submitted by the effectiveness groups in different departments, although that would be the simplest method, free from bureaucracy and also the fastest way. The contradiction here made it necessary to build a hierarchical structure of management also for the executed programme (effectiveness groups, advisory unit, implementation unit, Council of Company Consensus) so that it might correspond to the company's structure.

Proposals prepared by the effectiveness groups were passing up the subsequent levels of the programme's structure until decisions were taken about them. Next they were returning in the form of formal instruction, this time, however, down the levels of the company's structure. Both these structures had to meet at the decision-making level to make it possible to implement submitted proposals. It could be added that such solutions do not ensue from the existing regulations but from the mentality of the people who have become a part of this structure. That concerns mainly the middle-level managers who avoid making decisions and prefer to execute their superiors decisions.

Such a solution was adapted to the existing structure of the company but simultaneously it negated the programme's ideal. Difficulties connected with implementing the proposals submitted by the groups were undermining the advisability of its further execution as groups came to understand that the relative attractiveness of submitted proposals was of no importance here. They were also reluctantly discussed by members of both the advisory unit and the implementation unit. They placed the effectiveness groups in the role of a suppliant, who attempts to have something arranged while the two groups were defending themselves against him effectively. Those persons, or at least most of them, were unable to abandon their previous mode of thinking. They could not understand that instead of blocking initiatives springing from below such initiatives should be supported for the company's benefit.

The discussion held by us with the programme's advisers led to suggestions of another way to implement proposals submitted by the groups. The new solutions consisted in integrating particular elements of this structure and reversing the roles performed by them so far. Now the most important entity in the programme was to become the effectiveness groups, which had identified a problem, undertaken its analysis, prepared a solution, conducted consultations with the persons able to express their opinion about a proposed solution, as well as with the persons who may eventually participate in implementing them and with the persons able to make decisions on these issues.

The resulting talks and consultations should pave the way for the modification of the proposed solution so that it is better adapted to existing conditions and needs. Such activities result in preparing an implementation plan by a group, which constitutes an integral part of submitted proposals. Next, a given group invites all the above mentioned persons to discuss a submitted proposal. Participation in the meeting of all the interested persons should allow for comprehensive evaluation of the proposal, explaining all doubts on the spot and taking a decision. Such meetings should also be attended by an appointed person responsible for the proposal implementation and a deadline for it should be fixed. The decision about implementing the proposal does not mean that a group ends its contact with a given proposal. It should supervise its implementation until it is completed.

New tasks presented to the groups appeared more difficult than old ones. Hitherto a group's role would end, in principle, once a proposal was prepared, now a group is also involved in drafting a detailed implementation plan. Some of the groups assimilated the new methodology without encountering great difficulties, and their earlier experience proved very helpful here. Some groups found it more difficult and took a little longer to adapt to the new conditions. The first meetings held recently on the groups initiative showed that the new methodology is more effective than the old one. And although the process of preparing proposals is longer, the time of making a decision and implementing a proposal has been shortened. The programme in question is being executed at the moment and it is difficult to determine precisely its course in the future.

This paper is too short to present the proposals submitted by particular effectiveness groups. Suffice it to say that almost all of them deserve to be implemented, with a few representing a real breakthrough. Their implementation should contribute to a marked improvement of the company's financial status. The main obstacle, apart from the above mentioned mode of thinking, is lack of funds for investment. Improved effectiveness, which is contained in the title of the programme, does not constitute its basic goal. I consider the latter to be a change in the company's structure and its adaptation to demands posed by the market economy. The proposals in this area are an object of interest of one of the groups (the so-called organization group), which has prepared several variant solutions in this field.

The work of the remaining effectiveness groups may play an important role in preparing such changes because, through exerting an influence on the way of thinking of the company's personnel, the groups lay the foundations for these changes. At the same time, owing to their increasingly higher position, these groups may create a reform lobby to be taken seriously in the company. In as much as nobody previously had a sufficient power to effect such changes in the company today the existing reformatory groups may find an important ally just in the effectiveness groups. The future will show whether the position held by this ally is strong enough.

5. Summing up

The experience derived from the execution of the programme in question and earlier deliberations allow one to formulate some more general conclusions. This programme may be treated as a proof that there are no formal obstacles or constraints in reforming an enterprise today. That which was still not possible two or three years ago is possible now. The political changes occurring in Poland afford favourable possibilities for effecting the already mentioned changes in an enterprise, but they do not force such changes. As a result, only very few enterprises introduce these changes.

A major impediment for such changes is the critical stance of the present government towards the institution of self-management and employee codetermination. The otherwise just criticism of self-management forms operating in Poland unjustly overshadows the benefits, which an enterprise may reap from employee participation decision making. At the same time, it is hard to imagine any decentralization of management without a wider participation of employee in making decisions. Only in such a case can an enterprise reckon with their fuller involvement and increased responsibility for their work.

Another conclusion arising here is that it will be very difficult to effect any structural changes in enterprises without assistance provided by consultants from outside. Possibilities of obtaining such assistance are very limited due to a dearth of these consultants. This problem will not be solved by foreign consultants due to the language barrier and lack of their familiarity with conditions prevailing in Poland. The only solution seems to be the training of Polish consultants, including their training with the help of foreign consultants. Such a process may be aided by different types of management-training centres so fashionable in Poland these days, if they encompass in their programmes also this problem area.

Note: The research reported here is based on the International Research and Implementation Project on Improvement in Efficiency and Savin Workplaces Carried out in the Fagum-Stomil Factory Lodz, Lodz: University of Lodz.

Bibliography

Janowska, Z. (1984) *Organizacyjne formy humanizacji pracy produkcyjnej*, Warszawa: PWE.

Lazes P. and Constanzk, T. (1990) 'Xerox Cuts Costs Without Layoffs Through Union-Management Collaboration', *Labor-Management Brief*, July.

Lazes, P. (1985) 'Innovative Approaches to Saving and Creating Jobs', *National Productivity Review*, Spring.

Rudolf, S. and Piotrowski, S. (1988) 'Grupowe formy organizacji pracy i wynagradzania', Warszawa: Centrum Studiw Samorzodowych.

Rudolf, S. (1988) 'The Objective Nature of the Democratization Process in the Workplace', *Comparative Labour Law*, 3.

Rudolf, S. (1989a) 'Alternative Management Model in Polish Enterprises', Lodz: University of Lodz.

Rudolf, S. (1989b) 'Polish Experiments with Group Forms of Work', Warsaw: Centre for Self-Government Studies.

14 Prospects for employee ownership in the process of privatizing the Polish economy

Julian Pankow

This chapter reviews selected questions concerning privatization of the economy seen primarily from the vantage point of enterprises and their employees. My argument is based on empirical material and observations from my personal experience. This material has been accumulated during consulting done together with the staff of the Research Institute for Employee Self-Management, as part of the effort to prepare enterprises for privatizing.

1. Disputes concerning the concept

The adoption of the privatization bill by Parliament in July 1990 was preceded by an extensive political campaign. It can be viewed as yet another paradox of history; for it was none other than Marx who constructed his vision of human history assuming the dominant role of ownership relations in the historical process. The dispute concerning the shape of privatization involved every political force in the country, irrespective of its political provenance or position on Marxist philosophy.

There was really no questioning of the very idea of privatizing, considered as a sine qua non for introducing market relations in the Polish economy. The battle over privatization did not bring fully to light the game of interests, since the political map did not become any less muddled and illegible. Nor do institutional arrangements in the political area regarding privatization really reflect the political interests of any specific segment of the Polish society.

What was the crux of the protracted contest surrounding the privatization bill?

The concept of civic stock ownership pushed by local neo-liberals aimed at enfranchising everyone. This seems as attractive as a political slogan as it is ineffectual as an economic programme. This is evident both from surveys into attitudes on privatization and from the available monetary reserves of the population. For instance, findings by the DEMOSKOP Agency (survey commissioned by Minister K. Lis, the government commissioner for ownership changes) indicate that only 9 per cent of those surveyed would advise the purchase of stock in privatized enterprises, even considering that nearly three-quarters of those questioned voiced support for privatization ('Gazeta Wyborcza' of May 23, 1990).

Another poll, this time carried out in early 1990 by CBOS (Centre for Public Opinion Polling) indicates that, whilst 56 per cent believe that privatization as such is needed in Poland, as many as 65 per cent claimed to hold no savings which could be invested in stock. Of the remainder, some two-fifths, even though they have the available capital would not invest it in the securities of privatized firms ('Rzeczpospolita' of February 27, 1990). Shrinking real incomes and increasing pauperization still further reduce the purchasing power of the population. The problem is compounded by worries about a destabilizing political situation.

This state of affairs, confirmed by other surveys, leads to skepticism about the government's universal reliance on ESOP schemes to secure privatization. This skepticism is reinforced when one considers how the concept was promoted in the presidential campaign: for some quite absurd promises were made concerning the amount of so-called privatization certificates.

2. Dispute about the strategy

The main threats to the privatization process may come from its treatment as a largely formal-legal and economic-financial undertaking. This neglects how far privatization is an extremely complex social process taking place in a stormy political environment. What is more this treatment is accompanied by the conviction that privatization will in and of itself bring about all the necessary pro-efficiency changes. Practically no allowance is made for the organizational context, for the problems of management expertise, shortage of skilled personnel, general passivity in state enterprises, and so forth. State enterprises, their managements, and employees are all treated in the privatization process as objects to be shifted about. It is hardly surprising that they act accordingly in reality.

Hypothetically one could adopt a strategy of privatizing by administrative fiat, without going into the social context and consequences of the process. But in practice it is hard to imagine any reasonable person fully ignoring the social moods and attitudes. One has to reckon not only with passivity but also with resistance on the part of various social groupings, particularly those most directly involved, namely, employees of the privatized plants and their organizations. The above mentioned DEMOSKOP survey indicated that nearly every second person (47 per cent) thought that decisions to privatize should be taken by the employees; by the employee self-management according to 16 per cent, by the patron organization according to 9 per cent, by Parliament in the view of another 9 per cent, of 6 per cent by the state treasury, of 5 per cent by the management board, of 3 per cent by the Minister of Finance and to the same number by a bank.

In effect, nearly two-thirds of those polled believe that decisions concerning privatization should be taken by the employees or their formal representatives. These attitudes reflect not only biases and fears, but also real interests. Without opportunities to voice these interests and without negotiations between government and employee representatives one should expect conflicts to surface, putting in question the success of intended change.

In order to create these opportunities it would be advisable to approach ownership changes from the vantage point of an enterprise.

A fundamental problem is the question of pricing the assets of a privatized enterprise. Before a capital market emerges along with its appropriate financial institutions, such pricing will be done largely through subjective bargaining, given the lack of relatively objective criteria.

The simplest and (for most enterprises) practically the only available form of pricing involves accepting the book value of assets, even following their reassessment in accordance with the rules applicable to financial management. This is not a satisfactory method considering the objectives of privatization. Were one to go for the replacement value (with certain elements of pricing according to the market value), the result would be a valuation well above the book value (in cases actually studied between 2 and 5 times), which may in turn discourage potential investors, partners and shareholders.

The most promising approach would be to apply revenue methods, that is, capitalized profits. These methods, possible provided that the enterprises develop viable and alternative-path business plans, would result in defining the value of an enterprise in a way which, firstly, would be acceptable to the present owner, that is the state treasury and, secondly, would promise investors and shareholders a decent rate of return.

Another area for agreement concerns negotiations within the organization. This concerns both the formally required negotiations between the agents of the enterprise, namely the management board and the employee self-management council, and probably the less formalized agreements with the local trade unions.

Reaching agreement between all the groups concerned within an enterprise may prove a problem in itself. From the management board, this problem would arise because privatization offers no guarantees for the managers of continuing in their present jobs. From the self-management council, problems arise because the decision to go ahead and privatize will in effect be its very last decision ever, a self-destruct type move. From the trade unions, because once a firm is privatized, the earlier social benefits and perks will no longer apply.

Eliminating these hazards is not possible. The only solution is to have each party involved view its interests in such a way that decisions would be taken on the basis of a reasonably conceived risk. The prerequisite for that is access to every type of information and good communications. There is no more effective way of agreeing on this complicated interplay of interests than negotiations.

With respect to the major enterprises, the basic division over privatizing is that between viable enterprises and those on the verge of bankruptcy. In the first, i.e., the enterprises in a sound economic-financial position, the employees and their organizations stand to loose too much if they agree unreservedly to accept the risks inherent in privatizing. From their point of view, the only argument for privatization is the prospect of higher pay (and that is in no case certain). Practically all else would provide fuel for arguments against privatizing: the end of social perks, elimination of self-management structures, to say nothing about the uncertainty linked with the unknown scope of new employment policy, organization and labour discipline, possibilities of redundancies, etc.. In such circumstances the initiators of ownership transformations may find it hard to come up with arguments to allay the fears of employees and induce them to give up their comfortable status quo under the old state enterprise system.

The situation will differ for enterprises in poor standing, facing possible bankruptcy. Here the threat of possible loss of jobs could provide an incentive for more determined support of privatization. This will occur particularly in areas where a true labour market has started to develop, where unemployment has become a fact of life, particularly, for instance, in large enterprises in relatively small towns.

3. Debate surrounding employee stock ownership

In privatizing good and bad enterprises alike, the architects of change will probably have to confront the issue of employee stock ownership. Irrespective of where the initiative for privatization originated, be it from agencies within the enterprise or from outside, its execution will affect the people employed there. The people realize this only too well.

This is the truth which, if ignored, could fuel many a conflict. According to the surveys mentioned earlier, in cases where the decision to privatize is taken by outside forces, one-third of those surveyed expect some form of passive resistance from the employees, and another third expect strikes to break out. Only 8 per cent claim that nothing could be expected to happen.

There is much controversy over the employee stock ownership plans. Champions of this form of privatization have failed to present convincing economic arguments that ESOPs could become the prevalent form of privatization in Poland. But it is difficult to find rational arguments for ignoring the possibility of transforming the money holdings of employees of privatized enterprises into effective equity.

It is not possible to break completely with ideology when considering this question. Yet, a pragmatic approach is certainly possible: instead of trying to decide whether employee stock ownership is the right prescription for the Polish version of privatization, it would be more pertinent to consider the possible scope and forms of ESOPs. To foreign observers, and not necessarily those with left-wing leanings, it is a total mystery why the government economic team, deriving from a mass social movement and the Solidarity trade union, rejects out of hand the chance to reduce the contradiction between labour and capital. Why does it ignore the motivational function of linking employment to ownership? Why is it being assumed that the say of employees in shaping the destinies of the companies in which they work and would also hold stock would be something sinister? Such questions are bound to come up in negotiations between the architects of ownership change and employees of the enterprises scheduled for privatization.

The relatively strong support for the idea of privatization (anywhere between one-half and three-quarters of participants in various surveys) is generally accompanied by lesser willingness to participate in it. This willingness is higher when employee ownership is being considered. In the earlier cited DEMOSKOP survey, employees of state enterprises asked if 'they would buy stock in their company' answered positively in 47 per cent of cases and in 38 per cent negatively.

The basic questions: what will there be in it for me, is being asked by everyone facing a decision concerning investment of his or her own money. This is irrespective of whether it concerns a capitalist with a turnover of several million dollars or an employee in an enterprise for whom the equivalent of a month's wages represents a significant nest egg. Nonetheless, the latter's situation is special in the sense that this is not an anonymous business for the employee but his or her work place. Hence the risk involved is greater, and not just psychologically: failure of the company may put into jeopardy not only the person's savings but also his or her job.

It comes as no surprise, then, that employees are looking for the sort of solutions which will offer them a chance for at least a limited say concerning the functioning of the enterprise in which they work. With few exceptions no reasonable person questions the significance of professional, expert management. Thus having a say in day-to-day management decisions is not at issue; at stake is some say on the fundamental decisions pertaining to the company's future and those employed in it.

Under the terms of the relevant commercial code, decisions of this kind in joint stock companies are to be taken by the general assembly of shareholders by a qualified (2/3 or 3/4) majority vote. Accumulation of a traditionally defined control packet of stock is beyond the capacity of employees. One may expect them to strive to hold a significant packet of stock which would lay open the field to negotiations in case of decisions to be taken by such qualified majority vote. From the point of view of employees-shareholders this would mean a stock packet giving above 1/4 (or 1/3) of votes.

Amassing so much stock by employees on regular market terms would be highly improbable. Thus one may expect that in the negotiations concerning privatization employees will press demands for various concessionary terms, such as preferential rates for stock on offer and voting preferences.

The DEMOSKOP survey indicates that 80 per cent of those polled are in favour of selling stock (as opposed to 9 per cent who opt for giving it away free). But nearly two-thirds of those polled believe that preferential terms should be offered to specified categories of stock purchasers. Thus 41 per cent believe that preferential terms should be offered to all employees of the privatized enterprises, 23 per cent believe that such terms should go to employees with long work records, and 25 per cent that these should go to the people with the lowest earnings on the national scale. Similar positions are voiced in projects to prepare specific enterprises for privatization.

It is obvious that privileged stock status curtails the freedom of stock trading and discourages those who must buy stock on normal market terms. This has prompted efforts at compromise solutions and the setting up of special financial institutions to support ESOPs (foundations, employee ownership banks, etc.).

Western experience indicates that in situations where bankruptcy, redundancy and similar problems threaten, the employees who decided to buy stock in their companies are willing to accept considerable denials and hardships. There were frequent examples where the employee shareholders, to secure the competitiveness of their company's products, were willing to accept major cuts in their wages (an example was provided by the 18 per cent reduction in Weirton Steel, the US). Also there is no confirmation of the thesis about the reduced propensity to invest by companies with employee stock ownership - a case in point is Britain's National Freight Consortium transportation company, where 80 per cent of the share capital was held by employees, and where for several years running the shareholders voted to forego dividends, ploughing back the profits to expand and modernize their company. The feasibility of such an approach under Polish circumstances will depend largely on the situation in local labour markets.

Social awareness concerning privatization is marked by large areas of uncertainty. Such uncertainty is due to very poor knowledge about the workings of market economy mechanisms and institutions, ignorance of the basic categories. Ignorance gives rise to fears and bias, both concerning government policy and concerning domestic and foreign capital investment.

Government information policy does little to reduce these areas of uncertainty. Little promotional support was given to government policies in the area of privatization. Discussions are limited to narrow groups of specialists, without any real involvement of the enterprises affected. Neither of the two major trade unions has bothered to present its position on privatization. In this context, the self-management councils present a welcome contrast, particularly in presenting their views about the role of employee stock ownership in moves to transfer ownership.

4. Concepts of employee ownership

The privatization bill adopted by parliament, already representing a compromise with employee communities, offers relatively little opportunity to employees of privatized enterprises who wish to purchase stock in their companies. The bill offers a concession in the form of possible purchase of stock certificates at 50 per cent of their face value, with the total value of such stock not to exceed 20 per cent of the company's share capital, and at the same time the value of stock purchased by any one employee on concessional terms cannot exceed the average pay in the preceding 12 months in the 5 main branches of the national economy (depending on the situation, the more restrictive of the two provisions applies).

Such preferential terms remain in force for one year following the first offering of stock to company employees. Regardless of the ownership formula, the bill stipulates that one-third of the membership in the supervisory council is to be elected by the employees, and this right will continue in force as long as the state treasury holds a majority of shares in the company (51 per cent of the stock).

Simulation models calculated for several enterprises and initial employee reactions to the government proposals both indicate that with this range of options the share of employees in privatizing will be negligible if not practically zero.

In contrast to the capital formula preferred by the government, which calls for the privatizing of state enterprises through their transformation into single-owner companies of the state treasury, the concept proposed by the Research Institute on Employee Self-Management proposes to privatize enterprises through their liquidation and replacement by entirely new companies. The founders here would be the state treasury, investing as its equity share the assets of the liquidated enterprise, plus employees of the former enterprise and a foundation for employee ownership.

The foundation is to be set up by the enterprise even before launching the privatization proceedings, under the terms of the 1984 Foundations Act, with funds transferred from the gross profits of the enterprise (the law allows for transferring up to 10 per cent of the gross profit for such purposes).

Since both the employees and the foundation would be paying cash into the company, it is possible to apply the founder's privilege provisions of the Commercial Code. Under these provisions it is possible to acquire stock on credit, at one-fourth of its face value. The debt so contracted to the company would be repayable in, say, three yearly instalments, mainly out of the dividends received.

Until full repayment of the stock amount, the employee stock certificates would have the form of assigned shares, hence the freedom to trade them would be temporarily confined within the company. This in-company trading would be carried out by the foundation. Such restrictions on trade would not apply to the ordinary shares held by the state treasury. Trading in these would from the very outset be based on regular market rules.

This is one possible concept to embrace employee ownership. In addition to the foundations, other institutions are being considered (such as the Association of Future Employee Shareholders, also benefiting from a 10 per cent transfer of gross enterprise profits) as well as mechanisms bolstering employee participation in privatizing.

Experience accumulated to date indicates that privatization proposals with elements of employee ownership require particularly careful preparation. It will not be enough to address the economic, financial and legal issues involved. It is equally important to carry out parallel preparatory efforts addressing the social issues, identifying the arrangement of forces in enterprises, identifying the promoters of change, taking stock of possible barriers and sources of conflict, the problems linked with organization, restructuring efforts, and many other issues.

All these represent vast areas of uncertainty. The only way to reduce such uncertainties is to have efficient communications and adequate information. In privatizing projects with the active involvement of employees, it is a sine qua non for success that practically every member of the given organization is supplied with the basic facts pertaining to privatizing. This is of course a necessary condition, but in and of itself it is far from enough. Yet, ignoring it could make the whole process of privatizing that much more difficult and increase the social hardships involved.

15 The drifting society

Jerzy Mikulowski Pomorski

1 Farewell to the communist haven

In an earlier article (Pomorski 1991) I reflected upon the peculiar phenomenon that, despite declarations to the contrary, life goes on in the shadow of communism. This seemed to me so characteristic of the present fin de siècle that I identified it with Post-Communism. Evidence for this phenomenon could be found not only in Eastern Europe, but throughout the world; a world whose centres had previously learned to co-exist peacefully with the communist brand of totalitarianism. I also suggested that this reluctance to enter the new epoch could be related to other influential currents and phenomena, including, above all, postmodernism.

To illustrate this situation my previous article deployed the metaphor of a ship, which despite having been cut loose from its moorings at the quayside, cannot yet begin its journey. That is how it seemed in 1990. Has anything really changed in the meantime? It undoubtedly has. For the ship is now further from the shore but, instead of moving forward with a purpose, it is drifting aimlessly. Drifting is movement where a body is not subject to its own forces but responds to currents and other external influences. It involves an absence of spontaneous activity.

2. Where can we find authentic values?

In 1988, when I began to take a closer interest in societal changes at the global level, and in Polish society in particular, it struck me that during the present century Polish society has been able to create its own values. These in turn have defined the direction of its active adaptation to difficult historical conditions. On examining the contemporary history of Poles, one could say that society (please excuse this personification) was always aiming at something. Such a statement would amount to very little - one could say the same about the society of any nation - were it not for the fact that in every instance the reaction of Poles was an authentic one. In other words these ideas were not imported or instilled from a foreign source, but were native conceptions and inventions, which disagreed with or even contradicted what was suggested by the surrounding world, regardless of the extent to which such ideas were put forward in good faith.

Every important change in the historical conditions of national existence, even if transitory, was accompanied by the appearance of certain social values in a particular sequence. An older value gave way to a new one, which was more appropriate to the prevailing conditions. It is also significant that the cost of choosing and adopting a new value was resignation from the former which was placed, as it were, on the altar of history. I regard this older value as suspended, rather than abandoned: for, as we know from experience, its proponents will sooner or later come to the fore, while the non-realization of the value creates tension and eventually leads to its effective political articulation. One can say that both those values that society decided to realize, as indeed those it agreed to abandon, have remained in the repertoire of national aspirations.

We thus find, in every period of history, three categories of values: (a) introduced values (either introduced externally or previously developed) which must give way to (b) created values (created in the autonomous process of adapting to prevailing conditions), while (c) suspended values remain in the collective memory awaiting realization. These ideas are usually defined and identified in generational terms because it is generations that introduce them, defend them, and feel responsible for them. One can present the approximate sequence of values of Polish generations in the 20th century as follows:

Table 2.1 Poland: Main Generational Values

Generation linked with historical period (in years)	Implemented Values	Suspended Values
1918-1939	Introduced: emotional attachment to newly regained independence Created: endeavours to develop the new State	Social justice and equitable distribution of benefits
1939-1945	Introduced: struggle for independence Created: striving for biological survival	Personal development
1945-1956	Introduced: efforts aiming at reconstruction of the country Created: efforts to vindicate political subject-rights and overcome isolation from the world	Satisfaction of economic needs
1957-1970	Introduced: "Positivist" organic work for future development Created: efforts to modernize the country	Satisfaction of economic needs
1971-1979	Introduced: tendencies to secure higher living standards and enhanced consumption Created: resistance to political manipulation	Subject rights
1980-1981	Introduced: efforts to maintain living standards Created: efforts to	Satisfaction of consumption needs

	vindicate subject-rights for the nation	
1981-1988	Introduced: efforts to regain subject rights Created: privatization of life	Participation in public life
1989-	Introduced: return to civilized standards Created: ?	Equality

It is significant that the values associated with the remote past can return to the repertoire of national aspirations as values which are remembered to have been formerly esteemed, in which case they cease to be neutral. During the years that preceded the changes later to be known as the anti-communist revolution, these once-dominant values came under review in the course of national debate. The revolution's social and political programme was essentially a conglomeration of these values, which people had striven for in the past but which they had never been quite able to achieve. It was thus a maximalist programme which encompassed slogans that were fundamental to the past: national independence; prosperity; the end of isolation; civic responsibility; freedom; justice; further sacrifices for the common good and private satisfaction. All this was to be realized in a programme of normal living which would take control when society started to develop in a normal manner. Whereas the former values were characterized by a certain repertoire of behaviour (or habitus) that could guide action, the current programme turned out to be maximalist, and by consequence unrealizable. Whereas before people concentrated either on biological survival, the cultivation of Statehood, or ultimately on escaping from the public sphere to the security of private life, the current programme, as it is perceived today, demands too much for the values that it affirms to stand any chance of being fulfilled.

For the same reason one is struck by the vagueness of the current programme's point of departure; namely, a value called the return to the standards of European civilization. The thesis of the 'drifting society' is directly connected to the catalogue of contemporary values (post 1989) which have not been fully listed in figure 1. We may nonetheless observe how the introduced value of a return to the standards of civilization, i.e., to European normality, is greeted by the abandonment of concerns with social and economic equality.

3. European standards

Nowadays both these values are, from the outset, interpreted ideologically. Equality is identified with communism; standards of civilization with hopes of a free and prosperous Poland. In agreeing with what are hailed as European standards we accept values which society has neither evaluated nor accepted and, various declarations notwithstanding, which society has not claimed as its own. The substitution of an introduced value by a created one, as has regularly happened in the past, is undoubtedly prompted by the former's imperfection and inappropriateness to current conditions. But is the value of restoring the standards of civilization really imperfect?

Without a shadow of doubt. Contrary to appearances, this value, returning to the standards of civilization (European, it is often added), is decidedly vague. If we were to resort to other values, our subjective experience of them would be significantly easier to validate and more certain. It is less difficult for a person trying to report his experiences to say that he felt free, fulfilled, or powerful in performing an action, than to say that he acted as a civilized person or European, because the latter demands an external evaluation. To rely on the arbitrary judgement of the external world, especially for a nation as vain as Poles, can hardly be the aim of sacrifices and strategies of development.

A closer analysis of this alleged Europeanness, or civilization, reveals that it is more a construct of scholars of whom this continent has never been short; scholars like Pierre du Bois, the Italian humanists, Comenius, Balthazar Gracian, or the writers of the Enlightenment. Writing about common European virtues and the national division of labour amongst the countries of this continent, remains the pleasant and invigorating preoccupation of utopians, while the vitality of these ideas is once again proven in the context of imminent Western European integration.

Our own recent survey of how the Polish press dealt with the European theme between 1989 and 1991 shows that the protagonists of the European idea were initially ready to accept this conception of the European Arcadia, in which they linked the much sought-after standards of civilization with a selectively and sycophantically interpreted vision of the European cultural heritage. Yet towards the end of the period in question, this aim was already being identified with participation in Europe's inter-state structures, while the programme alone was supposed to fulfil the desired criteria of approval. Once this formal ticket to

Europe is issued one can expect that the matter of entering Europe will be resolved; future politicians will dispel this myth and remember that Attila, Nero and Hitler were part of Europe's past, that the present is characterized by demographic depression, and that the future lies with the muslim family. Those who remind us of these things will be stimulating the awakening of the post-communist East.

The drifting societies of the European East have succumbed to the myth of a just continent, participation in which will ensure a proper and affluent existence. In their maximalism these societies have allowed themselves to be lulled to sleep by the myth of Europe. Now they drift in this dream. Yet the experience may not be forgotten. New values, created values, will question this myth.

If new values are to be introduced by the new generation, as has always been the case hitherto, then the declarations that the anarchists and skinheads make at their rallies, even if they are just a verbal expression of feeling and do not amount to programmes, sound like the worst nationalist slogans of the past. Regardless of the degree to which it might prove valid, the claim that this is just a defence of integrity, and that these slogans should not be mistaken for fascistic promises, is as absurd as the old assurances that Hitler did not mean what he said.

4. International partnership

Before discussing international partnership, the reader is owed a few words on the author's first-hand experience of these matters. A major, though thankfully temporary change has occurred in my life, namely, that from being a social observer not at all engaged in public life, I now find myself in the position of a state employee in charge of a medium-sized Polish academic institution.

As director of this institution I concentrate on its contacts with the external world understood both as the internal, domestic market and the various networks of foreign partners. In terms of external policy I am endeavouring to adapt the structure of the institution so that it might be as broadly open to the external world as possible. In performing this function I am aware of the fact that, in my field of activity, post-communist Poland, at least in the initial period, was ill-prepared for negotiation with the foreign partners with whom it had established contact, and was unable to articulate its needs. Treating contact with the Western world as a good in itself, post-communist Poland was ready to accept whatever this world could offer. It drifted.

As I learned how to be more active in this co-operation, my western interlocutors learned how to distance themselves from their dependent partner. Now I was not asked, as had happened a year earlier: What do you want? Instead they told me what could could be given and indicated that, if I did not accept it, someone else would. Our conversations became increasingly less pleasant and our paths began to diverge.

In 1992, as I write these words, any post-communist European country seen through the eyes of my western partners is better if: (a) it is small in size, because then it is easier to govern and investment is less risky, if only from the point of view of the scale of undertakings; (b) it is monocentric, with decision-making and basic resources should be centralized in one institution; (c) it is administered efficiently, which, in a situation where one cannot count on a competent bureaucracy, means administered autocratically; (d) it is urbanized, because this implies a more highly developed infrastructure, a more concentrated population and greater receptiveness to marketing initiatives; and (e) it can keep its cheap labour force within its well-protected borders.

It is not difficult to see that most of these conditions were actually fulfilled in these countries by communism. Of course, one can point to a few desired goals that communism could not provide, namely: (a) a high level of privatization; (b) a well-developed transport and telecommunications system; (c) an efficient banking system; (d) convertible currency; and (e) access to the media.

Concluding my text two years ago I ventured the optimistic opinion that the future of Europe lies in its diversity. I still hold to this view but now I must reckon with the fact that this future is a distant one. And this is not because diversity will not prove necessary at some future date; but because the immediate need of the countries of Europe is to strive to limit their separateness so as not to complicate an already complex system of continental partnership.

5. Awakening from the European dream

The post-communist countries have, as it were, momentarily lost their ability to create authentic values. This can be interpreted as another way of saying that they have suspended their national integrity. It does not seem that, in a country with a traditionally strong intelligentsia responsible for its national goals, such a situation can last for long.

For our European partners such an awakening may become more of a problem than an interesting challenge. It seems that a young member of the intelligentsia of these countries will attack the European myth in the name of national integrity. This may yet become the first clash of two different civilizations within the bounds of the same continent.

Bibliography

Pomorski, J. (1991) 'New Challenge for a New Europe', in J. Hausner, B. Jessop, and K. Nielsen, eds., *Markets, Politics and the Negotiated Economy - Scandinavian and Post-Socialist Perspectives*, Cracow: Cracow Academy of Economics, 113-124.

Index

Accumulation strategy 25, 33, 39f, 203ff
Advantage, competitive 30, 31, 40, 161
Allocation 92, 124, 220ff, 224, 237ff, 250, 255
Arbitration 102
Autonomous groups 261, 267f

Bargaining 112, 187f, 196, 237ff (see also collective bargaining)
Borrowing 14, 70f, 73
Branch corporation 12, 17, 225ff, 232f, 237ff
Britain 37, 40, 50, 52, 59,
Bureaucracy 4, 16, 217, 225, 269, 289
Business influence 135f, 149ff (see also employer organizations, interest groups)

Campaign institutions 102, 184ff, 195f, 201ff, 211
Capital market 202ff, 253
Church, Catholic 241f, 247
CIS 56f (see also Soviet Union)
Citizenship 10
City of London 28, 53
Civil society 7, 10, 136, 227, 229
Class conflict 6, 175, 277
Class cooperation 101, 142
Coalition, political 53, 155, 187
Collective bargaining 106, 110, 138ff, 172ff, 195 (see also wage formation)
COMECON 7, 41
Commercialization 9
Commodification 171
Commons, tragedy of 115
Communication 95, 108, 110f,

183f, 190, 195ff, 212f
as social partnership 187
Competition 9, 11, 26ff, 255
discourse 23, 29, 36, 207ff
forms 29-30, 251
international 24, 41, 71, 75, 127
national 14
structural 23, 40
Competitiveness 14, 23ff, 27, 29, 160, 185, 187, 194, 207f
national 14 (see also competition)
structural 30, 38, 160, 184f, 195
Compromise 95, 135f (see negotiated economy)
Concentration, economic 157ff
Concertation 15, 133ff, 142, 159, 162 (see also corporatism)
Concessions 117ff
Conflict 107, 136, 219, 269
Consciousness, social 217f, 221, 226, 252
Consensus 95, 102, 196
company 267f
Consumer policy 15, 143-47
Cooperation 11, 221
Co-optation 178f
Coordination 104f, 171f, 177f, 179f, 219ff, 224
problem 101, 105, 177f, 196, 224
Corporate forms 29, 49f
Corporatism 10, 11, 13, 16-17, 35, 37, 58, 143f, 155, 171f, 178f, 188, 221, 224, 244f
enterprise 232f, 261ff, 264, 267f, 277
Councils, employee 232, 264
Crisis 14
Czechoslovakia 61

Decentralization 10, 54, 140, 162, 178f
De-institutionalization 132, 138, 143, 162
Demand management 92 (see also Keynesianism)
Democracy 3, 7, 10-11, 13, 247
Democratization 10ff, 16, 226, 261
Denmark 6, 16, 34, 79, 82, 101, 152, 169-210
Deregulation 10
Dilemma 13, 116
Dirigisme 29, 36, 37, 250f (see state intervention, statism)
Discursive practice 5, 6, 36, 100, 105, 108, 162, 190
Discourse institutions 101, 211
Distribution (see allocation)
Dominant competitive force 29

Effectiveness groups 267f
Efficiency 27, 47, 72, 107, 111,124, 237
dynamic 72
institutional 107
static 72
types 32, 33
Embeddedness 4
Employee stock ownership 278ff
Employer organizations 136f, 142f, 170f (see also trade associations)
Enterprises 18, 262f, 272f
Entrepreneurial firm 26, 199f, 241, 248
European Commission 29
European Community 42, 72f, 152f, 160, 208

Evolutionary theory 75f, 82f
Extensive growth 7
Externality 118f

Family 224, 227, 229f
Financial institutions 7
Flexibility 6, 12, 31, 35, 41, 59, 112, 170, 178, 209, 255
Flexible manufacturing systems 26
Fordism 9, 24, 26, 35, 47, 60
Foreign actors 14, 46ff
Foreign capital 256-7
Frame of meaning 101f, 106, 110
France 29, 50f

Games 99f, 102, 106, 109, 238
language 97, 99
strategy 106
Gas 15, 115ff
Germany 4, 26, 29, 42, 48, 54, 58f, 152
Globalization 7, 12, 16, 23ff, 26, 33 (see also internationalization, transnational companies)
Governance 13, 230
Government failure 106, 236
Growth strategy 7

Hegemony 26, 33, 58
Hollowing out 35, 40
Horizontal integration 49
Household 224, 251
Housing policy 145ff
Hungary 3, 61

Ideology 99, 101, 137, 183, 185
Imperialism 30
Implementaton 13, 14, 16, 46ff, 53, 100, 121ff, 270ff
Incomes policy 102
Individualism 171
Industrial policy 17, 23, 119, 134, 194-212, 183, 230, 240 (see also private industrial policy, structural policy)
Industrial relations 15, 139-42
Informal negotiation 96
Infrastructure 251
Innovation 26, 32, 70f, 74, 80f, 201
Innovation system 77f, 83f
Internal market 29, 72, 205
Institutional learning 78, 103f
Institutional selection 45, 70
Institutional theory 46, 56, 98f
Institutionalization 101, 170, 174
Institutions 3f, 100
economic 54-6
negotiation 111
political 53-4, 96, 102
Intensive growth 7
Interest groups 3, 4, 12, 17f, 108, 218, 223ff
business interest groups 141ff, 146ff, 151f
Interest representation 12, 177f, 215ff (see also representation)
International Monetary Fund 56f, 252
Internationalization 3, 5, 7, 15, 17, 23-26, 34f, 134f, 157, 160, 256 (see also globalization)
Investment strategy 58-9
Isomorphism 14, 46ff
forms 15, 47

Japan 25, 27, 33, 48ff, 54, 58f, 69, 77
Juridification 89, 171, 174

Keynes 53
Keynesianism 47, 50, 52ff, 93, 106, 181, 199
Keynesian welfare state 34f, 92, 135
Knowledge-intensive industry 24, 27, 30, 121
Korea, South 33

Labour, division of 218
Labour market 9, 95, 101, 137, 140ff, 144, 238, 250, 254
Labour process 9, 32, 262
Language 100
Language game 97, 99
Law 17, 34, 49, 117f, 171ff, 252, 256, 262
martial 261
Learning 15, 38, 71
interactive 75ff
Legitimacy 47, 55, 227
Liberalization 7, 9, 232
Liberal state 37
Licences 121
Local state 3, 11, 232

Management 238, 264ff, 269
self- 223, 228, 277
training 272
Market 4, 251
agent 93
economy 3f, 169, 195f, 249, 251ff
failure 93, 106, 198, 252
mechanism 7, 92, 95, 250ff, 255f
world 9ff, 25
Marketization 3, 7, 9ff, 15ff, 27
forms 9
Marshall Plan 48, 51, 81
Meta-market 28
Mixed economy 92-6, 105, 168, 177-80, 194f
Monopoly 9, 49, 225, 251
Monopoly competition 28
Multinational firms (see internationalization, transnational companies)

National economy 25, 34, 42, 197f, 232
Nationhood 7
Nation state 25, 30, 35f, 157
Negotiated economy 4ff, 16-17, 92-112, 117, 124f, 133, 135ff, 142, 157, 169ff, 188ff, 195ff, 212ff, 232
defined 94
Negotiation 45, 99, 144, 178
Negotiation institution 102
Neo-classical economics 70, 74
Neo-corporatism 245ff
Neo-liberalism 5, 13, 29, 36, 56, 58ff, 108, 136, 142, 228, 249
Neo-mercantilism 27, 29, 41
Network 54, 177f, 181f, 208ff, 212
New Democracy 134
NIC 25, 33, 41f
Nomenklatura capitalism 11, 241ff
Norms 99f, 109-11, 212f, 245

Oil 15f, 115ff
Oil industrial complex 130
OPZZ unions 243
Optimization mechanism 110
Opinion, public 18, 224f, 227, 245ff, 275ff
Organizational theory 46ff, 56, 218 (see also institutional theory)
Ownership,
employee, 274ff

private 249, 254
state 92, 241ff, 250, 258, 263f

Paradigm 9, 26
Parliament 10, 14, 177, 244
minority parliamentarianism 152f, 187
Party system 7, 135, 148ff, 224, 226ff, 244f, 262
Planning, central 7, 17, 41, 74, 76, 92, 236, 249, 252ff, 257, (see also shortage economy)
Pluralism 10, 14, 221, 230
Poland 3f, 7, 10, 12, 56, 60f, 236-90
Policy analysis 100
Political change 17
Polycentrism 180
Post-communism 283
Post-Fordism 9, 12, 24, 26, 35, 58f
Post-modernism 283
Post-socialism 5, 7, 14, 17-18, 41, 45, 56ff, 73, 224, 229f, 248, 252, 254, 258
Power 6, 91, 111, 137, 237f
elite 218, 222ff, 243f
functions 220ff
negative 219
political 47
struggle 107
system 217ff
Preferences 108, 197, 229
Price mechanism 4, 251, 255f
Price controls 146
Prison's dilemma 115
Private sector 249, 253
Private industrial policy 16, 194-212
Privatization 9, 17, 58, 137, 155, 231, 242, 245ff, 254, 256, 258, 274ff, 289
Productivity 69, 71, 73
Profit 237, 241f
Property rights 3, 106, 119, 231, 241

R&D 24, 34, 50, 76, 209
Rationality 107f, 110, 182
expressive 110
procedural 110
Recentralization 9
Reflexivity 27, 32, 38
Reform 262f
Reform discourse 12, 15, 45f, 53, 60f, 135, 138
Regional bloc 9, 42
Regional dimension 14, 17, 27, 200ff, 232
Rent (economic, technological) 27, 118, 129, 251
Rent (housing) negotiations 146
Representation 10, 12f, 217ff, 222f, 227f (see also corporatism, interest representation)
Resource allocation 4
Risk 121, 237
Round table 99, 106, 109, 144f (see also negotiation, negotiated economy)
Rumania 56

Saltsjöbaden Agreement 140ff
Scale, economies 26
Scandinavia 4f, 12, 15, 40, 58f, 98, 100, 103, 138f, 158f, 231, 261
Schumpeterian workfare state 35, 135, 154, 183, 199 (see also Keynesian welfare state, welfare state)
Scope, economies 26
Search processes 7, 19
Segmentation 179f
Shock therapy 60

Shortage economy 236ff (see also planning, central)
Social Democracy 134, 136, 140, 144, 150ff, 159
Social Market Economy 13
Social movement 11, 228
Socialism, state 250, 253
Societal corporatism 16, 156, 183ff, 222, 230f, 244 (see also corporatism, state corporatism, negotiated economy)
Solidarity 57, 228, 241ff, 245, 256, 264, 267, 278
  NSSZ Solidarity 241, 243
Soviet Union 7, 41, 47, 255 (see also CIS)
Spain 152
State capacities 23, 36, 38, 182, 194ff, 201f
State corporatism 16, 223, 227, 229ff (see also corporatism, societal corporatism, negotiated economy)
State form 12, 34, 178-90
State intervention 3, 16, 39, 116, 170f, 209f, 242, 249, 252, 256ff (see also dirigisme, industrial policy)
State policy 249
State reform 13f
State regulation 95
State, role of 229, 257-60, 286
State selectivity 23
Statism 36 (see also dirigisme, state intervention)
Statoil 121, 129
Strategy 12, 27, 38, 138, 194f, 197ff, 208ff
  first vs second-order 197f, 212f
  state 36
Structural competitiveness 30, 38, 159, 184f, 194f (see also competitiveness)
Structural policy 16, 182f, 186, 199f (see also industrial policy)
Structural selectivity 23
Supply-side - see Schumpeterian workfare state
Supra-regulation 103
Sweden 34, 52, 53, 77, 82, 134-63, 223
Swedish model 16, 134ff, 139, 157, 231f
Systęmic vacuum 7, 10, 12-13

Taiwan 33
Taxpayers 153f
Technology
  Board (Denmark) 184, 191, 199f
  new 24, 30, 33-4, 41, 50, 59, 72f, 77, 178, 199f
  transfer 24, 34, 35, 71, 73, 206ff
Thatcherism 4
Third Italy 4, 209
Trade association 11 (see also interest groups)
Trade union 11, 136ff, 149ff, 159, 163, 243, 255, 264, 267 (see also Solidarity)
Transnational companies 24, 26, 28-9, 120, 160, 163, 242 (see also internationalization)
Triad power 24, 27, 35, 42

USA 26, 27, 30f, 33f, 45, 49f, 52, 58, 71, 77, 153, 280

Vacuum, system 7, 10, 12-13
Values 284ff
Vertical integration 49, 58

Wage formation 15, 170f

Wage policy 102
Welfare state 4, 9, 17, 35f, 93, 130, 134, 138, 153, 179f, 181 184f (see also Keynesian welfare state)
Welfare policy 252
Welfare theory 93, 106